Real-Resumes for
Retailing, Modeling, Fashion & Beauty Jobs...
including real resumes used to change careers
and transfer skills to other industries

Anne McKinney, Editor

PREP PUBLISHING

FAYETTEVILLE, NC

PREP Publishing
1110½ Hay Street
Fayetteville, NC 28305
(910) 483-6611

Library of Congress Cataloging-in-Publication Data

Real-resumes for retailing, modeling, fashion & beauty jobs : including real resumes used to change careers and transfer skills to other industries / Anne McKinney, editor.
     p. cm. -- (Real-resumes series)
   ISBN 1-885288-31-X (trade pbk.)
    1. Résumés (Employment) 2. Retail trade. 3. Models (Persons). 4. Fashion merchandising. 5. Beauty operators. I. McKinney, Anne, 1948- II. Series.

   HF5383 .R3959 2002
   650.14'2--dc21
                                          2002027087
                                                    CIP

Printed in the United States of America

By PREP Publishing

Business and Career Series:

RESUMES AND COVER LETTERS THAT HAVE WORKED

RESUMES AND COVER LETTERS THAT HAVE WORKED FOR MILITARY PROFESSIONALS

GOVERNMENT JOB APPLICATIONS AND FEDERAL RESUMES

COVER LETTERS THAT BLOW DOORS OPEN

LETTERS FOR SPECIAL SITUATIONS

RESUMES AND COVER LETTERS FOR MANAGERS

REAL-RESUMES FOR COMPUTER JOBS

REAL-RESUMES FOR MEDICAL JOBS

REAL-RESUMES FOR FINANCIAL JOBS

REAL-RESUMES FOR TEACHERS

REAL-RESUMES FOR STUDENTS

REAL-RESUMES FOR CAREER CHANGERS

REAL-RESUMES FOR SALES

REAL ESSAYS FOR COLLEGE & GRADUATE SCHOOL

REAL-RESUMES FOR AVIATION & TRAVEL JOBS

REAL-RESUMES FOR POLICE, LAW ENFORCEMENT & SECURITY JOBS

REAL-RESUMES FOR SOCIAL WORK & COUNSELING JOBS

REAL-RESUMES FOR CONSTRUCTION JOBS

REAL-RESUMES FOR MANUFACTURING JOBS

REAL-RESUMES FOR RESTAURANT, FOOD SERVICE & HOTEL JOBS

REAL-RESUMES FOR MEDIA, NEWSPAPER, BROADCASTING & PUBLIC AFFAIRS JOBS

REAL-RESUMES FOR RETAILING, MODELING, FASHION & BEAUTY JOBS

REAL-RESUMES FOR HUMAN RESOURCES & PERSONNEL JOBS

Judeo-Christian Ethics Series:

SECOND TIME AROUND

BACK IN TIME

WHAT THE BIBLE SAYS ABOUT...Words that can lead to success and happiness

A GENTLE BREEZE FROM GOSSAMER WINGS

BIBLE STORIES FROM THE OLD TESTAMENT

Table of Contents

A WORD FROM THE EDITOR:
ABOUT THE REAL-RESUMES SERIES

Welcome to the Real-Resumes Series. The Real-Resumes Series is a series of books which have been developed based on the experiences of real job hunters and which target specialized fields or types of resumes. As the editor of the series, I have carefully selected resumes and cover letters (with names and other key data disguised, of course) which have been used successfully in real job hunts. That's what we mean by "Real-Resumes." What you see in this book are *real* resumes and cover letters which helped real people get ahead in their careers.

The Real-Resumes Series is based on the work of the country's oldest resume-preparation company known as PREP Resumes. If you would like a free information packet describing the company's resume preparation services, call 910-483-6611 or write to PREP at 1110½ Hay Street, Fayetteville, NC 28305. If you have a job hunting experience you would like to share with our staff at the Real-Resumes Series, please contact us at preppub@aol.com or visit our website at www.prep-pub.com.

The resumes and cover letters in this book are designed to be of most value to people already in a job hunt or contemplating a career change. If we could give you one word of advice about your career, here's what we would say: Manage your career and don't stumble from job to job in an incoherent pattern. Try to find work that interests you, and then identify prosperous industries which need work performed of the type you want to do. Learn early in your working life that a great resume and cover letter can blow doors open for you and help you maximize your salary.

This book is dedicated to those seeking jobs in the retailing, modeling, fashion, and beauty fields. We hope the superior samples will help you manage your current job campaign and your career so that you will find work aligned to your career interests.

Real-Resumes for
Retailing, Modeling, Fashion & Beauty...
including real resumes used to change careers
and transfer skills to other industries

Anne McKinney, Editor

As the editor of this book, I would like to give you some tips on how to make the best use of the information you will find here. Because you are considering a career change, you already understand the concept of managing your career for maximum enjoyment and self-fulfillment. The purpose of this book is to provide expert tools and advice so that you *can* manage your career. Inside these pages you will find resumes and cover letters that will help you find not just a job but the type of work you want to do.

Introduction:
The Art of
Changing
Jobs...
and Finding
New Careers

Overview of the Book

Every resume and cover letter in this book actually worked. And most of the resumes and cover letters have common features: most are one-page, most are in the chronological format, and most resumes are accompanied by a companion cover letter. In this section you will find helpful advice about job hunting. Step One begins with a discussion of why employers prefer the one-page, chronological resume. In Step Two you are introduced to the direct approach and to the proper format for a cover letter. In Step Three you learn the 14 main reasons why job hunters are not offered the jobs they want, and you learn the six key areas employers focus on when they interview you. Step Four gives nuts-and-bolts advice on how to handle the interview, send a follow-up letter after an interview, and negotiate your salary.

The cover letter plays such a critical role in a career change. You will learn from the experts how to format your cover letters and you will see suggested language to use in particular career-change situations. It has been said that "A picture is worth a thousand words" and, for that reason, you will see numerous examples of effective cover letters used by real individuals to change fields, functions, and industries.

The most important part of the book is the Real-Resumes section. Some of the individuals whose resumes and cover letters you see spent a lengthy career in an industry they loved. Then there are resumes and cover letters of people who wanted a change but who probably wanted to remain in their industry. Many of you will be especially interested by the resumes and cover letters of individuals who knew they definitely wanted a career change but had no idea what they wanted to do next. Other resumes and cover letters show individuals who knew they wanted to change fields and had a pretty good idea of what they wanted to do next.

Whatever your field, and whatever your circumstances, you'll find resumes and cover letters that will "show you the ropes" in terms of successfully changing jobs and switching careers.

Before you proceed further, think about why you picked up this book.
- Are you dissatisfied with the type of work you are now doing?
- Would you like to change careers, change companies, or change industries?
- Are you satisfied with your industry but not with your niche or function within it?
- Do you want to transfer your skills to a new product or service?
- Even if you have excelled in your field, have you "had enough"? Would you like the stimulation of a new challenge?
- Are you aware of the importance of a great cover letter but unsure of how to write one?
- Are you preparing to launch a second career after retirement?
- Have you been downsized, or do you anticipate becoming a victim of downsizing?
- Do you need expert advice on how to plan and implement a job campaign that will open the maximum number of doors?
- Do you want to make sure you handle an interview to your maximum advantage?

- Would you like to master the techniques of negotiating salary and benefits?
- Do you want to learn the secrets and shortcuts of professional resume writers?

Using the Direct Approach

As you consider the possibility of a job hunt or career change, you need to be aware that most people end up having at least three distinctly different careers in their working lifetimes, and often those careers are different from each other. Yet people usually stumble through each job campaign, unsure of what they should be doing. Whether you find yourself voluntarily or unexpectedly in a job hunt, the direct approach is the job hunting strategy most likely to yield a full-time permanent job. The direct approach is an active, take-the-initiative style of job hunting in which you choose your next employer rather than relying on responding to ads, using employment agencies, or depending on other methods of finding jobs. You will learn how to use the direct approach in this book, and you will see that an effective cover letter is a critical ingredient in using the direct approach.

The "direct approach" is the style of job hunting most likely to yield the maximum number of job interviews.

Lack of Industry Experience Not a Major Barrier to Entering New Field

"Lack of experience" is often the last reason people are not offered jobs, according to the companies who do the hiring. If you are changing careers, you will be glad to learn that experienced professionals often are selling "potential" rather than experience in a job hunt. Companies look for personal qualities that they know tend to be present in their most effective professionals, such as communication skills, initiative, persistence, organizational and time management skills, and creativity. Frequently companies are trying to discover "personality type," "talent," "ability," "aptitude," and "potential" rather than seeking actual hands-on experience, so your resume should be designed to aggressively present your accomplishments. Attitude, enthusiasm, personality, and a track record of achievements in any type of work are the primary "indicators of success" which employers are seeking, and you will see numerous examples in this book of resumes written in an all-purpose fashion so that the professional can approach various industries and companies.

The Art of Using References in a Job Hunt

You probably already know that you need to provide references during a job hunt, but you may not be sure of how and when to use references for maximum advantage. You can use references very creatively during a job hunt to call attention to your strengths and make yourself "stand out." Your references will rarely get you a job, no matter how impressive the names, but the way you use references can boost the employer's confidence in you and lead to a job offer in the least time.

Using references in a skillful fashion in your job hunt will inspire confidence in prospective employers and help you "close the sale" after interviews.

You should ask from three to five people, including people who have supervised you, if you can use them as a reference during your job hunt. You may not be able to ask your current boss since your job hunt is probably confidential.

A common question in resume preparation is: "Do I need to put my references on my resume?" No, you don't. Even if you create a references page at the same time you prepare your resume, you don't need to mail, e-mail, or fax your references page with the resume and cover letter. Usually the potential employer is not interested in references until he meets you, so the earliest you need to have references ready is at the first interview. Obviously there are exceptions to this standard rule of thumb; sometimes an ad will ask you to send references with your first response. Wait until the employer requests references before providing them.

An excellent attention-getting technique is to take to the first interview not just a page of references (giving names, addresses, and telephone numbers) but an actual letter of reference written by someone who knows you well and who preferably has supervised or employed you. A professional way to close the first interview is to thank the interviewer, shake his or her hand, and then say you'd like to give him or her a copy of a letter of reference from a previous employer. Hopefully you already made a good impression during the interview, but you'll "close the sale" in a dynamic fashion if you leave a letter praising you and your accomplishments. For that reason, it's a good idea to ask supervisors during your final weeks in a job if they will provide you with a written letter of recommendation which you can use in future job hunts. Most employers will oblige, and you will have a letter that has a useful "shelf life" of many years. Such a letter often gives the prospective employer enough confidence in his opinion of you that he may forego checking out other references and decide to offer you the job on the spot or in the next few days.

With regard to references, it's best to provide the names and addresses of people who have supervised you or observed you in a work situation.

Whom should you ask to serve as references? References should be people who have known or supervised you in a professional, academic, or work situation. References with big titles, like school superintendent or congressman, are fine, but remind busy people when you get to the interview stage that they may be contacted soon. Make sure the busy official recognizes your name and has instant positive recall of you! If you're asked to provide references on a formal company application, you can simply transcribe names from your references list. In summary, follow this rule in using references: If you've got them, flaunt them! If you've obtained well-written letters of reference, make sure you find a polite way to push those references under the nose of the interviewer so he or she can hear someone other than you describing your strengths. Your references probably won't ever get you a job, but glowing letters of reference can give you credibility and visibility that can make you stand out among candidates with similar credentials and potential!

The approach taken by this book is to (1) help you master the proven best techniques of conducting a job hunt and (2) show you how to stand out in a job hunt through your resume, cover letter, interviewing skills, as well as the way in which you present your references and follow up on interviews. Now, the best way to "get in the mood" for writing your own resume and cover letter is to select samples from the Table of Contents that interest you and then read them. A great resume is a "photograph," usually on one page, of an individual. If you wish to seek professional advice in preparing your resume, you may contact one of the professional writers at Professional Resume & Employment Publishing (PREP) for a brief free consultation by calling 1-910-483-6611.

Part One: Some Advice About Your Job Hunt

What if you don't know what you want to do?

Your job hunt will be more comfortable if you can figure out what type of work you want to do. But you are not alone if you have no idea what you want to do next! You may have knowledge and skills in certain areas but want to get into another type of work. What *The Wall Street Journal* has discovered in its research on careers is that most of us end up having at least three distinctly different careers in our working lives; it seems that, even if we really like a particular kind of activity, twenty years of doing it is enough for most of us and we want to move on to something else!

That's why we strongly believe that you need to spend some time figuring out ***what interests you*** rather than taking an inventory of the skills you have. You may have skills that you simply don't want to use, but if you can build your career on the things that interest you, you will be more likely to be happy and satisfied in your job. Realize, too, that interests can change over time; the activities that interest you now may not be the ones that interested you years ago. For example, some professionals may decide that they've had enough of retail sales and want a job selling another product or service, even though they have earned a reputation for being an excellent retail manager. We strongly believe that interests rather than skills should be the determining factor in deciding what types of jobs you want to apply for and what directions you explore in your job hunt. Obviously one cannot be a lawyer without a law degree or a secretary without secretarial skills; but a professional can embark on a next career as a financial consultant, property manager, plant manager, production supervisor, retail manager, or other occupation if he/she has a strong interest in that type of work and can provide a resume that clearly demonstrates past excellent performance in *any* field and *potential* to excel in another field. As you will see later in this book, "lack of exact experience" is the last reason why people are turned down for the jobs they apply for.

How can you have a resume prepared if you don't know what you want to do?

You may be wondering how you can have a resume prepared if you don't know what you want to do next. The approach to resume writing which PREP, the country's oldest resume-preparation company, has used successfully for many years is to develop an "all-purpose" resume that translates your skills, experience, and accomplishments into language employers can understand. What most people need in a job hunt is a versatile resume that will allow them to apply for numerous types of jobs. For example, you may want to apply for a job in pharmaceutical sales but you may also want to have a resume that will be versatile enough for you to apply for jobs in the construction, financial services, or automotive industries.

Based on more than 20 years of serving job hunters, we at PREP have found that your best approach to job hunting is **an all-purpose resume** and **specific cover letters tailored to specific fields** rather than using the approach of trying to create different resumes for every job. If you are remaining in your field, you may not even need more than one "all-purpose" cover letter, although the cover letter rather than the resume is the place to communicate your interest in a narrow or specific field. An all-purpose resume and cover letter that translate your experience and accomplishments into plain English are the tools that will maximize the number of doors which open for you while permitting you to "fish" in the widest range of job areas.

Figure out what interests you and you will hold the key to a successful job hunt and working career. (And be prepared for your interests to change over time!)

"Lack of exact experience" is the last reason people are turned down for the jobs for which they apply.

Your resume will provide the script for your job interview.
When you get down to it, your resume has a simple job to do: Its purpose is to blow as many doors open as possible and to make as many people as possible want to meet you. So a well-written resume that really "sells" you is a key that will create opportunities for you in a job hunt.

This statistic explains why: The typical newspaper advertisement for a job opening receives more than 245 replies. And normally only 10 or 12 will be invited to an interview.

But here's another purpose of the resume: it provides the "script" the employer uses when he interviews you. If your resume has been written in such a way that your strengths and achievements are revealed, that's what you'll end up talking about at the job interview. Since the resume will govern what you get asked about at your interviews, you can't overestimate the importance of making sure your resume makes you look and sound as good as you are.

So what is a "good" resume?
Very literally, your resume should motivate the person reading it to dial the phone number or e-mail the screen name you have put on the resume. When you are relocating, you should put a local phone number on your resume if your physical address is several states away; employers are more likely to dial a local telephone number than a long-distance number when they're looking for potential employees.

If you have a resume already, look at it objectively. Is it a limp, colorless "laundry list" of your job titles and duties? Or does it "paint a picture" of your skills, abilities, and accomplishments in a way that would make someone want to meet you? Can people understand what you're saying? If you are attempting to change fields or industries, can potential employers see that your skills and knowledge are transferable to other environments? For example, have you described accomplishments which reveal your problem-solving abilities or communication skills?

How long should your resume be?
One page, maybe two. Usually only people in the academic community have a resume (which they usually call a *curriculum vitae*) longer than one or two pages. Remember that your resume is almost always accompanied by a cover letter, and a potential employer does not want to read more than two or three pages about a total stranger in order to decide if he wants to meet that person! Besides, don't forget that the more you tell someone about yourself, the more opportunity you are providing for the employer to screen you out at the "first-cut" stage. A resume should be concise and exciting and designed to make the reader want to meet you in person!

Should resumes be functional or chronological?
Employers almost always prefer a chronological resume; in other words, an employer will find a resume easier to read if it is immediately apparent what your current or most recent job is, what you did before that, and so forth, in reverse chronological order. A resume that goes back in detail for the last ten years of employment will generally satisfy the employer's curiosity about your background. Employment more than ten years old can be shown even more briefly in an "Other Experience" section at the end of your "Experience" section. Remember that your intention is not to tell everything you've done but to "hit the high points" and especially impress the employer with what you learned, contributed, or accomplished in each job you describe.

Your resume is the "script" for your job interviews. Make sure you put on your resume what you want to talk about or be asked about at the job interview.

The one-page resume in chronological format is the format preferred by most employers.

Once you get your resume, what do you do with it?
You will be using your resume to answer ads, as a tool to use in talking with friends and relatives about your job search, and, most importantly, in using the "direct approach" described in this book.

When you mail your resume, always send a "cover letter."

A "cover letter," sometimes called a "resume letter" or "letter of interest," is a letter that accompanies and introduces your resume. Your cover letter is a way of personalizing the resume by sending it to the specific person you think you might want to work for at each company. Your cover letter should contain a few highlights from your resume—just enough to make someone want to meet you. Cover letters should always be typed or word processed on a computer—never handwritten.

Never mail or fax your resume without a cover letter.

1. Learn the art of answering ads.
There is an "art," part of which can be learned, in using your "bestselling" resume to reply to advertisements.

Sometimes an exciting job lurks behind a boring ad that someone dictated in a hurry, so reply to any ad that interests you. Don't worry that you aren't "25 years old with an MBA" like the ad asks for. Employers will always make compromises in their requirements if they think you're the "best fit" overall.

What about ads that ask for "salary requirements?"
What if the ad you're answering asks for "salary requirements?" The first rule is to avoid committing yourself in writing at that point to a specific salary. You don't want to "lock yourself in."

What if the ad asks for your "salary requirements?"

There are two ways to handle the ad that asks for "salary requirements."
First, you can ignore that part of the ad and accompany your resume with a cover letter that focuses on "selling" you, your abilities, and even some of your philosophy about work or your field. You may include a sentence in your cover letter like this: "I can provide excellent personal and professional references at your request, and I would be delighted to share the private details of my salary history with you in person."

Second, if you feel you must give some kind of number, just state a range in your cover letter that includes your medical, dental, other benefits, and expected bonuses. You might state, for example, "My current compensation, including benefits and bonuses, is in the range of $30,000-$40,000."

Analyze the ad and "tailor" yourself to it.
When you're replying to ads, a finely tailored cover letter is an important tool in getting your resume noticed and read. On the next page is a cover letter which has been "tailored to fit" a specific ad. Notice the "art" used by PREP writers of analyzing the ad's main requirements and then writing the letter so that the person's background, work habits, and interests seem "tailor-made" to the company's needs. Use this cover letter as a model when you prepare your own reply to ads.

Date

Mr. Arthur Wise, Regional Manager
Steve Madden Shoes
9439 Goshen Lane
Dallas, TX 22105

Dear Mr. Wise:

I would appreciate an opportunity to show you in person, soon, that I am the energetic, dynamic individual you are looking for as your General Manager for the Steve Madden Shoe Store In Dallas.

Here are just three reasons why I believe I am the effective management professional you seek:

- *I offer experience in store management.* In my current position, I manage a diversified upscale women's fashion boutique which caters to an exclusive clientele. While I enjoy my colleagues and the product line, I love shoes more than any other product. It would be an honor to manage a store which specializes in one of the finest shoe lines in the world.

- *I offer extensive expertise related to ladies shoes.* As you will see from my resume, I excelled in selling ladies' shoes for the Dillard's store in Ft. Worth, TX, and prior to that for Macy's in New York.

- *I understand the buying business, the reality of changing fashions in women's shoes, and the business of retailing.* Highly computer proficient, I am skilled at utilizing various software programs for analyzing inventory levels and product sell-through. Early in my retailing career, I worked as a buyer, and that experience has helped me work with and understand buyers as I have progressed in management. I am well known for my business management skills, and I have boosted the boutique's profitability 25% in the last year.

I am fortunate to have the natural energy, industry, and enthusiasm required to put in the long hours necessary for effective retailing. You will find me, I am certain, a friendly, good-natured person whom you would be proud to call part of your "team." I would enjoy the opportunity to share my proven sales techniques and extensive knowledge with other junior sales professionals in a management and development position.

I hope you will call or write me soon to suggest a convenient time when we might meet to discuss your needs further and how I might serve them. I can provide outstanding references at the appropriate time.

Yours sincerely,

Your Name

Employers are trying to identify the individual who wants the job they are filling. Don't be afraid to express your enthusiasm in the cover letter!

2. Talk to friends and relatives.

Don't be shy about telling your friends and relatives the kind of job you're looking for. Looking for the job you want involves using your network of contacts, so tell people what you're looking for. They may be able to make introductions and help set up interviews.

About 25% of all interviews are set up through "who you know," so don't ignore this approach.

3. Finally, and most importantly, use the "direct approach."

The "direct approach" is a strategy in which you choose your next employer.

More than 50% of all job interviews are set up by the "direct approach." That means you actually mail, e-mail, or fax a resume and a cover letter to a company you think might be interesting to work for.

To whom do you write?

In general, you should write directly to the *exact name* of the person who would be hiring you: say, the vice-president of marketing or data processing. If you're in doubt about to whom to address the letter, address it to the president by name and he or she will make sure it gets forwarded to the right person within the company who has hiring authority in your area.

How do you find the names of potential employers?

You're not alone if you feel that the biggest problem in your job search is finding the right names at the companies you want to contact. But you can usually figure out the names of companies you want to approach by deciding first if your job hunt is primarily geography-driven or industry-driven.

In a **geography-driven job hunt,** you could select a list of, say, 50 companies you want to contact **by location** from the lists that the U.S. Chambers of Commerce publish yearly of their "major area employers." There are hundreds of local Chambers of Commerce across America, and most of them will have an 800 number which you can find through 1-800-555-1212. If you and your family think Atlanta, Dallas, Ft. Lauderdale, and Virginia Beach might be nice places to live, for example, you could contact the Chamber of Commerce in those cities and ask how you can obtain a copy of their list of major employers. Your nearest library will have the book which lists the addresses of all chambers.

In an **industry-driven job hunt,** and if you are willing to relocate, you will be identifying the companies which you find most attractive in the industry in which you want to work. When you select a list of companies to contact **by industry,** you can find the right person to write and the address of firms by industrial category in *Standard and Poor's, Moody's,* and other excellent books in public libraries. Many Web sites also provide contact information.

Many people feel it's a good investment to actually call the company to either find out or double-check the name of the person to whom they want to send a resume and cover letter. It's important to do as much as you feasibly can to assure that the letter gets to the right person in the company.

On-line research will be the best way for many people to locate organizations to which they wish to send their resume. It is outside the scope of this book to teach Internet research skills, but librarians are often useful in this area.

What's the correct way to follow up on a resume you send?

There is a polite way to be aggressively interested in a company during your job hunt. It is ideal to end the cover letter accompanying your resume by saying, "I hope you'll welcome my call next week when I try to arrange a brief meeting at your convenience to discuss your current and future needs and how I might serve them." Keep it low key, and just ask for a "brief meeting," not an interview. Employers want people who show a determined interest in working with them, so don't be shy about following up on the resume and cover letter you've mailed.

It pays to be aware of the 14 most common pitfalls for job hunters.

STEP THREE: Preparing for Interviews

But a resume and cover letter by themselves can't get you the job you want. You need to "prep" yourself before the interview. Step Three in your job campaign is "Preparing for Interviews." First, let's look at interviewing from the hiring organization's point of view.

What are the biggest "turnoffs" for potential employers?

One of the ways to help yourself perform well at an interview is to look at the main reasons why organizations *don't* hire the people they interview, according to those who do the interviewing.

Notice that "lack of appropriate background" (or lack of experience) is the *last* reason for not being offered the job.

The 14 Most Common Reasons Job Hunters Are Not Offered Jobs (according to the companies who do the interviewing and hiring):

1. Low level of accomplishment
2. Poor attitude, lack of self-confidence
3. Lack of goals/objectives
4. Lack of enthusiasm
5. Lack of interest in the company's business
6. Inability to sell or express yourself
7. Unrealistic salary demands
8. Poor appearance
9. Lack of maturity, no leadership potential
10. Lack of extracurricular activities
11. Lack of preparation for the interview, no knowledge about company
12. Objecting to travel
13. Excessive interest in security and benefits
14. Inappropriate background

Department of Labor studies have proven that smart, "prepared" job hunters can increase their beginning salary while getting a job in *half* the time it normally takes. (4½ months is the average national length of a job search.) Here, from PREP, are some questions that can prepare you to find a job faster.

Are you in the "right" frame of mind?

It seems unfair that we have to look for a job just when we're lowest in morale. Don't worry *too* much if you're nervous before interviews. You're supposed to be a little nervous, especially if the job means a lot to you. But the best way to kill unnecessary fears about job hunting is through 1) making sure you have a great resume and 2) preparing yourself for the interview. Here are three main areas you need to think about before each interview.

Do you know what the company does?
Don't walk into an interview giving the impression that, "If this is Tuesday, this must be General Motors."

Find out before the interview what the company's main product or service is. Where is the company heading? Is it in a "growth" or declining industry? (Answers to these questions may influence whether or not you want to work there!)

Research the company before you go to interviews.

Information about what the company does is in annual reports, in newspaper and magazine articles, and on the Internet. If you're not yet skilled at Internet research, just visit your nearest library and ask the reference librarian to guide you to printed materials on the company.

Do you know what you want to do for the company?
Before the interview, try to decide how you see yourself fitting into the company. Remember, "lack of exact background" the company wants is usually the last reason people are not offered jobs.

Understand before you go to each interview that the burden will be on you to "sell" the interviewer on why you're the best person for the job and the company.

How will you answer the critical interview questions?
Put yourself in the interviewer's position and think about the questions you're most likely to be asked. Here are some of the most commonly asked interview questions:

Anticipate the questions you will be asked at the interview, and prepare your responses in advance.

Q: *"What are your greatest strengths?"*
A: Don't say you've never thought about it! Go into an interview knowing the three main impressions you want to leave about yourself, such as "I'm hard-working, loyal, and an imaginative cost-cutter."

Q: *"What are your greatest weaknesses?"*
A: Don't confess that you're lazy or have trouble meeting deadlines! Confessing that you tend to be a "workaholic" or "tend to be a perfectionist and sometimes get frustrated when others don't share my high standards" will make your prospective employer see a "weakness" that he likes. Name a weakness that your interviewer will perceive as a strength.

Q: *"What are your long-range goals?"*
A: If you're interviewing with Microsoft, don't say you want to work for IBM in five years! Say your long-range goal is to be *with* the company, contributing to its goals and success.

Q: *"What motivates you to do your best work?"*
A: Don't get dollar signs in your eyes here! "A challenge" is not a bad answer, but it's a little cliched. Saying something like "troubleshooting" or "solving a tough problem" is more interesting and specific. Give an example if you can.

Q: "What do you know about this organization?"

A: Don't say you never heard of it until they asked you to the interview! Name an interesting, positive thing you learned about the company recently from your research. Remember, company executives can sometimes feel rather "maternal" about the company they serve. Don't get onto a negative area of the company if you can think of positive facts you can bring up. Of course, if you learned in your research that the company's sales seem to be taking a nose-dive, or that the company president is being prosecuted for taking bribes, you might politely ask your interviewer to tell you something that could help you better understand what you've been reading. Those are the kinds of company facts that can help you determine whether or not you want to work there.

Q: "Why should I hire you?"

A: "I'm unemployed and available" is the wrong answer here! Get back to your strengths and say that you believe the organization could benefit by a loyal, hard-working cost-cutter like yourself.

In conclusion, you should decide in advance, before you go to the interview, how you will answer each of these commonly asked questions. Have some practice interviews with a friend to role-play and build your confidence.

STEP FOUR: Handling the Interview and Negotiating Salary

Now you're ready for Step Four: actually handling the interview successfully and effectively. Remember, the purpose of an interview is to get a job offer.

Eight "do's" for the interview

According to leading U.S. companies, there are eight key areas in interviewing success. You can fail at an interview if you mishandle just one area.

1. **Do wear appropriate clothes.**

You can never go wrong by wearing a suit to an interview.

2. **Do be well groomed.**

Don't overlook the obvious things like having clean hair, clothes, and fingernails for the interview.

3. **Do give a firm handshake.**

You'll have to shake hands twice in most interviews: first, before you sit down, and second, when you leave the interview. Limp handshakes turn most people off.

4. **Do smile and show a sense of humor.**

Interviewers are looking for people who would be nice to work with, so don't be so somber that you don't smile. In fact, research shows that people who smile at interviews are perceived as more intelligent. So, smile!

5. **Do be enthusiastic.**

Employers say they are "turned off" by lifeless, unenthusiastic job hunters who show no special interest in that company. The best way to show some enthusiasm for the employer's operation is to find out about the business beforehand.

Go to an interview prepared to tell the company why it should hire you.

A smile at an interview makes the employer perceive of you as intelligent!

6. **Do show you are flexible and adaptable.**

   An employer is looking for someone who can contribute to his organization in a flexible, adaptable way. No matter what skills and training you have, employers know every new employee must go through initiation and training on the company's turf. Certainly show pride in your past accomplishments in a specific, factual way ("I saved my last employer $50.00 a week by a new cost-cutting measure I developed"). But don't come across as though there's nothing about the job you couldn't easily handle.

7. **Do ask intelligent questions about the employer's business.**

   An employer is hiring someone because of certain business needs. Show interest in those needs. Asking questions to get a better idea of the employer's needs will help you "stand out" from other candidates interviewing for the job.

8. **Do "take charge" when the interviewer "falls down" on the job.**

   Go into every interview knowing the three or four points about yourself you want the interviewer to remember. And be prepared to take an active part in leading the discussion if the interviewer's "canned approach" does not permit you to display your "strong suit." You can't always depend on the interviewer's asking you the "right" questions so you can stress your strengths and accomplishments.

An important "don't": Don't ask questions about salary or benefits at the first interview.
Employers don't take warmly to people who look at their organization as just a place to satisfy salary and benefit needs. Don't risk making a negative impression by appearing greedy or self-serving. The place to discuss salary and benefits is normally at the second interview, and the employer will bring it up. Then you can ask questions without appearing excessively interested in what the organization can do for you.

Now...negotiating your salary
Even if an ad requests that you communicate your "salary requirement" or "salary history," you should avoid providing those numbers in your initial cover letter. You can usually say something like this: "I would be delighted to discuss the private details of my salary history with you in person."

Once you're at the interview, you must avoid even appearing *interested* in salary before you are offered the job. Make sure you've "sold" yourself before talking salary. First show you're the "best fit" for the employer and then you'll be in a stronger position from which to negotiate salary. **Never** bring up the subject of salary yourself. Employers say there's no way you can avoid looking greedy if you bring up the issue of salary and benefits before the company has identified you as its "best fit."

Interviewers sometimes throw out a salary figure at the first interview to see if you'll accept it. You may not want to commit yourself if you think you will be able to negotiate a better deal later on. Get back to finding out more about the job. This lets the interviewer know you're interested primarily in the job and not the salary.

When the organization brings up salary, it may say something like this: "Well, Mary, we think you'd make a good candidate for this job. What kind of salary are we talking about?" You may not want to name a number here, either. Give the ball back to the interviewer. Act as though you hadn't given the subject of salary much thought and respond something like this: "Ah, Mr. Jones, I wonder if you'd be kind enough to tell me what salary you had in mind when you advertised the job?" Or ... "What is the range you have in mind?"

Employers are seeking people with good attitudes whom they can train and coach to do things their way.

Don't appear excessively interested in salary and benefits at the interview.

Don't worry, if the interviewer names a figure that you think is too low, you can say so without turning down the job or locking yourself into a rigid position. The point here is to negotiate for yourself as well as you can. You might reply to a number named by the interviewer that you think is low by saying something like this: "Well, Mr. Lee, the job interests me very much, and I think I'd certainly enjoy working with you. But, frankly, I was thinking of something a little higher than that." That leaves the ball in your interviewer's court again, and you haven't turned down the job either, in case it turns out that the interviewer can't increase the offer and you still want the job.

Salary negotiation can be tricky.

Last, send a follow-up letter.

Mail, e-mail, or fax a letter right after the interview telling your interviewer you enjoyed the meeting and are certain (if you are) that you are the "best fit" for the job. The people interviewing you will probably have an attitude described as either "professionally loyal" to their companies, or "maternal and proprietary" if the interviewer also owns the company. In either case, they are looking for people who want to work for *that* company in particular. The follow-up letter you send might be just the deciding factor in your favor if the employer is trying to choose between you and someone else. You will see an example of a follow-up letter on page 16.

A follow-up letter can help the employer choose between you and another qualified candidate.

A cover letter is an essential part of a job hunt or career change.

Many people are aware of the importance of having a great resume, but most people in a job hunt don't realize just how important a cover letter can be. The purpose of the cover letter, sometimes called a **"letter of interest,"** is to introduce your resume to prospective employers. The cover letter is often the critical ingredient in a job hunt because the cover letter allows you to say a lot of things that just don't "fit" on the resume. For example, you can emphasize your commitment to a new field and stress your related talents. The cover letter also gives you a chance to stress outstanding character and personal values. On the next two pages you will see examples of very effective cover letters.

A cover letter is an essential part of a career change.

Please do not attempt to implement a career change without a cover letter such as the ones you see in Part Two of this book. A cover letter is the first impression of you, and you can influence the way an employer views you by the language and style of your letter.

Special help for those in career change

We want to emphasize again that, especially in a career change, the cover letter is very important and can help you "build a bridge" to a new career. A creative and appealing cover letter can begin the process of encouraging the potential employer to imagine you in an industry other than the one in which you have worked.

As a special help to those in career change, there are resumes and cover letters included in this book which show valuable techniques and tips you should use when changing fields or industries. The resumes and cover letters of career changers are identified in the table of contents as "Career Change" and you will see the "Career Change" label on cover letters in Part Two where the individuals are changing careers.

Date

Exact Name of Person
Exact Title of Person
Company Name
Address
City, State Zip

Dear Sir or Madam:

    With the enclosed resume, I would like to make you aware of my strong desire to become a part of your organization.

    As you will see from my resume, I recently earned my Bachelor of Science in Fashion Merchandising degree at the University of Georgia. Since it has always been my childhood dream to become a prominent merchandiser in a retail environment, my college graduation was an especially meaningful event in my life.

    While earning my college degree, I completed internships with major retailers, and I successfully assumed the duties of an assistant merchandising manager, buyer, and merchandiser. During one of those internships, under the guidance of an experienced general manager, I wrote a strategic plan for introducing new electronics products which was recommended for review by senior officials.

    In summer jobs while earning my college degree, I held part-time jobs as a retail sales clerk and professional actor. I have been fortunate to live in a state which is the third most active in filmmaking, and I have been used as an extra in various movies filmed in North Carolina. That professional acting experience has greatly refined my communication skills and has enabled me to become a self-confident professional.

    If you can use a highly motivated young professional with unlimited personal initiative as well as strong personal qualities of dependability and trustworthiness, I hope you will contact me to suggest a time when we might meet to discuss your needs. I can provide excellent personal and professional references, and I am eager to apply my natural creativity and merchandising knowledge to benefit an outstanding firm.

          Sincerely,

          Melanie Thompson

Alternate final paragraph:
    I hope you will welcome my call soon when I contact you to try to arrange a brief meeting to discuss your needs and how my talents might help you. I appreciate whatever time you could give me in the process of exploring your needs.

Date

Exact Name of Person
Title or Position
Name of Company
Address (number and street)
Address (city, state, and zip)

Dear Exact Name of Person: (or Dear Sir or Madam if answering a blind ad)

I would appreciate an opportunity to talk with you soon about how I could contribute to your organization through my experience in hotel operations and banquet management. I am interested in pursuing opportunities to join your cruise ship team.

You will see from my resume that I began working when I was 16 years old while I was in high school. I became a skilled hospitality industry employee while working in numerous restaurants during the summer, and I had an opportunity to learn from veteran professionals.

Most recently I have worked as Assistant Banquet & Catering Manager for the college where I earned my degree, and I have become experienced in negotiating contracts with vendors. I am held in the highest regard by my current employer and can provide outstanding references at the appropriate time. I have become proficient at the process of hiring, training, and supervising restaurant and banquet workers.

Although I have been offered full-time employment in the banqueting department at my college when I graduate, I have decided to explore career opportunities with the cruiseship industry. I am seeking an employer who can use a highly motivated individual with strong communication skills and an outstanding reputation. I am single and would welcome the opportunity to travel as extensively as your needs require. I hold a valid passport.

If you can use a self-starter who could rapidly become a valuable part of your organization, I hope you will contact me to suggest a time when we might meet to discuss your needs and how I might serve them. I can provide outstanding references.

Sincerely,

Lonnie Patton

cc: Thomas Crane

Semi-blocked Letter

Date

Three blank spaces

Address

Salutation

One blank space

Body

One blank space

Signature

cc: Indicates you are sending a copy of the letter to someone

Date

Exact Name of Person
Title or Position
Name of Company
Address (number and street)
Address (city, state, and zip)

Follow-up Letter

A great follow-up letter
can motivate the
employer
to make the job offer,
and the salary offer may
be influenced by the
style and tone of your
follow-up
letter, too!

Dear Exact Name:

I am writing to express my appreciation for the time you spent with me on 9 December, and I want to let you know that I am sincerely interested in the position of Controller which you described.

I feel confident that I could skillfully interact with your 60-person work force in order to obtain the information we need to assure expert controllership of your diversified interests, and I would cheerfully travel as your needs require. I want you to know, too, that I would not consider relocating to Salt Lake City to be a hardship! It is certainly one of the most beautiful areas I have ever seen.

As you described to me what you are looking for in a controller, I had a sense of "déjà vu" because my current boss was in a similar position when I went to work for him. He needed someone to come in and be his "right arm" and take on an increasing amount of his management responsibilities so that he could be freed up to do other things. I have played a key role in the growth and profitability of his multi-unit business, and he has come to depend on my sound financial and business advice as much as my day-to-day management skills. Since Christmas is the busiest time of the year in the restaurant business, I feel that I could not leave him during that time. I could certainly make myself available by mid-January.

It would be a pleasure to work for a successful individual such as yourself, and I feel I could contribute significantly to your restaurant business not only through my accounting and business background but also through my strong qualities of loyalty, reliability, and trustworthiness. I am confident that I could learn Quick Books rapidly, and I would welcome being trained to do things your way.

Yours sincerely,

Jacob Evangelisto

In this section, you will find resumes and cover letters of retailing, modeling, fashion and beauty professionals—and of people who want to work in those fields. How do they differ from other job hunters? Why should there be a book dedicated to people seeking jobs in these areas? Based on more than 20 years of experience in working with job hunters, this editor is convinced that resumes and cover letters which "speak the lingo" of the field you wish to enter will communicate more effectively than language which is not industry specific. This book is designed to help people (1) who are seeking to prepare their own resumes and (2) who wish to use as models "real" resumes of individuals who have successfully launched careers in the restaurant, food service, or hotel field or who have advanced in the field. You will see a wide range of experience levels reflected in the resumes in this book. Some of the resumes and cover letters were used by individuals seeking to enter the field; others were used successfully by senior professionals to advance in the field.

Newcomers to an industry sometimes have advantages over more experienced professionals. In a job hunt, junior professionals can have an advantage over their more experienced counterparts. Prospective employers often view the less experienced workers as "more trainable" and "more coachable" than their seniors. This means that the mature professional who has already excelled in a first career can, with credibility, "change careers" and transfer skills to other industries.

Retailing, modeling, fashion, and beauty industry professionals might be said to "talk funny." They talk in lingo specific to their field, and you will find helpful examples throughout this book.

Newcomers to the field may have disadvantages compared to their seniors. Almost by definition, the inexperienced professional—the young person who has recently earned a college degree, or the individual who has recently received certifications respected by the industry—is less tested and less experienced than senior managers, so the resume and cover letter of the inexperienced professional may often have to "sell" his or her potential to do something he or she has never done before. Lack of experience in the field she wants to enter can be a stumbling block to the junior manager, but remember that many employers believe that someone who has excelled in anything—academics, for example—can excel in many other fields.

Some advice to inexperienced professionals...
If senior professionals could give junior professionals a piece of advice about careers, here's what they would say: Manage your career and don't stumble from job to job in an incoherent pattern. Try to find work that interests you, and then identify prosperous industries which need work performed of the type you want to do. Learn early in your working life that a great resume and cover letter can blow doors open for you and help you maximize your salary.

Special help for career changers...
For those changing careers, you will find useful the resumes and cover letters marked "Career Change" on the following pages. Consult the Table of Contents for page numbers showing career changers.

Date

Exact Name of Person
Title or Position
Name of Company
Address (no., street)
Address (city, state, zip)

ASSISTANT BOOKSTORE MANAGER
for Barnes and Noble

Dear Exact Name of Person: (or Dear Sir or Madam if answering a blind ad.)

I would appreciate an opportunity to talk with you soon about how I could contribute to your organization through my purchasing, financial management, and inventory control experience, along with my excellent public relations and writing skills.

As you will see from my resume, I excelled in the business administration program at Eastern College, graduating *cum laude*. My coursework emphasized personnel, financial, and production management in addition to business policy and strategic planning.

You would find me to be an organized, results-oriented professional who works well with others and who also has a special knack for working with numbers. I sincerely enjoy contributing to my employer's "bottom line."

I hope you will welcome my call soon to arrange a brief meeting at your convenience to discuss your current and future needs and how I might serve them. Thank you in advance for your consideration.

Sincerely yours,

Andrea J. Hopkins

Alternate last paragraph:
I hope you will call or write me soon to suggest a time convenient for us to meet and discuss your current and future needs and how I might best serve them. Thank you in advance for your time.

ANDREA JOY HOPKINS

1110½ Hay Street, Fayetteville, NC 28305　　•　　preppub@aol.com　　•　　(910) 483-6611

OBJECTIVE	To benefit an organization through my purchasing, financial management, and inventory experience, along with my excellent communication and organizational skills.
EDUCATION	**B.S.** in **Business Administration/Finance**, Eastern College, St. Davids, PA, 2001. • Completed a rigorous degree program in 3 1/2 years with a 3.33 GPA, graduated *Cum Laude*. • Awarded a **Certificate of Achievement** for maintaining exceptional scholarship.
EXPERIENCE	**ASSISTANT BOOKSTORE MANAGER**. Barnes and Noble, Philadelphia, PA (2003-present). In this fast-paced position, conduct day-to-day financial transactions and supervise up to 10 employees at one of the nation's largest retail booksellers. • Responsible for store operations, including loss prevention, in-store audits, cash handling and reconciliation. Assist with set-up and opening of new stores. • Developed an effective style in dealing fairly and patiently with the public in both sales and customer relations. • Acquired skills in marketing, merchandising displays, and personnel administration. • Gained professional poise while learning to use my time effectively. **MERCHANDISE MANAGER**. The White Shop at the Hilton, Erie, PA (2002-03). Played a key role in the set-up and opening of this popular retail clothing store. • Gained valuable "hands-on" experience in business administration, cash flow, and inventory control management. • Supervised up to eight employees in planning and executing daily operations. • Acquired skills in clothing merchandising and marketing. **RETAIL MANAGER**. Michael's Designs, Erie, PA (1999-02). Supervised day staff and managed inventory while developing a loyal clientele for this retail business. • Assisted management in most facets of branch operation. • Applied my creative design skills in developing decorations for both individual customers and business promotions. • Gained valuable skills in buying, ordering, and merchandising store product. **MANAGER'S AIDE**. Pier Imports, Davids, PA (1996-99). With little or no supervision, handled numerous details in the daily operations of this retail business. • Supervised and managed a small staff of 3 to 4 people. • Learned how to handle cash transactions quickly and accurately. • Responsible for daily bank deposits and drawer reconciliations. *Highlights of other experience*: • Tutor, Fairley High School, St. Davids, PA (1995-1996). Created and used lesson plans to teach three dyslexic children. • Special events volunteer, Braxton County United Way, St. Davids, PA (1995). Developed my public relations and communication skills during the planning and coordinating of special events.
COMPUTERS	Have experience with Microsoft Word, Excel, PowerPoint, and PageMaker.
PERSONAL	Am a self-directed innovative thinker with high personal and professional standards. Work well under pressure and enjoy working closely with others to achieve a common goal.

Exact Name of Person
Title or Position
Name of Company
Address (no., street)
Address (city, state, zip)

ASSISTANT MANAGER
for the Wal-Mart
Corporation

Dear Exact Name of Person: (or Dear Sir or Madam if answering a blind ad.)

I would appreciate an opportunity to talk with you soon about how I could contribute to your organization through my versatile experience in retailing and product line management, customer service and public relations, as well as sales, inventory control, and financial management.

As you will see from my resume, I am currently enjoying a track record of promotion within the Wal-Mart Corporation, which is grooming me for further rapid promotion into store management. Since graduating from the Marymount University of Arlington, Virginia with a B.A. degree, I have become a valuable asset to Wal-Mart and have been commended for my creativity, resourcefulness, and problem-solving ability.

After doing well at stores in several states, I was selected for special assignments related to troubleshooting a "problem" store, starting up new Wal-Marts, and reengineering existing operations. I am known for the careful eye I keep on the bottom line, and I am proud that in my current store the area I manage has shown increasing profitability while several other store areas have been sluggish.

I credit one of my early jobs with teaching me much about management and motivation. In one grueling summer job with the Byrd Enterprises Inc., I sold books door to door and essentially excelled in an entrepreneurial role through hard work and personal stamina. Of the more than 30 sales representatives that started that summer, I was one of the 22 who returned, and I came away from that job with a renewed awareness that a positive mental attitude is the key to success in most areas of life.

If we meet in person, I feel confident that you would find me to be an enthusiastic and congenial individual who offers highly refined skills in getting along with people. I believe I have learned how to strike a balance between aggressively pushing sales and profitability while maintaining excellent working relationships with customers, employees, and vendors. I am certain I could make valuable contributions to your organization as I have to Wal-Mart.

I hope you will welcome my call soon when I try to arrange a brief meeting at your convenience to discuss your current and future needs and how I might serve them. Thank you in advance for you time.

Sincerely yours,

Tyler J. Nahra

TYLER J. NAHRA

1110½ Hay Street, Fayetteville, NC 28305 • preppub@aol.com • (910) 483-6611

OBJECTIVE

To benefit an organization that can use a dedicated young professional who offers versatile skills in sales, customer service, and product line management along with experience in computer operations, inventory control, and retailing.

EDUCATION

Earned a **B.A. in Political Science**, Marymount University, Arlington, VA, 1998.

EXPERIENCE

Have excelled in the following track record of promotion within the Wal-Mart Corporation at stores in VA, TX, and SC (2003-present):

2003-present: ASSISTANT MANAGER. At store #5165 in Richmond, VA, store #4684 in Houston TX, and store #4712 in Charleston, SC, am responsible for all aspects of softlines merchandising including sales, special promotions, displays, stock rotation, filling, and stockroom management.

- Experienced an increased growth rate in softline goods even while sales of other store products were sluggish. Continuously meet all targeted goals for gross sales, and am being groomed for promotion into store management.
- As a Closing Manager, am frequently the only person in the store late at night and must often make decisions that maintain customer goodwill while observing company policy.
- Work with vendors representing product lines from many companies. Monitor planning, ordering, receiving, stocking, displaying, and rotation with a "bottom line" orientation.
- Utilize company software for inventory ordering and control purposes.

2002-03: FASHIONS MANAGER. After excelling in the Richmond, VA, store, was selected to troubleshoot operations and profitability problems in the Charleston, SC, store; greatly contributed to this store's timely opening through my expertise, dedication, and hard work.

- After being placed in charge of personnel, effectively handled the hiring, firing, training, and scheduling of personnel while also troubleshooting problems in these areas:

merchandising and layout	sales promotions	freight unloading
inventory control	theft and pilferage control	inventory purchasing

- Was credited with producing valuable bottom-line results.

2000-02: ASSISTANT FASHIONS MANAGER. While working as an Operations Assistant and being groomed for promotion into softlines and store management positions, learned the "nuts and bolts" of retailing behind the scenes.

- Was responsible for stockrooms; oversaw the transport of freight to the store floor; handled damaged goods including paperwork; labeled counters; signed racks.

2000: ASSISTANT PROJECT COORDINATOR. Was specially selected to assist project coordinators in various locations while being based in Houston, TX.

- Coordinated the building and refurbishment of new and old Wal-Marts. Worked with carpenters, electricians, service representatives, store personnel, and company executives.

Other experience:

- Worked briefly as an Assistant Manager at Home Depot and learned to handle every detail of retail management.
- As an Orders Operator with Virginia Medical Supplies Company, worked in the front office and in the warehouse.

PERSONAL

Am single and will relocate according to my employer's needs. Can provide outstanding personal and professional references. Believe in the relentless pursuit of excellence.

CAREER CHANGE

Date

Exact Name
Title or Position
Name of Company
Address (no., street)
Address (city, state, zip)

ASSISTANT SALES MANAGER

with the Lerner Store Chain. This individual plans to change careers into the accounting field.

Dear Exact Name of Person: (or Dear Sir or Madam if answering a blind ad.)

I would appreciate an opportunity to talk with you soon about how I could contribute to your organization through my education in accounting as well as through my experience related to retail management, customer service, and sales.

I attend Jacksonville University majoring in Business Administration with a concentration in Accounting, as you will see from my resume. I enjoy working with figures and have always excelled in math. As a junior high and high school student I studied in an accelerated math program and was recognized throughout school for my aptitude for math and interest in accounting.

My experience in retail management has given me opportunities to apply my mathematical skills and accounting education by processing deposits, handling payroll accounts, balancing registers, and maintaining records in multimillion-dollar operations.

I am a mature hard-working young professional who offers extensive customer service and sales experience to complement my office, training, and management abilities.

I hope you will call or write soon to suggest a time convenient for us to meet and discuss your current and future needs and how I might serve them. Thank you in advance for your time.

Sincerely yours,

LaFonda Costner

LAFONDA T. COSTNER

1110½ Hay Street, Fayetteville, NC 28305　　•　　preppub@aol.com　　•　　(910) 483-6611

OBJECTIVE

To apply my education and experience related to accounting to an organization that can use a hard-working young professional with a proven talent for working with figures as well as customer service and management abilities.

EDUCATION

Am studying **Business Administration** with a concentration in **Accounting**, Jacksonville University, Jacksonville, FL, degree anticipated 2004.
Was an honor student at Winter Park High School, Winter Park, FL.
- Placed in accelerated math program from seventh grade through high school.
- Graduated in the top 10% and was a Beta Club member for five years.
- Maintained a perfect 100% average in accounting all through high school.

EXPERIENCE

Advanced in the following "Track Record" with the Lerner Store Chain:
2003-present: ASSISTANT SALES MANAGER. Jacksonville, FL. Was promoted to assist in managing a $1 million-dollar store and handle numerous functional areas such as merchandising, opening and closing the store, interviewing and hiring new employees, controlling inventory, and managing seven employees.
- Process deposits, handled payroll accounting, and balanced registers. Manage a "bad check" account: contacted people and completed paperwork.
- Conduct customer service training for new employees.
- Played a key role in the store's recognition as "the best" of eight.

2002-03: STORE SALES MANAGER. Jacksonville, FL. Was promoted from associate manager to supervise eight people in a million-dollar store. Increased sales 30%.

2000-02: ASSOCIATE SALES MANAGER. Tampa, FL. Filled in during absences of the manager; supervised 30 employees in a $3 million-dollar store.

1997-00: STORE SALES MANAGER. Tampa, FL. Was placed in charge of an eight-employee store which had been without a manager for several months.
- Guided the store to its first sales increase in more than a year.

Other experience:
DEPARTMENT MANAGER. Jean Nicole's Fashions, Daytona Beach, FL (1996-97). Was promoted from sales clerk to control operations in a $1 million-dollar store with ten employees; made bank deposits and balanced registers.
- Was selected as the interim manager for a $1.5 million-dollar store with 20 employees.

SALES AND CUSTOMER SERVICE SPECIALIST. Jean Nicole's Fashions, Winter Park, FL (1994-96). Worked with customers to help them find the items they were looking for in addition to handling inventory control. Learned procedures for operating cash registers, making sales, and providing good service in a retail environment.

ACCOUNTS RECEIVABLE CLERK. M. M. Kahn, Winter Park, FL (1994). Hired on a temporary basis to fill in for an ill employee, was asked to stay for the entire summer.
- Handled hundreds of thousands of dollars in payments daily, made deposits, applied payments to the proper invoices, compared computer listings to amounts received, and prepared daily balance sheets.

PERSONAL

Knowledgeable use of IBM registers, Microsoft Word, and Excel.

Date

Exact Name of Person
Title or Position
Name of Company
Address (no., street)
Address (city, state, zip)

ASSISTANT SHOE STORE MANAGER

for the Rack Room

Dear Exact Name of Person: (or Dear Sir or Madam if answering a blind ad.)

Can you use an aggressive young manager and sales professional with a background in high-volume retail sales environments and a reputation as a "go getter" who excels in developing employees, increasing sales, and creating interesting merchandising displays?

Through training and experience, I have built a work history which includes training and supervising up to 25 employees while controlling inventory, directing merchandising, coordinating sales and payroll, and opening/closing stores.

I am presently an Assistant Manager for the Rack Room in Jersey City, NJ, where I am refining managerial and supervisory abilities while further refining time management, sales, and merchandising skills in a busy "better" shoe store. As you will see from my resume, I also have exposure in clothing and intimate apparel settings.

I hope you will welcome my call soon to arrange a brief meeting at your convenience to discuss your current and future needs and how I might serve them. Thank you in advance for your time.

Sincerely yours,

Helen T. Dotson

Alternate last paragraph:
I hope you will call or write soon to suggest a time convenient for us to meet and discuss your current and future needs and how I might serve them. Thank you in advance for your time.

HELEN THERESA DOTSON

1110½ Hay Street, Fayetteville, NC 28305   •   preppub@aol.com   •   (910) 483-6611

OBJECTIVE   To contribute managerial, sales, training, and motivational abilities in a retail management position where my experience in high-volume retail sales environments will be beneficial to a company that can use a flexible "go getter" who adapts easily to new situations.

EDUCATION   **B.A. in Business Management**, Thomas Edison State College, Trenton NJ, 2001.

EXPERIENCE   **ASSISTANT SHOE STORE MANAGER.** The Rack Room, Jersey City, NJ (2003-present). Was moved from the Trenton location to help build up a store with "sagging" sales; am applying my skills and knowledge in areas including training and supervising employees in a high-quality shoe store.
- Sold an average of $3,000 in merchandise a week in a store which has reached a quarter million dollar level in annual sales. Supervise approximately 20 employees with additional time spent in preparing payroll figures and overseeing inventory control.
- Gained experience in developing and setting up attractive merchandise displays.
- Learned the importance and proper methods of fitting children's shoes.

RETAIL MANAGEMENT TRAINEE. Parisienne's, Trenton, NJ (2002-2003). Handled functional operations including making bank deposits, opening and closing the store, and preparing payroll for an average of 10 employees in this store specializing in "moderate-range" men's wear; measured suits for alterations.
- Contributed to repeat sales through my well-developed skills.
- Used creativity and an understanding of merchandising to prepare displays.

DEPARTMENTAL SUPERVISOR. Halston's, Trenton, NJ (1999-2002). Polished time management skills while overseeing operations and supervising and preparing time cards for around 20 employees in four departments.
- Gained knowledge of inventory control procedures while accepting and in-processing shipments of new merchandise.
- Received additional experience in floor management as well as merchandising.
- Was invited to share my knowledge as a sponsor for high school students who were members of the Distributive Education Clubs of America (DECA).

CO-MANAGER. The Limited, Trenton, NJ (1997-1999). As co-manager, shared the supervision and managerial responsibilities in a 15-employee women's intimate apparel location. Developed excellent organizational and time management skills while training employees, supervising sales associates, and preparing payroll.

ASSISTANT MANAGER and **SALES ASSOCIATE.** Sak's Fifth Avenue, New York City, NY (1994-1997). Displayed my adaptability while progressing from a sales position to assist the manager of the intimate apparel and children's departments.
- Was selected to run the specialty Christmas Shop for the 1997 season which gave me increased opportunities to create attractive displays.

Other experience: Summer jobs as a camp counselor, retail sales associate, receptionist.

TRAINING   Completed corporate training programs emphasizing customer relations, management.

PERSONAL   Am very effective in training employees and helping them develop their own abilities. Offer exceptionally strong sales skills and the proven ability to motivate others.

Exact Name of Person
Title or Position
Name of Company
Address (no., street)
Address (city, state, zip)

AUTO PARTS STORE MANAGER
for Advance Auto Parts

Dear Exact Name of Person: (or Dear Sir or Madam if answering a blind ad.)

With the enclosed resume, I would like to confidentially express my interest in exploring management opportunities in your organization. I can provide outstanding references at the appropriate time, and I am held in the highest regard and am considered to be on the "fast track" by my current employer. However, I would ask that you treat my interest in your organization in confidence until we have a chance to talk in person.

As you will see from my enclosed resume, I began my retail management career with Champs Athletic Store where I was a Manager in Training and Assistant Manager. I developed excellent retail management skills while working for the largest athletic footwear retailer in the country.

In 2003, I was recruited by Advance Auto Parts, and I have been promoted from Sales Associate, to Commercial Specialist and Assistant Manager, to Store Manager. I am currently being groomed for promotion into higher management levels.

As a Store Manager, I have made numerous contributions to several stores. At the Advance Auto Parts store in Macon, I managed 20 employees and a $1.5 million annual sales volume while transforming that store into a model operation which hosted the district's Leadership Training seminars. On my own initiative, I prospected for outside commercial accounts and brought them up to a sufficient volume. As a Commercial Specialist, I managed to handle and grow that segment of Advance's business. I personally have won numerous sales awards within Advance Auto Parts, and I have trained employees in techniques designed to boost sales and maximize profitability.

One of my strong abilities is the ability to troubleshoot problems, and recently I have been selected to take over the management of a troubled store in Columbus. I am already correcting numerous problems related to inventory and shrink, personnel and staffing, store standards, as well as sales and profitability.

If you can use a top producer to join your management team, I hope you will contact me to suggest a time when we might meet to discuss your needs. Thank you in advance for your time.

Sincerely,

Victor W. Jennings, Jr.

VICTOR WILLIAM JENNINGS, JR.

1110½ Hay Street, Fayetteville, NC 28305   •   preppub@aol.com   •   (910) 483-6611

OBJECTIVE

To benefit a company that can use an experienced retail manager who has enjoyed a track record of rapid promotion based on my ability to troubleshoot problems, select and train quality employees, control inventory and reduce shrink, and increase sales.

EDUCATION

A.A., in Business Administration, Macon State College, Macon, GA, 2001.
Was selected for intensive **leadership training** sponsored by Advance Auto Parts, 2003.
- Only the top store managers across the U.S. were chosen for this elite training in Atlanta emphasizing recruiting, interviewing, and hiring of employees as well as other topics.

Completed extensive **retail management training** sponsored by Champs Athletic Wear, 2002.
Completed **product service management training,** General Electric, 2000.

EXPERIENCE

AUTO PARTS STORE MANAGER. Advance Auto Parts, locations in Columbus, Savannah, and Macon, GA (2003-present). Began with Advance Auto Parts as a Sales Associate, then advanced to Commercial Specialist and Assistant Manager, and then was promoted to Store Manager; am being groomed for further promotion to higher management levels.
- At the Macon store, manage 20 employees and a store with sales of $1.5 million yearly; establish many commercial accounts and manage a Commercial Specialist to prospect for and serve large outside commercial accounts.
- After we transformed the Macon store into what was considered a "model" operation, we created and hosted Leadership Training seminars for management in the district.
- Recently was handpicked to troubleshoot and correct a wide variety of problems at the Columbus store, which has 18 employees producing $1.75 million yearly in sales; corrected numerous problems related to plan-o-grams, staffing, and loss prevention.
- Have distinguished myself within Advance Auto Parts for excellent skills related to inventory control; while the district goal is 1.4% shrink, I have averaged 1.1% shrink. At the Abercorn Road store in Savannah, reduced shrink from 2.3% to .97%. Achieved this change through rigorous analyzing paperwork, conducting physical audits to assess truck shortages, and performing intensive follow-through of inventory credits.
- Have become skilled at recruiting, hiring, training, and managing employees as well as retraining employees in sales, and store standards which led to winning sales contests.
- Won Shrinkage Reduction Awards for catching shoplifters and warehouse shortages.

MANAGER IN TRAINING. Champs Athletic Store, Atlanta, Savannah, Macon, and Columbus (2001-03). Have developed excellent retail management skills while working for the largest athletic footwear retailer in the country after graduating from Macon State.
- At the Macon location, developed excellent retail selling and customer service skills; fine-tuned my retail management skills in a $3 million per year store.
- In Atlanta, Savannah, and Macon, served as Assistant Manager; opened and closed the store, handled shipping and receiving, and managed store operations including personnel and finance; refined merchandising, marketing, and recruiting techniques.

Highlights of other experience:
PAYROLL CLERK. U. S. Post Office. Macon, GA (1998-00). Worked in finance processing payroll for 3,000 employees and also handled responsibilities related to training employees.

COMPUTER SKILLS

Computer-related coursework included PASCAL, BASIC, and RPG languages. Working knowledge of Microsoft Word, Excel, Access and PowerPoint.

PERSONAL

Highly motivated self starter and go getter. Outstanding personal and professional references.

Date

Exact Name of Person
Exact Title
Exact Name of Company
Address
City, State, Zip

**BEAUTY CONSULTANT
with Fashion
Merchandising Degree**
working for Dillard's
department store

Dear Exact Name of Person (or Dear Sir or Madam if answering a blind ad)

With the enclosed resume, I would like to make you aware of my extensive cosmetics and cosmetology knowledge as well as my desire to put that knowledge to work for your organization in some role in which I could contribute to your bottom line.

As you will see from my resume, I have completed extensive training related to numerous premier-line cosmetics courses and seminars from cosmetic industry firms such as Revlon, Fashion Fair, Infusium and Clairol. I am an Louisiana State Board licensed Cosmetologist, and I am the graduate of a 1500-hour Cosmetology certification course. I also hold an Associate of Arts degree in Fashion Merchandising.

Currently working as a freelance Beauty Consultant/Makeup Artist, I worked previously for Dillards in Louisiana, where I created innovative displays and merchandising concepts while coordinating fashion shows and special events to market Fashion Fair products. I also worked for Merle Norman Cosmetics from 2000-03 in New Orleans, where I played a key role in the sales team which generated the highest sales within the company.

In earlier experience in the cosmetology industry, I excelled as a Cosmetologist with Macias Angela's Hair Design in Monroe, LA and I also worked as a Salon Manager and Cosmetologist. While at the Hilton Hotel & Salon, I interviewed and hired employees while managing all aspects of a salon catering to high-end customers.

If you can use my considerable customer service experience as well as my expertise in all aspects of cosmetology, I hope you will contact me to suggest a time when we might meet to discuss your needs. I can assure you in advance that I can provide excellent references.

Sincerely,

Amelia J. Pennington

AMELIA J. PENNINGTON

1110½ Hay Street, Fayetteville, NC 28305 • preppub@aol.com • (910) 483-6611

OBJECTIVE   To benefit an organization that can use an enthusiastic young professional with exceptional communication and organizational skills who offers a track record of accomplishment as a premier-lines cosmetics advisor, consultant, aesthetician, and salon manager.

EDUCATION   **Associate of Arts in Fashion Merchandising**, Delgado Community College, New Orleans, LA, 2002.

Graduated from 1500-hour Cosmetology certification course, Monroe Technical College, Monroe, LA 1996.

Completed numerous premiere-lines cosmetics courses and seminars, including:
- *Revlon Beauty Seminar,* 40-hour course in product line, sales, and productivity, 1996.
- *Fashion Fair Cosmetics Beauty Seminars,* 120 hours; trained in proper application, developed knowledge of product lines, learned sales and merchandising techniques.
- *New Image Color Class,* 80 hours; learned application, product lines, sales techniques.
- *Infusium Hair Academy,* 160 hours; trained in product lines, sales techniques, and proper application of Infusium Cosmetics products.
- *Clairol Color Class & Color Analysis,* 80 hours; learned hair coloring, highlighting, and color-matching techniques.

EXPERIENCE   **BEAUTY CONSULTANT & MAKEUP ARTIST.** Monroe, LA (2003-present). Freelance.

BEAUTY ADVISOR and **FREELANCE MAKEUP ARTIST.** Dillard's, New Orleans, LA (2003). Performed cosmetic makeovers and facials, presenting Fashion Fair's premier line of cosmetics to customers and training them in proper techniques for applying makeup.
- Created innovative and effective displays and merchandising concepts; coordinated fashion shows and other special events to present Fashion Fair products.
- Developed strong relationships with clients, generating repeat customers and sales of Fashion Fair products; met or exceeded all store, district, and regional sales quotas.
- Provided service to Fashion Fair clients, averaging eight makeovers per 4-hour shift.

MARKETING REPRESENTATIVE. Merle Norman, Monroe, LA (2000-03). Performed inventory control, merchandising, customer service, bookkeeping, and events promotion while professionally representing Fashion Fair's premiere line of cosmetics.
- Provided makeovers, manicures, facials, and Personal Image Consulting to new and existing Fashion Fair customers, generating sales of premiere line cosmetics; developed innovative merchandising and marketing strategies, arranging fashion shows and other special events to promote the company's products and services.
- Was a key member of a sales team which generated the highest sales of all Merle Norman stores in the United States; met and exceeded all weekly sales quotas.

COSMETOLOGIST. Macias Angela Hair Design, Monroe, LA (1998-00). Provided a full range of cosmetology, hair care, manicure/pedicure, and therapeutic massage services.

SALON MANAGER and **COSMETOLOGIST.** Hilton Hotel & Salon, Monroe, LA (1996-1998). Interviewed, hired, and trained all new employees; managed inventory; ordered supplies.

AFFILIATIONS   Member, Monroe Area Chamber of Commerce, 1999-2003.
Patron, Louisiana Museum of Arts, 1996-1999.

PERSONAL   Excellent personal and professional references are available upon request.

Exact Name of Person
Title or Position
Name of Company
Address (no., street)
Address (city, state, zip)

BUSINESS OFFICE CLERK

for Target in Ohio

Dear Exact Name of Person: (or Dear Sir or Madam if answering a blind ad.)

I would appreciate an opportunity to talk with you soon about how I could contribute to your organization through my education and strong interest in the area of banking and finance.

As you will see from my resume, I attend the University of Toledo where I have completed approximately 75 semester hours. I have maintained a 3.0 GPA while displaying my time management skills working and attending school simultaneously. Majoring in Business with a concentration in Banking and Finance.

During the last five years I advanced in a "track record" of promotions with a division of the retail giant Target. My last position was as a Business Office Clerk following earlier jobs in sales and customer service. Working for this large organization gave me opportunities to learn and increase my practical skills in computer operations and the use of a wide variety of office equipment.

I feel that I am a mature and dependable young professional with a background of adaptability and a talent for problem-solving sure to make me a valuable asset to your organization.

I hope you will welcome my call soon to arrange a brief meeting at your convenience to discuss your current and future needs and how I might serve them. Thank you in advance for your time.

Sincerely yours,

Jamie M. Shoop

Alternate last paragraph:
I hope you will call or write soon to suggest a time convenient for us to meet and discuss your current and future needs and how I might serve them. Thank you in advance for your time.

JAMIE MARIE SHOOP

1110½ Hay Street, Fayetteville, NC 28305   •   preppub@aol.com   •   (910) 483-6611

OBJECTIVE   I want to apply my educational concentration in banking and finance to an organization that can use a young professional with a reputation for outstanding problem-solving, sales, and organizational abilities along with practical computer and office experience.

EDUCATION   **B.S. in Business** with a concentration in **Banking** and **Finance**, University of Toledo, Toledo, OH, 2001.
Completed Principles of Banking (Teller Course), Owens Community College, Toledo, 2000.

EXPERIENCE   *Helped finance my education while gaining practical work experience and advancing in this "track record" with Target in Toledo, OH:*
2003-present: BUSINESS OFFICE CLERK. Am skilled in accounting for maintaining records of large sums of money while handling a variety of day-to-day functions in this retail location's main office.
- Utilize office equipment including the bill counter and check encoder while increasing my speed and skill with the 10-key adding machine.
- Am entrusted with important responsibilities including: counting cash receipts, recording hourly sales figures, encoding checks for deposit, and making deposits.
- Make regular "cash pulls" and counted and recorded them.
- Audit cash registers on a regular basis and make loans to cash registers as needed.

2001-03: CUSTOMER SERVICE SPECIALIST. Polished my "people skills" while accepting and processing individual memberships; prepared monthly budget allocations.
- Named as the "Associate of the Month," was honored for my initiative and leadership skills as well as my initiative in building sales.
- Entered data into the computer system for new members; typed membership cards and took the customer's picture to attach to the card.
- Collected data on the number of new memberships accepted and processed as well as the amounts received and compiled daily reports.
- Increased my typing speed and began to learn to use the 10-key adding machine.

1998-01: SALES REPRESENTATIVE. Represented the company to a broad and diverse section of area businesses while "selling" the advantages of corporate memberships.
- Applied my knowledge of the broad range of merchandise available while communicating with professionals effectively.
- Used my analytical skills and knowledge while making sales projections.

1998: CASHIER. Provided friendly and efficient service to customers while becoming familiar with the store's wide range of merchandise.
- Became skilled in maintaining accuracy with no shortages or overages.
- Was honored as "Cashier of the Month" for June 1998 on the basis of my customer service skills and accuracy.

COMPUTER   Offer knowledge of computers and office equipment including the following:
&   Am familiar with Microsoft Word and PageMaker software.
OFFICE   - Use equipment such as 10-key adding machines, typewriters, copiers, fax machines,
SKILLS   check encoding machines, and money/bill counters.

PERSONAL   Completed seminars in franchise operations and business communications. Am known for my ability to remain calm under pressure and handle difficult situations with tact.

Date

Exact Name of Person
Exact Title
Exact Name of Company
Address
City, State, Zip

BUYER

for J. C. Penney's

Dear Exact Name of Person: (or Dear Sir or Madam in answering a blind ad)

With the enclosed resume, I would like to make you aware of my extensive sales, merchandising, and management skills as well as my interest in exploring the possibility of utilizing my experience to benefit your organization.

After earning a B.S. degree (cum laude) from Seattle Pacific University, I was recruited by the J C Penney organization as an Associate Buyer in 1999. I achieved unusually rapid advancement to Buyer after only one year and four months, and since then I have excelled in handling a $10 million volume while buying for 22 stores. The buying function had been handled in New York City for the previous five years, and I instituted a major reorganization of the buying process which led to increased sales.

My sales and gross margin results have been consistently superior, and I have never received anything less than "above average" on annual performance evaluations of my business, sales, marketing, merchandise planning, and inventory control skills. I am well known for my ability to establish and maintain effective working relationships with people at all levels, from top-level buying and merchandising experts in New York City to store managers and vendors in Washington. I pride myself on my ability to react quickly to emerging trends and to respond decisively in averting problems before they happen.

If you can use a dynamic and results-oriented individual with excellent communication skills, I hope you will contact me to suggest a time when we can meet to discuss your goals and needs and how I might help you. I can provide excellent references. Thank you in advance for your time and professional courtesies.

Yours sincerely,

Julia F. Palchek

JULIA FAITH PALCHEK

1110½ Hay Street, Fayetteville, NC 28305　　•　　preppub@aol.com　　•　　(910) 483-6611

OBJECTIVE

I want to contribute to an organization that can use a dynamic and results-oriented young professional who has enjoyed promotion to increasing responsibilities because of an ability to produce outstanding bottom-line results.

EDUCATION

Bachelor of Science Degree in Criminal Justice, cum laude, Seattle Pacific University, Seattle, WA, 2000.
- Named to Social Science Honor Society (Pi Gamma Mu), the freshman Honor Society (Phi Eta Sigma), and Who's Who Among College Students.
- Worked as a Writing Lab Tutor; elected Vice President of Criminal Justice Club; was honored by selection as a University Ambassador.

Excelled in numerous professional development courses related to purchasing, sales, merchandising, and finance sponsored by J.C. Penney Department Stores.

COMPUTERS

Highly proficient with computers including Microsoft Word, Excel, Access, and PowerPoint; utilize LAN to provide timely information; also proficient with all merchandise systems including POM, Markdown, IMS, Store SKU Database, MPO/MPT, and SAR.

EXPERIENCE

Have excelled in the following track record of advancement with J C Penney Department Stores, Seattle, WA (2002-present).
2002-present. BUYER. Was promoted to Buyer because of my exceptional performance as an Associate Buyer. Am now responsible for a $10 million sales volume while buying for the Juniors departments for 22 stores.
- **Superior sales results:** Increased sales 1.1% in 2002 compared to the previous year; am currently showing an 8.9% sales increase in 2003 compared to 2002; reorganized the Juniors area and increased sales after taking over buying which had been handled in New York City for the previous five years.
- **Gross margin increase:** Increased GM from 36.2 in 2002 to 37.1 in 2003.
- **Sales and marketing management:** Consistently maintain "above average" on annual performance evaluations, and have been verbally commended for my insightful sales and marketing management.
- **Business and professional management:** React prudently to changing market trends to maximize sales; work with vendors to build profitable relationships.
- **Merchandise planning and inventory management:** Am skilled in planning and achieving balanced assortments that meet customer demands.

1999-02: ASSOCIATE BUYER. In unusually rapid advancement, was promoted to buyer after only 1 year and four months in this job and was given responsibility for a $10 million sales volume; learned the duties of a buyer while working with Ladies Ready to Wear, Ladies Sportswear, Accessories, Cosmetics, Fragrances, Lingerie, Jewelry, and Hosiery.

Other experience: *Partially financed college education working up to 30 hours a week.*
1997-99: Sales Representative & Sales Support Specialist. The Gap, Seattle, WA. In addition to sales, handled additional responsibilities which included maintaining security and adhering to a strict theft reduction system.

1997 Internship: Seattle Police Department, Seattle, WA. Observed finger printing process, crime scene photography, and subsequent paper work; observed proper police procedures.

PERSONAL

Outstanding decision maker and problem solver who thrives on multiple responsibilities.

Exact Name of Person
Exact Title
Exact Name of Company
Address
City, State, Zip

BUYER, CLOTHING INDUSTRY
for Kohn's Department Store

Dear Exact Name of Person: (or Dear Sir or Madam in answering a blind ad)

    With the enclosed resume, I would like to make you aware of my experience in (and love for) the business of buying, merchandising, and retailing.

    As you will see from my resume, I have been involved in retail buying in various capacities. Currently as a Buyer for Kohn's Department Store, I worked with established retailers as well as startups. I played a key role in the startup of a successful high-end ladies' apparel store in Santa Barbara and handled all the buying while hiring and managing a staff of six. In another job as a Retail Buyer for a 112-year-old store in La Jolla, I worked closely with manufacturers in Los Angeles to develop exclusive merchandise for a retailer of women's and men's clothes.

    In a previous position as a Sales Representative for a Verizon Wireless, I met or exceeded a sales goal of $1.5 million yearly while also participating in trade shows and preparing in-store trunk shows for clients. I have also worked in retailing as a Counter Manager for Lancome, and I managed a crew of three while performing as a certified makeup analyst, planning monthly events for sales promotions, and handling all aspects of sales, inventory, and scheduling.

    Although I have excelled in all my jobs and have thoroughly enjoyed them all, I have held numerous positions in different states because I relocated frequently with my former husband, who was a human resources executive with a Fortune 500 company. I can provide outstanding references from all previous employers.

    I thoroughly enjoy all aspects of the business of selling and merchandising better clothing, and I have developed an extensive network of friends and contacts within the garment industry worldwide. Naturally outgoing with an instinctive sales personality and a flair for fashion merchandising, I am widely respected for my good taste and my fashion "instincts" about the future. I am single and accustomed to working the long hours required to be successful in retail, and I can travel as extensively as your needs require. I have recently relocated to Lake Tahoe, where my extended family lives, and I am excited about being back on my "home turf."

    If my considerable talents and skills interest you, I hope you will contact me by phone to suggest a time when we might meet. I am sure that it would be an honor to be associated with your fine company, and I hope I will have the pleasure of meeting you.

Yours sincerely,

Stephanie C. Parisi

STEPHANIE C. PARISI

1110½ Hay Street, Fayetteville, NC 28305   •   preppub@aol.com   •   (910) 483-6611

OBJECTIVE

I want to contribute to an organization that can use an outgoing and highly effective professional who has excelled in business development through resourcefully applying my strong communication, sales, and relationship-building skills.

EDUCATION

Bachelor of Arts in Elementary Education, University of California, La Jolla, CA, 2002.
Associate of Science in Business Technology, Lake Tahoe Community College, South Lake Tahoe, CA, 2000.
Extensive training related to sales, customer service, merchandising, and buying.

EXPERIENCE

BUYER & SALES ASSOCIATE. Kohn's Department Store, La Jolla, CA, (2002-present). Make numerous regular buying trips to New York and routinely attend trunk shows and style shows while consistently meeting or exceeding sales as a buyer of sportswear and dress apparel while attending college on a full-time basis. Manage a staff of 10.
- Work closely with manufacturers in New York to develop exclusive merchandise for this 112-year-old retail business with two stores of women's and men's clothes.
- Am knowledgeable of retail clothing as well as store operations and purchasing.

SALES REPRESENTATIVE. Verizon Wireless, Lake Tahoe, CA (2001-2002). As a sales rep in a multi-line showroom, met or exceeded sales goal of $1.5 million yearly while also participating in trade shows and preparing in-store trunk shows for clients.
- Handled a heavy volume of phone sales and telephone customer service.

COUNTER MANAGER. Lancome (Macy's-Southland Mall), La Jolla, CA (1999-2001). Managed a crew of three while performing as a certified makeup analyst, planning monthly events for sales promotions, and handling all aspects of sales, inventory, and scheduling.

SALES MANAGER. Allen A. Knoll Publishers, Santa Barbara, CA (1996-1999). Sold patient education materials, such as brochures explaining various illnesses and procedures, to hospitals, clinics, and doctors' offices.
- Established an excellent reputation within the medical community. Gained an understanding of medical terminology while learning how doctors handle buying decisions.

FIRST GRADE TEACHER. Lansing County Schools, Santa Barbara, CA (1994-1996). Served as Grade Level Chairperson during the 1995-96 year; was a First Grade Teacher.

MANAGER & BUYER. Lord & Taylor, Santa Barbara, CA (1993-1994). Played a key role in the start-up of a high-end ladies' apparel store, and then became its primary buyer, which involved frequent buying trips to Los Angeles. Selected, trained, and managed a staff of six.

FIRST GRADE TEACHER. Brisbane Elementary School, Lake Tahoe, CA (1991-1993). Introduced multi-level first grade students to reading and mathematics; individualized the curriculum to encourage the development of each child.

COMPUTERS

Computers: Working knowledge of Microsoft Word, Excel, and Access.
Office Equipment: Operate a variety of equipment used in office operations including calculators, multi-line phones, copiers and fax machines.

PERSONAL

Grew up in Lake Tahoe and have resettled here, where my extended family lives.

Exact Name of Person
Title or Position
Name of Company
Address (no., street)
Address (city, state, zip)

CASHIER
for Home Depot
in Chicago

Dear Exact Name of Person: (or Dear Sir or Madam if answering a blind ad.)

I am happy to provide the copy of the resume which you asked me for, and I am very interested in sitting down with you at your convenience to discuss the possibility of my becoming involved in Best Buy's management training program.

I have long been impressed with your organization's philosophy and corporate style, and it was my deliberate plan after graduating from college with a B.S. degree to join your staff in an entry-level position. My experience in cashiering has given me insight into how important that "front line" job is, since it is the customer's "last impression" of the store and, once the customer is leaving, our main goal is to keep him or her coming back. I have also been involved in customer service as needed.

In a previous position as a Merchandise Manager for Rich's, I was rapidly identified as a young leader and groomed for rapid promotion into management. While training, motivating, supervising, and evaluating a small team of employees, I led our team to be named "the best" in competition with other outstanding communications teams. I won prestigious acknowledgments for my selling expertise and management skills.

You would find me to be a congenial and industrious person who thrives on new challenges and who has a realistic and mature understanding of what is involved in management. I understand that management involves long hours, personal sacrifices, and a willingness to travel and relocate as the company needs.

I look forward to our having the opportunity to sit down to discuss your organization's management training program and how I might become a part of it.

Yours sincerely,

Samuel J. Fowler

SAMUEL J. FOWLER

1110½ Hay Street, Fayetteville, NC 28305 • preppub@aol.com • (910) 483-6611

OBJECTIVE

To contribute to the increasing success and financial health of an organization that can use a hard-working young professional who offers unlimited executive ability and management potential along with experience in sales, customer service, and communications operation.

EDUCATION

A.S., degree in Business Management, Rock Valley College, Rockford, IL, 2003.

EXPERIENCE

CASHIER. Home Depot, Rockford, IL (2003-present). Made the decision to join this company after college graduation because of my admiration for its philosophy and corporate image; have excelled in these and other areas related to store operation:

Cashiering:Have become very aware of the importance of politely and accurately performing the cashiering function since this is the customer's "last impression" of the store and is the "front line" of store operations.

Customer service: Am frequently asked by management to assist customers in answering questions and solving problems.

Employee relations: In my brief time as a part-time employee, have become extremely well-liked and respected by my co-workers; am regarded as a leader by my peers and am sought out on occasion for my counsel on personal and job-related matters. Have gained insight into all aspects of the assistant manager's job, especially the "art" of satisfying customers, keeping them happy, and ensuring that they always come back to Home Depot.

MERCHANDISE MANAGER. Rich's, Chicago, IL (2001-03). Rapidly advanced into management while employed by Rich's. Praised for showing initiative in merchandising projects. Supervised 8 people within the Women's Apparel Department:

Supervision and management: Trained, motivated, supervised, and evaluated eight people on customer service skills, merchandise displays, and transaction operations.

Project management: Was handpicked for numerous storewide merchandise display projects and assignments because of my reputation as a thoroughly reliable hard worker with excellent decision-making and problem-solving skills along with an attitude of "attention to detail."

Inventory control: Accounted for assets valued at $200,000.

Was commended for my leadership in the women's apparel department to be evaluated as Manager of the Month in a competition among nine other merchandising managers.

TRAINING

Completed extensive college-level technical and management training:
- While in college, was involved in a Home Depot sponsored organization known as National Student Awareness Program, which aims to educate the general public on matters including the federal debt, national deficit, and waste public spending.
- In 2001, participated in a six-person panel of students which gave an oral presentation with slides to six judges at Rock Valley College about the budget deficit.
- Also as a member of the Veterans Club, raised money for disaster relief.

COMPUTERS

Working knowledge of computers; familiar with Microsoft Word, Excel and PowerPoint.

PERSONAL

Will provide excellent personal and professional references upon request. Have a mature understanding of the long hours and other personal sacrifices involved in management. Am single and am willing to travel and relocate as needed.

CAREER CHANGE

Date

Exact Name of Person
Exact Title
Exact Name of Company
Address
City, State, Zip

**CLOTHING SALES
REPRESENTATIVE**

for the Limited

Dear Exact Name of Person: (or Dear Sir or Madam if answering a blind ad)

With the enclosed resume, I would like to make you aware of my interest in exploring employment opportunities with your organization. I would like an opportunity to talk with you soon about how I can contribute to your organization through my education and strong interest in the area of merchandising and retail.

As you will see from my resume, I have been working as a Clothing Sales Representative for the Limited in this position, I became skilled at merchandising with planograms; contributed numerous ideas which improved customer relations and boosted repeat business.

I am highly regarded in my current position and have enjoyed contributing my communication skills and management abilities to a profit-making company. While working in previous sales jobs, I became accustomed to having my results measured on the bottom line, and I would like to be a part of dynamic organization with ambitious goals. I am confident that my outgoing personality and ambitious nature would be well suited to an organization which values initiative, discipline, and resourcefulness.

If you can use a hard-working young professional with strong written and oral communication skills, I hope you will contact me soon to suggest a time when we might meet to discuss your needs. I can provide outstanding references at the appropriate time.

Sincerely,

Brenda Menefee

BRENDA S. MENEFEE

1110½ Hay Street, Fayetteville, NC 28305   •   preppub@aol.com   •   (910) 483-6611

OBJECTIVE

To benefit an organization that can use an articulate young professional with strong communication, marketing, and public relations skills who excels in transmitting ideas to others while handling multiple responsibilities and deadlines in a resourceful manner.

EDUCATION

A.A. in English, Trident Technical College, Charleston, SC, 2000.
Graduated from Stratford High School, Charleston, SC, 1997.

EXPERIENCE

CLOTHING SALES REPRESENTATIVE. The Limited, North Charleston, SC (2003-present). Partially financed my college education in this job which strengthened my sales, customer service, merchandising, and inventory control skills.
- Am skilled at merchandising with planograms; contribute numerous ideas which improved customer relations and boosted repeat business.
- Learned the art of fashion merchandising while gaining excellent sales skills.
- Was commended for my strong motivational abilities, and have been strongly encouraged to enter company's management trainee program after college graduation.

ADJUNCT FACULTY MEMBER. Mt. Pleasant High School, Charleston, SC (2002-03). While completing my A.A. degree, worked as an Adjunct Faculty Member; promoted educational programs and registered students for classes; maintained attendance statistics and substituted for teachers in various classes.

SALES REPRESENTATIVE & CUSTOMER SERVICE REPRESENTATIVE. Walgreens, Mt. Pleasant (1999-02). Began working when I was 15 years old, and became a dedicated and reliable employee of this small drug store.
- Was frequently commended by customers for my sunny disposition and helpful style.
- Learned how to merchandise a store for maximum sales and inventory turnover.
- Handled receiving functions; operated a cash register; learned to work well with the public.

ACCOUNT EXECUTIVE. Swedenborg Association, Charleston, SC (1996-98). For a medical publishing company, was involved in performing research and prospecting for advertisers for six different publications; negotiated contracts, set up ads, and handled data entry.

Other experience: *While earning my college degree, worked part-time in these jobs which refined my sales, communication, and customer service skills.*
SALES ASSOCIATE/CASHIER. Belk, Charleston, SC (2002). For this major retailer, sold clothes, opened charge accounts, and operated a multi-line phone system.
FUNDRAISER. Medical University of South Carolina Foundation, Charleston, SC (2001). Called alumni to update them on current events, new building plans, new programs, and special financial needs of the university; sought donations and pledges. Because of my skill in fundraising, was assigned to the university's highest-priority campaign.
- Learned how to be assertive without being pushy.

PERSONAL

Enjoy reading, playing the piano, exercising, listening to music, spending time with family and friends, and writing. Am considered to be "a good listener." Can provide excellent references.

Date

Exact Name of Person
Title or Position
Name of Company
Address (no., street)
Address (city, state, zip)

CLUSTER MANAGER
for Burlington Shoe Store

Dear Exact Name of Person: (or Dear Sir or Madam if answering a blind ad.)

I would appreciate an opportunity to talk with you soon about how I could contribute to your organization through my versatile experience in retailing and product line management, customer service and public relations, as well as sales, inventory control, and financial management.

As you will see from my resume, I am currently enjoying a track record of promotion within the Burlington's Shoe Store, which is grooming me for further rapid promotion into store management. Since graduating from the Lansing Community College with a A.A. degree, I have become a valuable asset to Burlington and have been commended for my creativity, resourcefulness, and problem-solving ability.

I have attended numerous seminars and training programs related to managing nearly every area of retail operations. I have also received a Supervision Certificate from Burlington's Shoe Store and am currently in their District Manager's Training Program. I credit one of my earlier jobs for gaining management and motivational skills. One aspect that is most beneficial in the retail business is realizing that a positive mental attitude is the key to success in most areas of life.

If we meet in person, I feel confident that you would find me to be an enthusiastic and congenial individual who offers highly refined skills in getting along with people. I believe I have learned how to strike a balance between aggressively pushing sales and profitability while maintaining excellent working relationships with customers, employees, and vendors. I am certain I could make valuable contributions to your organization.

I hope you will welcome my call soon when I try to arrange a brief meeting at your convenience to discuss your current and future needs and how I might serve them. Thank you in advance for you time.

Sincerely yours,

Doreen Louise Masterson

Alternate last paragraph:
I hope you will welcome my call soon to arrange a brief meeting at your convenience to discuss your current and future needs and how I might serve them. Thank you in advance for your time.

DOREEN LOUISE MASTERSON

1110½ Hay Street, Fayetteville, NC 28305   •   preppub@aol.com   •   (910) 483-6611

OBJECTIVE   I want to contribute to an organization that can use my management and organizational skills along with my reputation as a resourceful self starter with strong entrepreneurial instincts combined with an aggressive sales attitude.

EDUCATION   **A.A. in Business**, Lansing Community College, Lansing MI, 2000.
Received Supervision Certificate, Burlington Shoe Stores, 2003; am currently in District Manager's Training Program. Have attended numerous seminars and training programs.

EXPERIENCE   **CLUSTER MANAGER.** Burlington Shoe Store, Grand Rapids, MI (2003-present). Have rapidly advanced with this company, and am being groomed for promotion to District Manager.

- Travel with the District Manager or alone to document store visits, oversee special projects, and observe/audit special areas of concern.
- Oversee the operations of three stores in addition to my responsibilities for training managers in 15 different stores; have met or exceeded quarterly sales goals two out of four times and received the "Above and Beyond Duty Award" for the summer of 2004.
- Train and develop managers for placement in stores within 10 weeks; empower managers to successfully operate stores with little supervision. Coordinate training guidelines and follow-on training provided to assure compliance of 15 managers in 15 individual stores.
- Perform troubleshooting in 26 locations and have excelled in correcting problems related to shrinkage, staffing, and general store operations.
- On my own initiative, designed a Training Recap for the entire district which has greatly facilitated the proper development of staff.

ASSISTANT CO-MANAGE. Lerner, Grand Rapids, MI (2002-03). Recruited, hired, and trained new associates in an extensive three-day program; assigned duties to a 27-person staff while directing the fast pace of sales activities.

- Performed a wide range of administrative duties which included making deposits, preparing weekly and monthly paperwork, administering payroll, conducting performance and salary reviews, controlling inventory, organizing and leading store meetings, overseeing assets, and communicating store policies.
- Received 2003 award for "Best performance in a new position." Beat 2002 sales by 33%.

ASSISTANT MANAGER & COLLECTIONS MANAGER. Circuit City, Grand Rapids, MI (1999-02). Performed light accounting while handling the responsibility of approving or denying credit applications; developed financial contracts, started allotments, checked references and established client applications.

- Prepared and distributed collections letters; ran credit checks and handled all areas of collections including CBI and TRW. Developed numerous new forms and documents which became valuable parts of the company's credit and collections systems.
- Achieved seven days of taking in $18,000; consistently beat the previous year's sales.

SALES PACESETTER. Express, Lansing, MI (1998-1999). Began as a Sales Associate and was promoted to Pacesetter and trained for the Assistant Manager Position; set sales pace for this store which became upgraded to a superstore because of its 1999 sales increases.

- Was #4 sales associate in entire nation in sales volume and was #2 in our store's classification volume; was honored with various gifts including a trip to Chicago, IL.

PERSONAL   Skilled in using aggressive sales tactics and pride myself on achieving ambitious sales goals. Known for my ability to motivate, train, and develop others. Strategic thinker.

Exact Name of Person
Title or Position
Name of Company
Address (no., street)
Address (city, state, zip)

**COLLECTIONS AGENT
& ADMINISTRATIVE
ASSISTANT**
for Calhoun Finance
Company

Dear Exact Name of Person: (or Dear Sir or Madam if answering a blind ad.)

I would appreciate an opportunity to talk with you soon about how I could contribute to your organization through my education and strong interest in the area of collections.

As you will see from my resume, I received a B.A. in Business Administration from Emerson College in Boston, Massachusetts. During this time, I took courses in management, finance, and accounting while completing approximately 125 semester hours. I have developed my time management skills working and attending school simultaneously while majoring in Business with a concentration in Finance.

In my current position as a Collections Agent, I successfully applied a variety of resources in order to collect monies for up to 300 accounts per month. Working for this large organization gave me opportunities to learn and increase my practical skills in computer operations and the use of a wide variety of office equipment.

I feel that I am a mature and dependable young professional with a background of adaptability and a talent for problem-solving sure to make me a valuable asset to your organization. I hope you will welcome my call soon to arrange a brief meeting at your convenience to discuss your current and future needs and how I might serve them. Thank you in advance for your time.

Sincerely yours,

LaShonda V. Peltier

Alternate last paragraph:
I hope you will call or write soon to suggest a time convenient for us to meet and discuss your current and future needs and how I might serve them. Thank you in advance for your time.

LASHONDA V. PELTIER

1110½ Hay Street, Fayetteville, NC 28305 • preppub@aol.com • (910) 483-6611

OBJECTIVE

To benefit an organization that can use a dedicated and dependable young professional with proven leadership ability and experience in telemarketing, computer operations, and financial analysis.

EDUCATION

B.A. in Business Administration at Emerson College, Boston, MA, 2002.

EXPERIENCE

COLLECTIONS AGENT and **ADMINISTRATIVE ASSISTANT**. Calhoun Finance Company, Boston, MA (2003-present). Successfully apply a variety of resources in order to collect monies for up to 300 accounts per month including past due auto loan payments and checks with non-sufficient funds while cross-training in the credit department and handling routine clerical duties.

- Reduced bad debts from over 30% to about 3%.
- Develop research skills using a variety of materials such as city directories, cross-reference books, and land records.
- Am an expert at locating people who tried to disappear without paying their bills.
- Significantly increased my ability to "size up" a person's character as well as their ability and willingness to pay their bills.
- Learned valuable computer skills performing data entry daily.
- Process all paper work for accident and health claims, credit life claims, refinance contracts, repo notification, credit bureau inquiries, and small claims court.

COLLECTIONS SUPERVISOR. Financial Independent Group, Boston, MA (2001-03). Because of my outstanding leadership abilities, was rapidly promoted to supervise six employees recovering funds from returned checks for companies such as Walmart, Piggly Wiggly, and Pizza Inn.

- Created a control sheet for balancing computer accounts, accounts receivable, and the cash drawer at the end of each day.
- Trained collectors in telemarketing and in utilizing all resources available including the military chain of command to collect funds for military members who wrote bad checks.
- Was commended for my ability to motivate people to pay bills.
- Exceeded my quota of collecting on 50 checks per week; in one week, collected on 96 checks resulting in $34,000 revenue for the company.
- Played a key role in helping the company grow from two collectors and two managers to six collectors, one data entry employee, and three managers.
- Learned to use an adding machine and most other types of office equipment.

BANK TELLER. First Federal Bank, Boston, MA (1999-01). Became skilled in the accurate handling of cash, money orders, cashier's checks, and bonds in this position held as an internship while also attending high school.

- Learned basic computer operations.
- Was cross-trained in the commercial loans area.

COMPUTERS

Working knowledge Microsoft Word, Excel, and QuickBooks.

PERSONAL

Have a reputation as a friendly and outgoing employee with outstanding communication skills. Give "110%" in any task given to me and have the ability to motivate others to strive to reach my high standards.

CAREER CHANGE

Exact Name of Person (if known)
Title or Position
Name of Company
Address (no., street)
Address (city, state, zip)

**CONTRACTING
MANAGER**

for Access Equipment
Company

Dear Exact Name of Person: (or Dear Sir or Madam)

I would appreciate an opportunity to talk with you soon about how my public relations skills and "results-oriented" approach to management could benefit your organization.

As you will see from my resume, I earned a B.A. in Political Science from the Southwest Missouri State University in Springfield, Missouri. I can also offer extensive management and personnel supervisory experience that I have gained from previous employment with Lowe's as a Sales Area Manager.

In addition, my current experience as a contracting manager has provided me with a keen appreciation of the outstanding results that can be achieved when a flexible, creative, and empathetic approach is brought to managing and motivating others. This, I think, is one of the toughest, yet most rewarding challenges any manager can face. Also, I feel certain that you would find me to be a hard-working and reliable professional who prides myself on doing any job to the best of my ability.

I hope you will call or write me soon to suggest a time convenient for us to meet and discuss your current and future needs and how I might serve them. Thank you in advance for your time.

Sincerely,

Nicole Sheridan Hendrick

NICOLE SHERIDAN HENDRICK

1110½ Hay Street, Fayetteville, NC 28305 • preppub@aol.com • (910) 483-6611

OBJECTIVE

To contribute to an organization that can use a resourceful young professional experienced in contract negotiation, administration, and procurement, who offers excellent analytical, communication, and management skills.

EDUCATION

B.A. degree in Political Science, Southwest Missouri State University, Springfield, MO, 2001.
- Major: Political Science with emphasis in International Affairs
- Minor: Economics with emphasis in Comparative Economic Systems
- Internship: Served as an intern at the Attorney General's Office in Missouri, 1999.

MANAGEMENT TRAINING

In a "track record" of promotion with the Access Equipment Company, was selected for, and then excelled in, a rigorous management training/executive development program; also completed several courses in management, sales, and computer operations.

EXPERIENCE

CONTRACTING MANAGER (SUPERVISORY). Access Equipment Company, Springfield, MO (2003-present). Supervise and train one contract technician while negotiating contracts for the procurement of automotive parts and equipment, including vehicles; negotiate contracts ranging from $2,000 to millions of dollars.
- Procure items such as automotive parts, gas dispensers used at service stations, 18-wheelers, forklifts, and other equipment.
- Conduct interviews with vendors to review/obtain pricing, availability, and product data to expand sources, conduct market research, and identify market conditions.
- Resolve vendor invoicing problems; perform technical coordination worldwide.
- Negotiate and release purchase/delivery orders; prepare solicitations and amendments; evaluate proposals; prepare contract awards; negotiate/prepare amendments for approval; prepare warning, cure, show cause letters, and termination notices; prepare agreements.
- Perform liaison with vendors; analyze purchasing, replacement, and distribution patterns.

SALES AREA MANAGER. Lowe's, Springfield, MO (2001-03). Hired, trained, and supervised approximately 15 employees, including two supervisors, while handling all responsibilities of a store manager when required, including overseeing the daily opening and closing of the store; consistently met or exceeded all sales, productivity, and selling goals.
- Recommended changes to stock assortment to meet changing customer preferences; monitored inventory levels and supervised reorder associates.
- Maintained proper levels of merchandise display, and worked with visual merchandising personnel to achieve the best presentation; managed special promotional events while also disposing of clearance, damaged, or defective merchandise.
- Scheduled sales associates; performed routine store surveys to track customer/sales associate ratios; trained and developed employees to maintain a positive image.
- Prepared and maintained employee hour and cost budgets.

MANAGER TRAINEE. Lowe's, Springfield, MO (2001). Excelled in a seven-month management training/executive development program.

CASHIER/FLOOR SUPERVISOR. Sears, Springfield, MO (1998-2001). Excelled in serving customers, accounting for financial transactions, and monitoring cleanliness of retail areas.

PERSONAL

Am a high-energy, hard-working, loyal individual, who gives 100% to my job and my company. Can provide excellent personal and professional references. Familiar with Microsoft Word, Excel, and Access software programs.

CAREER CHANGE

Date

Exact Name of Person
Title or Position
Name of Company
Address (no., street)
Address (city, state, zip)

**CONVENIENCE STORE
ASSISTANT MANAGER**

for Exxon in Oklahoma.
This individual is switching
to the information
management and computer
operations field.

Dear Exact Name of Person: (or Dear Sir or Madam if answering a blind ad.)

Can you use a versatile and hard-working manager who is skilled in boosting the sale, profitability, efficiency, and overall vitality of food service operations?

As you will see from my resume, I offer "hands-on" management experience gained from a previous position in which I was rapidly promoted to a Department Supervisor and supervised over 80 employees through all stages of training them to produce high quality food products.

In my current position as an Assistant Manager from Exxon, I train and supervise a small staff of three while working toward a degree in Computer Information Systems from Cameron University on a full-time basis. I believe one of my greatest strengths is my ability to train people and develop plans/goals designed to maximize the productivity of each employee. Experience has taught me that "communication and follow up" in even the smallest job are the keys to successfully managing any business.

I hope you will welcome my call soon to arrange a brief meeting at your convenience to discuss your current and future needs and how I might serve them. Thank you in advance for your time.

Sincerely yours,

Charles Luther Eaton

Alternate last paragraph:
I hope you will call or write soon to suggest a time convenient for us to meet and discuss your current and future needs and how I might serve them. Thank you in advance for your time.

CHARLES LUTHER EATON

1110½ Hay Street, Fayetteville, NC 28305 • preppub@aol.com • (910) 483-6611

OBJECTIVE
To offer my computer expertise as well as my supervisory, management, and customer service skills for the benefit of an organization that can use a dedicated hard worker who is respected for the ability to creatively apply my knowledge in solving business problems.

EDUCATION
Bachelor of Science degree in **Computer Information Systems,** Cameron University, Lawton, OK, degree anticipated during the Spring of 2003.
A.A.S., Business Computer Programming, Oklahoma City Community College, Oklahoma City, OK, 2002; GPA 3.8.

COMPUTER EXPERTISE
Through training and experience, have developed proficiency related to the following:
Hardware: IBM System 36, IBM 370, IBM AS400, IBM PCs, and PC compatible.
Software: Microsoft Word, Excel, Access, dBase III+, dBase IV, ROSCOE, Turbo Pascal, PageMaker, and MS-DOS.
Operating systems: Windows, UNIX, and OS/MVS
Languages: BASIC, COBOL, C, UNIX, OS/MVS JCL, and Pascal
Other: system analysis, payroll processing, and data entry

EXPERIENCE
CONVENIENCE STORE ASSISTANT MANAGER. Exxon, Oklahoma City, OK (2003-present). Train and now supervise three employees in this busy convenience store while also taking charge of day-to-day activities such as inventory control and processing cash receipts.

DEPARTMENT SUPERVISOR and **INTERPRETER.** Tyson Foods, Oklahoma City, OK (2001-03). Because of my Spanish language skills, was originally hired as an interpreter and then rapidly moved into management; was selected to staff all jobs in a newly created department, and then achieved similar success in another new department.
- Supervised more than 80 employees through all stages of training and into their work assignments following training. Spoke fluent Spanish interpreting for Hispanic employees.

COMPUTER CONSULTANT. Automaxx, Oklahoma City, OK (1998-2001). While pursuing my degree in Computer Information Systems, provided this automobile dealership with support for their internal computer systems.
- Performed troubleshooting and maintenance on the dealership's computers while also assisting with customer service activities. Installed new software and upgrades.

COMPUTER OPERATOR/PAYROLL CLERK. JC Penney, Lawton, OK (1996-98). Worked in this job while working toward my B.S. degree in Computer Information Systems.

PAYROLL/PERSONNEL CLERK. Department of the Treasury, Lawton OK (1993-96). Supervised and trained 15 employees while overseeing the completion of payroll processing, administrative duties, and human resource services.
- In a formal Letter of Commendation was praised in this manner: "Such enthusiasm and aggressiveness in a job which requires methodical checklists is rarely seen."

Other experience: **INVENTORY CLERK.** Tandy, Inc., Lawton, OK (1993). Gained experience in a summer job creating and maintaining the inventory database.

PERSONAL
Can provide outstanding references from all of the above employers. Have a knack for producing precise and quality results in numerous technical areas where perfection is required including photography, video communications, and marksmanship.

Date

Exact Name of Person
Title or Position
Name of Company
Address (no., street)
Address (city, state, zip)

CONVENIENCE STORE SHIFT MANAGER
for 7-11

Dear Exact Name of Person: (or Dear Sir or Madam if answering a blind ad.)

Can you use a versatile and hard-working manager who is skilled in boosting the sale, profitability, efficiency, and overall vitality of food service operations?

As you will see from my resume, I offer "hands-on" experience in starting new food service operations, transforming underperforming units into "superstars," and maximizing the profitability of established units.

I believe one of my greatest strengths is my ability to train employees and develop training plans/goals designed to maximize the productivity of each employee. Experience has taught me that "communication and follow up" in even the smallest job are the keys to successfully managing any business.

I hope you will welcome my call soon to arrange a brief meeting at your convenience to discuss your current and future needs and how I might serve them. Thank you in advance for your time.

Sincerely yours,

Gary Culbertson

Alternate last paragraph:
I hope you will call or write soon to suggest a time convenient for us to meet and discuss your current and future needs and how I might serve them. Thank you in advance for your time.

GARY CULBERTSON

1110½ Hay Street, Fayetteville, NC 28305 • preppub@aol.com • (910) 483-6611

OBJECTIVE

To contribute to an organization that can use a dedicated and hard-working manager who has excelled in motivating people, starting new ventures, controlling costs, increasing profits, and managing operations for maximum customer satisfaction.

EDUCATION

A.S. in Civil Engineering, University of Kentucky Lexington Community College, KY, 2002. Excelled in intensive food service management training including:
- Burger King School of Training (two weeks)
- Hardee's Training School (six weeks)
- Chick-Fil-A Training School (two weeks)

EXPERIENCE

CONVENIENCE STORE SHIFT MANAGER. Seven Eleven, Lexington, KY (2003-present). Apply my knowledge of inventory control to help this convenience store retailer improve its ordering and stocking procedures; handle sales, customer service, and store maintenance.

STORE MANAGER. McDonald's Restaurant (Murray Enterprises), Lexington, KY (2002-03). Worked closely with the owner of a franchise operating four separate stores; took over management of a troubled restaurant with eroding profitability and improved sales and profits by 8% over the previous year.
- Was accountable monthly to the owner for the store's profit and loss position. After taking over the underperforming unit, retrained personnel and hired new employees.

STORE MANAGER. Chick-Fil-A (Jenkins Management Corp.), Lexington, KY (1999-02). Was commended for my ability to use versatile management approaches while supervising five different stores; managed up to 30 people.
- Excelled in decreasing food costs to the lowest possible level while assuring quality raw materials and quality preparation. Became accustomed to working long hours and tough schedules because of supervisory shortages.

STORE MANAGER. Cracker Barrel, Lexington, KY (1998-1999). Was promoted to store manager after only three months as a "manager trainee" with the company; learned how to operate every area of a full-service restaurant.
- Trained, motivated, and supervised a staff of up to 60 people. Managed store operations so that the unit was always ranked in the top 10% of other Cracker Barrel locations.

STORE MANAGER. Hardee's, Lexington, KY (1994-1998). Successfully opened two new restaurants for this franchise; substituted for the area supervisor in his absence in addition to overseeing all aspects for store operations including these: hiring and training employees, purchasing/inventory control, store maintenance, and customer relations.
- Learned the pitfalls involved in starting up new restaurants.

STORE MANAGER/AREA SUPERVISOR. Burger King Restaurant, Lexington, KY (1991-1994). Oversaw the profitability and consistent quality operation of five different stores; managed the units so that all showed gains in sales and profitability.
- Learned how to successfully manage a multiunit operation.
- Acquired extensive "hands-on" expertise in planning and administering budgets, preparing payroll, and analyzing profit-and-loss statements.

PERSONAL

Believe that "communication and follow up" are the keys to successful management. Pride myself on my ability to "size up" employees and determine training to stretch capabilities.

Date

Exact Name of Person
Title or Position
Name of Company
Address (no., street)
Address (city, state, zip)

**COSMETIC SALES &
MERCHANDISING
SPECIALIST**

for LaFayette Beauty
Supply

Dear Exact Name of Person: (or Dear Sir or Madam if answering a blind ad.)

I am sending my resume in response to the advertisement you recently placed for a Service Merchandiser.

As you will see from my resume, I have skills and abilities that could make me a valuable part of your team. In addition, I feel certain that you would find me to be a hard-working and reliable professional who prides myself on doing any job to the best of my ability.

In a current position as a Cosmetic Sales and Merchandising Specialist, I have increased sales of major cosmetic lines such as Maybelline, Revlon, and Fashion Fair within the Kansas City area. My extensive sales experiences expands over a period of ten years. I can provide excellent personal and professional references if you request them.

I hope you will call or write me soon to suggest a time convenient for us to meet and discuss your current and future needs and how I might serve them. Thank you in advance for your time.

Sincerely,

Kamala M. Miradesh

KAMALA M. MIRADESH

1110½ Hay Street, Fayetteville, NC 28305   •   preppub@aol.com   •   (910) 483-6611

OBJECTIVE

To contribute to an organization that can use my experience in sales and merchandising, my specialized knowledge of beauty and health care products, and my reputation as a professional who can work well independently.

EDUCATION & TRAINING

Studied **Business and Accounting**, Kansas City Community College, Kansas City, KS (2001-2002).

Completed numerous Revlon and Elizabeth Arden corporate-sponsored seminars in sales, management, marketing, and beauty advisory skills.

EXPERIENCE

COSMETIC SALES AND MERCHANDISING SPECIALIST. LaFayette Beauty Supply, Kansas City, KS (2003-present). Increase sales of several major cosmetic lines while covering the main retail store plus five other outlets throughout Kansas City.

- Handle sales and merchandising for a multiline corporation which marketed Maybelline, Revlon, and Fashion Fair cosmetics as well as Liz Claiborne fragrances.
- Advanced the Liz Claiborne line with award-winning sales promotions and displays.
- Supervise two employees who gave demonstrations and completed sales.
- Was credited with bringing about impressive increases in the sales of all lines: Maybelline by 11%, Revlon by 28%, Fashion Fair by 9%, and Liz Claiborne by 5%.
- Am skilled in judging correct amounts to stock to avoid running out of items or overstocking.
- Gained experience in ensuring proper stock rotation while servicing the military base's main commissary and 21 outlets.
- Process weekly orders, control a yearly inventory of $120,000, and set up sales promotions.
- Increased sales 17% by applying my product knowledge and sales skills.

REGIONAL SALES/MERCHANDISING MANAGER. VACO, Inc., Kansas City, KS (2001-2003). Supervised four employees and directed the merchandising for 24 accounts at five locations throughout Kansas.

- Became highly knowledgeable of product lines and refined communications skills working closely with clients throughout the region. Developed displays to promote products as well as conducting inventories, ordering, and stocking merchandise.

SALES REPRESENTATIVE. Inline Cosmetics, Kansas City, KS (1998-2001). Was promoted to the regional management team on the basis of my product knowledge, sales abilities, and performance while representing eight accounts. Represented Maybelline and Revlon which included preparing inventory reports, ordering and stocking merchandise, and promotions.

BEAUTY ADVISOR/ COORDINATOR. Merle Norman, Kansas City, KS (1995-1998). Promoted to oversee a marketing account with $130,000 in annual sales, earned many awards while developing excellent rapport with vendors, management, and retail personnel.

- Performed makeovers, conducted beauty seminars, assisted with the makeup for fashion shows, and set up attractive displays to promote merchandise sales.
- Increased annual sales from approximately $90,000. Scheduled three employees.

Highlights of other experience: **DENTAL ASSISTANT**. Appel & Appel Dentistry, Kansas City, KS (1992-1995). Displayed my versatility as a dental assistant performing additional tasks in the X-ray and oral surgery departments while also acting as a receptionist.

PERSONAL

Offer language skills including speaking, reading, and writing German and speaking conversational French. Am very effective in situations requiring a self-sufficient professional.

Exact Name of Person
Title or Position
Name of Company
Address (no., street)
Address (city, state, zip)

CUSTOMER SERVICE
SPECIALIST

for Ladies Footlocker

Dear Exact Name of Person: (or Dear Sir or Madam if answering a blind ad.)

I would appreciate an opportunity to talk with you soon about how I could contribute to your organization through my excellent public relations, customer service, and administrative skills.

As you will see from my resume, I have excelled in positions that have permitted me to develop my know-how in these and other areas: handling people and problems by telephone and in person; researching information and organizing materials for maximum usefulness and easy reference; and operating a variety of business machines.

You would find me to be a well-organized, reliable professional with a genuine customer-service orientation. Thoroughly flexible, I would cheerfully relocate according to your needs.

I hope you will welcome my call soon to arrange a brief meeting at your convenience to discuss your current and future needs and how I might serve them. Thank you in advance for your consideration.

Sincerely yours,

Molly E. Berriman

Alternate last paragraph:
I hope you will call or write me soon to suggest a time convenient for us to meet and discuss your current and future needs and how I might best serve them. Thank you in advance for your consideration.

MOLLY ELIZABETH BERRIMAN

1110½ Hay Street, Fayetteville, NC 28305 • preppub@aol.com • (910) 483-6611

OBJECTIVE

To contribute to an organization that can use my excellent skills in working with the public, along with my administrative and business equipment expertise.

EDUCATION

A.S., in Business Administration, Pima Community College, Tucson, AZ, 2002.

EXPERIENCE

CUSTOMER SERVICE SPECIALIST. Ladies Footlocker, Tucson, AZ (2002-present). In this fast-paced "meet-the-public" position, refined my problem-solving and customer relations know-how.

- **Purchasing transactions:** Handle merchandise credit, charge account credit, and cash refunds.
- **Customer relations:** Play a key role in maintaining customer satisfaction and ensuring repeat business.
- **Administration:** Issue gift certificates as well as hunting and fishing licenses.
- **Inventory control:** Account for sporting goods in stock and ensured merchandise was ticketed properly.
- **Management:** Was promoted after only 60 days on the job; became known for my professionalism and willingness to work "on call."

CUSTOMER SERVICE REPRESENTATIVE. Harris Teeter, Tucson, AZ (2001-2002). Acquired valuable skills in cash and credit transactions while efficiently managing my time and resources.

- Dealt extensively with the public in a courteous and efficient manner.
- Learned to use a wide range of office equipment.

SALES REPRESENTATIVE. Petite Sophisticate, Tucson, AZ (1999-2001). While learning the basics of retail management, developed top customer-service abilities in this direct contact role selling women's clothing.

Other experience:
CAREGIVER. Tucson, AZ (1997-1999). Provided round-the-clock care 4 to 7 days a week for an 2-year old child.
HEAD PHOTOGRAPHER. R. D. Morgan High School, Tucson, AZ (1996-1997). In this elected position, was responsible for producing all yearbook photographs for a 2000-student high school.

EQUIPMENT EXPERTISE

Have a strong working knowledge of the following equipment:
Office:

Calculator	Adding machine Cash register
Copier	Microfilm reader Typewriter (45 wpm)

Computer:
IBM-compatible and MacIntosh PCs
Microsoft Word, Excel, Access and PowerPoint.
Photographic:
Minolta, 35mm and Polaroid

PERSONAL

Have learned how to manage most customer service situations and "people problems" through working in a variety of environments. Am a cheerful professional who enjoys helping people. Am "cool, calm, and collected" in crisis or difficult situations. Have some limited reading and writing ability in Spanish.

Date

Exact Name of Person
Title or Position
Name of Company
Address (no., street)
Address (city, state, zip)

DEPARTMENT MANAGER

for Burdines Department
Store

Dear Exact Name of Person: (or Dear Sir or Madam if answering a blind ad.)

Can you use a resourceful young professional who offers a "track record" of accomplishment based on the ability to rapidly master new activities as well exceptional customer service skills?

As you will see from my enclosed resume, I have been promoted to increasing managerial responsibilities because of my unlimited personal initiative and strong "bottom-line" results. Working for Burdines has helped me to enhance my customer service skills. While supervising a six-person department, I became an in-store authority on customer service policies, and I also became known for my ability to tactfully and professionally resolve any customer relation problems.

I have come to believe that skillful customer service is the key to a company's survival and success in this competitive marketplace, and I pride myself on my ability to help my employer become "number one" in market share, customer satisfaction, and repeat business.

You would find me to be a reliable and hard-working young person who can always be counted on for exceptional results.

I hope you will welcome my call soon to arrange a brief meeting at your convenience to discuss your current and future needs and how I might serve them. Thank you in advance for your time.

Sincerely yours,

Charlotte K. Levine

Alternate last paragraph:
I hope you will call or write me soon to suggest a time convenient for us to meet and discuss your current and future needs and how I might serve them. Thank you in advance for your time.

CHARLOTTE K. LEVINE

1110½ Hay Street, Fayetteville, NC 28305   •   preppub@aol.com   •   (910) 483-6611

OBJECTIVE   To contribute to an organization that can use a skilled customer service professional who offers a "track record" of achievement and promotion based on proven management ability, strong problem-solving skills, as well as unlimited personal initiative and resourcefulness.

EXPERIENCE   *Have become known as a loyal and reliable employee while being promoted into key management positions by a giant corporation known for its emphasis on skillful customer service and merchandising creativity.*

2003-present: DEPARTMENT MANAGER and **FLOOR MANAGER**. Burdines, Orono, ME. Was "third in charge" of this 50-employee superstore while also managing a six-person department; excelled in handling responsibilities in these and other functional areas:

- **Customer service**: Am an in-store authority on customer service policies and procedures related to areas including making refunds and exchanges, resolve customer complaints and satisfy unhappy customers, as well as train and counsel employees and provide formal reprimands when appropriate; continuously promote the concept storewide that outstanding **customer service is the #1 priority.**

- **Budgeting and finance**: Responsible for the department's budgeting and for control of payroll costs; monitor cash flow and verify accounting related to bank deposits.

- **Employee training**: Train new department associates and maintain a weekly training session with all departmental employees in order to keep them acquainted with new products and changing procedures; am required to keep written training records of all employees under my supervision and always received outstanding reviews of my training records upon inspection by the District Human Resources Manager.

- **Planning and organizing**: Responsible for organizing, delegating, and following up on all departmental operations; prepared the weekly departmental schedule.

- **Store management**: Manage all store operations including opening and closing the store during the absence of top-level managers.

- **Computer operations**: In a store in which sales and inventory control matters were increasingly computerized, perform data entry/retrieval pertaining to shipments and purchase orders, mail orders, sales level, and nightly reports.

- **Merchandising**: Assure that new merchandise was displayed within 24 hours of receipt and set up department according to new floor plans/layouts; assembled displays for sales floor; became known for maintaining high standards of neatness and cleanliness.

- **Security**: Control the shipment/receipt of firearms while overseeing store security, including responding to alarm calls when the store was closed; dealt with shoplifters.

- **Sales achievements**: Out of 16 stores in the district, always maintained my department in the first or second position in number of extended warranties sold; commended for motivating others through my dedication to excellence and by setting the example.

Other experience:

2000-03: ASSISTANT DEPARTMENT MANAGER. Assisted the department manager in all areas; was selected for intensive management development training.

1998-00: SALES ASSOCIATE. Earned rapid promotion because of my customer service skills and product knowledge.

EDUCATION &   After excelling in high school, completed extensive professional training courses sponsored
TRAINING   by the Burdines company in operations management, employee supervision, customer service.

PERSONAL   Am known for my ability to rapidly master new activities and assume responsibility. Am proficient in using the full range of office equipment. Have operated an 8-line switchboard.

Exact Name of Person
Title or Position
Name of Company
Address (no., street)
Address (city, state, zip)

DEPARTMENT MANAGER & AREA SALES MANAGER

for a major department store in Arkansas

Dear Exact Name of Person: (or Dear Sir or Madam if answering a blind ad.)

Can you use a hard-working and dedicated young professional who offers a "track record" of advancement to a management role along with outstanding communication, motivational, and sales abilities?

While financing my college education working as a Sales Associate with Dillard's Department Stores, I consistently set sales records and upon college graduation moved into a full-time position which led to my acceptance into a management training program. My most recent position was as a Department Manager where I supervised six employees and directed operations in the home furnishings department.

As you will see from my resume, I am very experienced in managing time productively and earning my degree in Business Administration with a minor in Retail Management, gave me opportunities to refine my research and analytical skills. I am widely recognized as an articulate and mature person who works well with others.

I hope you will welcome my call soon to arrange a brief meeting at your convenience to discuss your current and future needs and how I might serve them. Thank you in advance for your time.

Sincerely yours,

Jacob H. Clay

Alternate last paragraph:
I hope you will call or write soon to suggest a time convenient for us to meet and discuss your current and future needs and how I might serve them. Thank you in advance for your time.

JACOB HENRY CLAY

1110½ Hay Street, Fayetteville, NC 28305 • preppub@aol.com • (910) 483-6611

OBJECTIVE

To apply my education and experience for the benefit of an organization that can use a hard-working and articulate young professional with a reputation for outstanding management skills and the ability to learn quickly.

EDUCATION

B.S. in Business Administration with a minor in **Retail Management**, Arkansas State University, Jonesboro, AR, 2002.
- Was selected to participate in the Retail Management Program and completed courses in Sales and Public Relations.
- Learned to handle pressure and maximize available time in management courses requiring extensive research on tight schedules.

COMPUTERS

Was part of the management team that installed a new software within Dillard's which has improved the timeliness of all accounting and inventory control functions.

EXPERIENCE

Earned promotion to Area Sales Manager after financing my education as a Sales Associate with Dillard's Department Stores, Jonesboro, AR:
2003-present: DEPARTMENT MANAGER and **AREA SALES MANAGER.** Recognized for my outstanding sales abilities and potential, was promoted to supervise six employees and ensure the smooth operation of the home furnishings department.
- Achieved sales figures 7% above the projected departmental goal.
- Reorganized floor space and set up a new section selling pictures and art work.
- Selected to attend a corporate management training program in Little Rock, spring 2003.
- Participated in a project to prepare a new store for opening: polished my organizational skills and learned to coordinate diverse elements in order to achieve a desired result.

2002-03: SALES ASSOCIATE. Won numerous awards for sales and customer service expertise while advancing from selling and stocking the men's department to overseeing men's accessories.
- Earned the 2002 "Pacesetter Award," the organization's highest honor for sales personnel.
- Was awarded the "Manager's Award" three consecutive years.
- Acquired computer skills while learning to use state-of-the-art equipment to make bar codes and to take inventory with a scanning system.

Other experience:
ENGINEERING AIDE. Mid-South Communications, Jonesboro, AR (2001-2002). Assisted an engineer during a summer job drawing cable locations and designing improvements to methods of getting service to customers.
- Learned the value of working as a productive team member while observing how different departments coordinated joint activities.
- Diversified my knowledge by acquiring technical drafting skills.

AFFILIATIONS

Member, Junior Retailers of America; member, Jonesboro Baptist Church. Former member, Junior Homemakers of America and Future Farmers of America.

PERSONAL

Am proud of my reputation as an honest and trustworthy young professional. Offer adaptability and the ability to handle pressure. Will relocate.

Exact Name of Person
Exact Title
Exact Name of Company
Address
City, State, Zip

DEPARTMENT STORE MANAGER
for Strawbridge's

Dear Exact Name of Person (or Dear Sir or Madam if answering a blind ad)

I would like to introduce you to a management professional who has built a reputation as a versatile and adaptable individual with wide-ranging knowledge, abilities, and skills.

As you will see from my enclosed resume, I have earned the respect of my superiors and peers while advancing in a track record of accomplishments with the Strawbridge's department store chain in various locations throughout Nevada. With experience in all aspects of retail operations from buying and inventory control, to human resources management, to budgeting and payroll oversight, I have always contributed to the bottom line profitability of each location.

The recipient of the prestigious Buyer-of-the-Year Award at Dillard's, I am one of only 1% of employees to win this highest honor and I received the first award given by the company in 1998. From my resume you will also see that in each location I played a major role in leading the way to notable increases in the levels of sales and profitability. I have consistently contributed creative ideas and found ways to improve operations while ensuring customer satisfaction which translates into repeat business.

Consistently described as a role model who works well with others both in managerial roles and while adding to the success of team efforts, I truly enjoy people and the opportunity to help them mature and build their own successful careers. My versatile abilities also include excellent planning, math, analytical, and research abilities and I am familiar with software such as Microsoft Word, PowerPoint, and Excel.

I have especially enjoyed the opportunity to recruit, train, coach, motivate, and develop junior associates, and I am a retailer who is skilled at imparting my extensive knowledge to others so that they will be able to produce outstanding bottom line results and achieve outstanding career success. My communication skills are outstanding, and I am proud that I have trained and developed many individuals who have gone on to become top-notch performers in their retailing specialties.

If you can use a mature, versatile, and adaptable professional with wide-ranging knowledge of retail operations, I hope you will call or write me soon to suggest a time when we might have a brief discussion of how I could contribute to your organization. I will provide excellent professional and personal references at the appropriate time.

Sincerely,

Laverne S. Hile

LAVERNE S. HILE

1110½ Hay Street, Fayetteville, NC 28305   •   preppub@aol.com   •   (910) 483-6611

OBJECTIVE

To contribute versatile, well-refined managerial abilities to an organization that can benefit from my knowledge and experience in building and managing sales as well as overseeing inventory control actions while creatively increasing sales and bottom line results.

EDUCATION & TRAINING

Completed two years of general studies, University of Nevada, Reno, NV.
Continuously attend programs, courses, and professional seminars which have included:
- Attended OSHA and sexual harassment seminars in July 2002.
- The Dillard's Store Manager Program, May 2000-May 2001.
- Retail Management Series emphasizing recruiting, interviewing, and coaching, 1999.
- Attended training in Advanced Marketing and Merchandising and inventory control.

EXPERIENCE

Have excelled in this track record of advancement with retailer Strawbridge's:
2003-present: DEPARTMENT STORE MANAGER. Reno, NV. Am continually implementing new operations procedures and improving sales results while supervising 36 employees including two Area Sales Managers in the Hickory Ridge Shopping Center location which achieved approximately $4 million in sales for the most recent year of business.
- Manage the operating budget while controlling payroll expenses, variable costs, and profitability which increased 5.6% for sales per hour; reduced payroll expenses 5%.
- Maintain a Web site, supervise blood drives, and handle newspaper/magazine advertising.

2002-03: REGIONAL BUYER, MODERATE SPORTSWEAR. Reno, NV. Held decision-making authority for a region with 22 store locations and $15 million in annual sales while keeping alert for trends, planning merchandise assortments, and obtaining clothing lines in the correct quantities to supply the stores with adequate stock.
- Developed the team buying concept which allowed buyers from different regions to work together to find the best buys; developed three new categories of merchandise.

2001-02: BUYER, BETTER SPORTSWEAR. Reno, NV. Earned promotion based on my achievements and creativity displayed while planning, buying, merchandising, and controlling inventories for 22 stores with $9 million in sales. Increased sales 25%.

1999-01: BUYER, ACCESSORIES. Reno, NV. Credited with bringing about a 6% increase in sales my second year after a first year increase of 2%, effected improvements to inventory control in support of 13 stores with $6 million in sales. Received a prestigious Merchandiser Award for "best item presentation" and in recognition of highest sales increases in the region.

Other experience:
DIVISION MANAGER. Dillard's, Reno, NV (1994-99). Supervised the Ladies Clothing Buyers for three stores with a $4 million sales volume while planning sales and inventory control procedures; acted as Assistant Manager of one store.
- Trained four buyers who each went on to move up rapidly in the company.
- Achieved a 7% sales increase despite the turmoil of a major renovation.
- Received the company's first **Buyer-of-the Year Award** in 1998 for outstanding performance based in part on a 25% increase in sales as a Division Manager (Accessories and Cosmetics); then was promoted to Division Manager, Ladies Clothing.

PERSONAL

Was honored by Governor Michael V. Spencer for volunteering as a reading and math tutor and by the American Cancer Society for encouraging Liz Claiborne (a major cosmetics company) to sponsor a golf tournament and contribute $10,000. Am positive/enthusiastic.

Exact Name of Person
Title or Position
Name of Company
Address (no., street)
Address (city, state, zip)

DINING ROOM MANAGER

for a country club

Dear Exact Name of Person: (or Dear Sir or Madam if answering a blind ad.)

Can you use a versatile and hard-working manager who is skilled in boosting the sales, profitability, efficiency, and overall vitality of food service operations?

As you will see from my resume, I offer "hands-on" management experience gained from a previous position in which I was a General Manager for Ryan's Steak House Corporation. I managed three store units producing an average of $750,000 annually in sales. I supervised over 80 employees through all stages of training them to produce high quality food products.

In my current position as a Dining Room Manager or the Ladson Country Club in Texas, I coordinate, direct, and manage all club house dining room functions and facilities. I also train and supervise a small staff of ten employees. I believe one of my greatest strengths is my ability to train people and develop plans/goals designed to maximize the productivity of each employee. My experience has taught me that "communication and follow up" in even the smallest job are the keys to successfully managing any business.

I hope you will welcome my call soon to arrange a brief meeting at your convenience to discuss your current and future needs and how I might serve them. Thank you in advance for your time.

Sincerely yours,

Caleb Trevor Woods

Alternate last paragraph:
I hope you will call or write soon to suggest a time convenient for us to meet and discuss your current and future needs and how I might serve them. Thank you in advance for your time.

CALEB TREVOR WOODS ("Trevor")

1110½ Hay Street, Fayetteville, NC 28305 • preppub@aol.com • (910) 483-6611

OBJECTIVE

To benefit an organization that can use a gracious and experienced club operations manager who offers a proven ability to make a profit and control costs while satisfying customers, solving problems, and building a team of well-trained and enthusiastic employees.

EDUCATION

Currently enrolled in the Associate degree Hotel and Restaurant Management program at Laredo Community College, Laredo, TX degree anticipated in 2003.

EXPERIENCE

DINING ROOM MANAGER/HOST. Ladson Country Club, Laredo, TX (2003-present). Coordinate, direct, and manage all club house dining room functions and facilities, in addition to overseeing picnics, barbecues, and other outdoor catering services.
- Provide catering service for a wide range of private functions, including wedding receptions, anniversaries, dinner theatre, big band dancing, golf luncheons, professional tennis and golf tournament dinners, award banquets, and civic club dinners.

BANQUET SET-UP MANAGER. Laredo Western Country Club, Laredo, TX (2001-03). Refined knowledge of club operations while serving as banquet set-up manager, host, and bartender at a private member-owned club.

ASSISTANT MANAGER. Ryan's Steak House Corporation, San Antonio, Tyler, and Laredo, TX (1999-01). Was specially recruited by Ryan's Steak House to act as a troubleshooter in three different "problem" stores in which high management turnover had resulted in staff problems which eventually led to sales and customer service problems.
- Helped each store "get back to basics": made sure each store was complying with company regulations and with product-producing specifications.
- Trained people to do their jobs instead of just hiring people and expecting them to do their jobs without training. Was offered a store management position in 2000 but declined.

GENERAL MANAGER. Ryan's Steak House Corporation, TX, NM, and LA (1989-99). For restaurants in three locations, managed units producing an average of $750,000 annually in sales; maintained food costs at approximately 38% of sales, labor costs at 14% of sales, and kept noncontrollables and controllables within set ranges while consistently producing a profit of between 16% to 19% of overall sales compared to the company average of 15%.
- For the Ryan's Steak House in Laredo, TX, was selected by the corporation for the honor of managing the company's first restaurant in the Southwest (1995-1999).
- Took over a Ryan's Steak House located in Albuquerque, NM, which had been unprofitable for four years and rapidly produced a first-year profit of $16,000; a second-year profit of $67,000; and a third-year profit of $120,000 (1992-1995): first restored internal operations according to company standards, and then focused on aggressive personal outside sales campaigns which induced "trial" and reestablished a loyal customer base.
- For a location in New Orleans, LA, in a "start-up" situation, established a new unit which made a profit its first year of operation (1989-1992) while aggressively managing:

personnel hiring/training	food preparation/ordering
customer relations	accounting
advertising	sales/financial reporting

HONORS

Won numerous awards for extraordinary sales and production, Ryan's Steak House Corp.

PERSONAL

Offer a proven ability to reduce costs in any operation while creating a customer-friendly place where workers feel strongly that they are an important link in the business chain.

Date

Exact Name of Person (if known)
Title or Position
Name of Company
Address (no., street)
Address (city, state, zip)

DISTRICT MANAGER
for Hancock Fabrics

Dear Exact Name of Person: (or Dear Sir or Madam)

With the enclosed resume, I would like to make you aware of my interest in your organization. If you feel that my well-developed managerial skills could be of value to you, I would appreciate the opportunity to talk with you in person about my considerable background in training, team building, and customer service as well as my track record of achievement in retail operations.

As you will see from my resume, I am known for my team building, time management, and organizational abilities. Since 2002, I have been employed as a District Manager with Hancock Fabrics, Inc. I am responsible for 14 locations producing in excess of 15 million dollars in annual sales volume while handling the responsibility for total merchandising and operations functions for all units. While controlling shrinkage to an average of 1.11 percent, I have significantly refined the skills and knowledge of our management staff through aggressive recruitment, training, and development.

In prior positions with Hamricks, Inc. and earlier with Ike's Stores, I was singled out to manage complex projects including overseeing store openings from hiring and staffing locations, to opening them, to operational oversight. I have been involved in managing projects to remodel multiple stores and as well as in corporate strategic planning.

I have gained experience in all operational environments in retail settings: human resources and personnel management, purchasing and inventory control, customer service, public relations, merchandising, office operations, and loss prevention. Having been in management for approximately 14 years, I offer expertise in numerous areas and am confident that I am a professional capable of contributing successfully to your organization's "bottom line."

If my considerable talents and skills interest you, I hope you will call or write me soon to suggest a time convenient for us to meet to discuss your needs and how I might serve them. I can provide outstanding personal and professional references at the appropriate time. Thank you in advance for your time.

Sincerely,

Gene F. Wallenberg

EUGENE F. WALLENBERG ("Gene")

1110½ Hay Street, Fayetteville, NC 28305 • preppub@aol.com • (910) 483-6611

OBJECTIVE

To contribute to an organization that can use an articulate management professional who excels in supervising, training, and communicating with others while building strong teams, exceeding sales goals, prioritizing tasks, and meeting schedules.

EXPERIENCE

DISTRICT MANAGER. Hancock Fabrics, Binghampton, NY (2002-present). Responsible for 14 locations producing in excess of $15 million in annual sales; oversee total merchandising and operation functions for all units.
- Recruited and developed an outstanding management team. Decreased shrinkage 1.11%.

STORE MANAGER and **DISTRICT TRAINING MANAGER.** Hamrick's, Binghampton, NY (2000-02). Completed two months of corporate familiarization training at the Brooklyn, NY, store before taking over a new location and building it to be recognized as one of the most profitable and successful locations in the 100-store region.
- Conducted interviews and selected the store's 130 associates including training and developing the management team which led to successful store operations.
- Handpicked as district training manager, personally carried out the training of all new store managers in a nine-store area. Achieved one of the ten lowest shrinkage percentages in a 100-store region while earning a 94% score during a corporate audit.
- Was cited by the Regional Manager as "by far one of the greatest managers that I had the opportunity to work with in my eleven years with the company."

Advanced in managerial roles with Ike's Stores, Inc., based in Binghampton, NY:
STORE MANAGER. Binghampton, NY (1996-00). Carried out daily planning as well as staffing and supervising employees and directing all phases of operations so that each store consistently reached high levels of profitability while averaging under 2% shrinkage throughout an 11-year period.
- Trained and supervised an average of 100 associates in each store.
- Singled out as the coordinator of special projects for the district, managed remodeling activities at 12 stores and was involved in corporate-level strategic planning.
- Earned awards including "Best Store Appearance in District" and "Best Sales Increase" in the zone, both in 1997.
- Consistently met sales goals of $7 million annually and controlled million dollar annual operating budgets.

Highlights of earlier experience with Ike's Stores, Inc.:
SENIOR ASSISTANT MANAGER. (1994-96). Assisted in employee supervision while overseeing merchandising, loss prevention, personnel staffing, and training for a store with 100 associates; special areas of emphasis were inventory shrinkage prevention and sales.
ASSISTANT STORE MANAGER. (1990-94). Provided leadership in merchandising and operational areas of the store while contributing to profitability of an 80-employee store.
MANAGEMENT TRAINEE. (1988-90). Completed assignments in merchandising and operations after being selected for management training based on my accomplishments during two years as a sales associate, stockroom manager, and department manager.

EDUCATION & TRAINING

A.S. in Business Administration, Broome Community College, Binghamton, NY.
Completed the Michael Adirondack Course in Effective Communication and Human Relations.

PERSONAL

Possess communication and motivational skills which result in sales goals being met and high quality customer service provided. Offer strong analytical and problem-solving skills.

Date

Exact Name of Person (if known)
Title or Position
Name of Company
Address (no., street)
Address (city, state, zip)

Dear Exact Name of Person: (or Dear Sir or Madam)

I would appreciate an opportunity to talk with you soon about how my excellent public relations skills and "results-oriented" approach to management could benefit your organization.

As you will see from my resume I offer extensive management and personnel supervisory experience from my current position as Supervisor/District Manager with CATO's Fashions. Also, I feel certain that you would find me to be a hard-working and reliable professional who prides myself on doing any job to the best of my ability.

In addition, my experience in sales management has provided me with a keen appreciation of the outstanding results that can be achieved when a flexible, creative, and empathetic approach is brought to managing and motivating others. This, I think, is one of the toughest, yet most rewarding challenges any manager can face.

You requested that I submit my salary requirements, and admittedly it is difficult to request a firm salary without the knowledge of what the expectations of the position are. I am willing to accept the mid to upper 20,000-dollar range and, of course, am willing to negotiate commensurate to the demands of the position.

I hope you will call or write me soon to suggest a time convenient for us to meet and discuss your current and future needs and how I might serve them. Thank you in advance for your time.

Sincerely,

Tannis R. Davidson

TANNIS R. DAVIDSON

1110½ Hay Street, Fayetteville, NC 28305   •   preppub@aol.com   •   (910) 483-6611

OBJECTIVE   I want to contribute my excellent public relations skills and managerial "know-how" to an organization in need of a dedicated, hard-working young professional with a proven ability to achieve outstanding results.

EDUCATION   **B. A. in Psychology with a minor Sociology,** Cosumnes River College, Sacramento, CA, 2002.

EXPERIENCE   *Advanced in this "track record" of achievements for this retail clothing chain in 12 locations of CATO Fashions throughout California and Oregon:*
2003-present: DISTRICT MANAGER & SUPERVISOR. Supervise all sales and personnel management for a staff of approximately 150.
- Contact and visit area colleges and high schools for recruitment possibilities. Travel to each facility and prepare individual store reports. Make decisions concerning hiring and terminating as well as promotions and raises.
- Perform functions of payroll, inventory control, and opening/closing facilities.
- Assist with preparations for the opening of a new store which included hiring staff and stocking merchandise.
- Visit the 12 stores in my district, checking merchandising levels to determine ordering needs; inspect and improve merchandising displays.
- Create guidelines for store managers and set goals for each store to obtain.
- Handle security problems which included working with local authorities as well as dismissing dishonest employees.
- Work with all employees to better understand their positions and limitations as well as for the benefit of being able to personally provide "back-up."

2002-03: AREA MANAGER. Traveled to the Ridgecrest, Hayward, and Santa Clara locations as troubleshooter and supervisor for as many as 35 employees.
2000-02: MANAGER. Ridgecrest, CA. Pushed this 15-person staff in becoming the #1 store in the company with a first-time $1 million in sales.
1996-00: MANAGER. Hayward, CA. Effectively managed a staff of up to 17 employees.
1995-96: ASSISTANT MANAGER. Ridgecrest, CA. Refined supervisory and management skills.

Highlights of other experience:
SALES REPRESENTATIVE: Consistently met and exceeded sales quotas to be awarded "Top Salesperson" honors.
- Was asked by the owners to travel to various stores to teach my sales techniques.

SPECIAL   Can effectively handle people who are displaying disorderly conduct.
SKILLS   Offer extensive security and theft detection skills including:
- shoplifting awareness
- counterfeit bill detection
- identifying quick change artists

TRAINING   Attended a number of seminars including "How to Interview," "Motivating Your Team," and "Memo Writing."

PERSONAL   Am highly motivated and dedicated to instilling in others that same willingness to work hard and meet any challenge. Understand the importance of detecting employee strengths and building on them. Have developed expert skills in supervising people. Thrive on new ways to accomplish tasks and adapt quickly to new environments.

Date

Exact Name of Person
Title or Position
Name of Company
Address (no., street)
Address (city, state, zip)

DISTRICT SUPERVISOR
for Save More, Inc.,

Dear Exact Name of Person: (or Dear Sir or Madam if answering a blind ad.)

Can you use a versatile and hard-working manager who is skilled in boosting the sale, profitability, efficiency, and overall vitality of convenience store operations?

As you will see from my resume, I offer "hands-on" management experience gained from a current position in which I am a District Supervisor and supervised over 42 employees and play a key role in interviewing and hiring key management personnel. With a reputation as a successful district supervisor, I routinely visit stores at all locations to personally interact with staff and perform spot checks on numerous control systems such as labor practices, merchandising methods, cash and inventory control and customer service techniques.

I have earned a B. S. in Business and Psychology from Rhode Island College in Providence. I believe one of my greatest strengths is my ability to train people and develop plans/goals designed to maximize the productivity of each employee. Experience has taught me that "communication and follow up" in even the smallest job are the keys to successfully managing any business.

I hope you will welcome my call soon to arrange a brief meeting at your convenience to discuss your current and future needs and how I might serve them. Thank you in advance for your time.

Sincerely yours,

Warren Edward Townsend

Alternate last paragraph:
I hope you will call or write soon to suggest a time convenient for us to meet and discuss your current and future needs and how I might serve them. Thank you in advance for your time.

WARREN EDWARD TOWNSEND

1110½ Hay Street, Fayetteville, NC 28305　　•　　preppub@aol.com　　•　　(910) 483-6611

OBJECTIVE

My goal is to offer potential investors an exciting profit opportunity in a business which is an excellent fit with my background as a successful entrepreneur and manager of a multiunit chain serving varying types of customers in differing market locations.

EDUCATION

B.S. in Business and Psychology, Rhode Island College, Providence, RI, 1999.
Previously attended Roger Williams University (transferred credits to Rhode Island College). H.S. Diploma from The Providence Academy where I was captain of two state soccer championship teams; lettered 13 times in tennis, baseball, basketball, and soccer; and was named MVP three times in baseball at the school, conference, and regional levels.

EXPERIENCE

Advanced in this "track record" of management experience at 10 locations of Save More Inc., convenience stores throughout Providence:
2003-present: DISTRICT SUPERVISOR. Produced a 16% increase in sales and a 19% increase in profit while overseeing annual sales of $8 million through 10 convenience stores.
- Have made strategic decisions about opening stores in new locations and closing stores in locations which did not meet profit expectations.
- Currently oversee 42 employees; play a key role in hiring key management personnel.
- With a reputation as a "hands-on" district supervisor, routinely visit stores at all locations to personally interact with staff and to provide spot checks on the chain's numerous control systems related to labor practices, merchandising methods, cash control, inventory control, and customer service.
- Negotiate contracts with vendors and maintain liaison with prime vendor accounts.
- Have been involved in solving nearly every type of problem including pilferage, determining the inventory mix for maximum customer satisfaction and profitability, and choosing sites and the product mix for new locations.
- Am known as a gifted motivator with a talent for recognizing individual strengths and weaknesses and for developing a stable work force in an industry known for high turnover.

2000-03: STORE MANAGER. Store #31 on Shelby Drive, Providence, RI. Increased sales by 27% while learning the "nuts and bolts" of convenience store management at the unit level; managed four employees while coordinating with vendors, controlling cash and inventory, and overseeing the product mix.

AFFILIATIONS

- Member, Board of Directors for Providence Arts Festival 2001; was a member of the festival's fundraising event.
- 1999 President Elect, Providence Academy Alumni Council.
- Member, Providence Chamber of Commerce.

EDUCATION

Have completed numerous executive development programs and training seminars designed to enhance management skills and teach specific technical knowledge:
- (1996-1997): Completed Providence Brewers Academy, Smithfield, RI; studied leasing and finance, government regulation, flow of operations, beer styles, equipment selection, product formulas, and brewing business/micro brewery business management.
- (1995-1996): At numerous seminars and training programs, studied shrinkage control and robbery prevention; worker compensation and human resource administration; as well as the strategy and implementation involved in "creating excellence" in business.

PERSONAL

Have a reputation for unquestioned business ethics and can provide outstanding business, credit, personal, and professional references.

Date

Exact Name of Person
Exact Title
Exact Name of Company
Address
City, State, Zip

**DIVISIONAL
MERCHANDISE
MANAGER**
for Sears & Roebuck

Dear Exact Name of Person (or Dear Sir or Madam if answering a blind ad):

With the enclosed resume, I would like to make you aware of my desire to become a Divisional Merchandising Manager of the Shoe Division.

As you will see from my resume, I offer a track record of achievements with Sears and Roebuck Department Stores, where I began working after high school. While excelling in numerous professional development and executive training programs, I feel as though I have earned my "Ph.D. in retailing" in my more than 20 years of experience with Sears.

I am proud of the significant contributions I have made to the organization's bottom line over the years, and I am known for my strong financial control and meticulous attention to detail. I am also respected for my aggressive emphasis on team building and relationship building among the buying team, between the buyers and stores, and with vendors. Through the years, I have acquired the know-how which enables me to foster a results-oriented environment while providing the kind of supervision which buyers thrive on. I have come to believe that buyers are very unusual individuals, and I excel in mentoring, coaching, interacting with, motivating, supervising, and inspiring buyers of different experience levels.

You will see from my resume that I have utilized my personal initiative and expert knowledge of the shoe business to produce valuable bottom-line results. I am a youthful, energetic, and highly computer-proficient manager who could certainly continue to produce valuable bottom-line results as a Divisional Merchandise Manager, and I would cheerfully relocate as your needs require. I believe in the intrinsic vitality of the Sears and Roebuck organization, and I want to continue to "make it happen" in shoes.

Sincerely,

Cyrus Lafferty

CYRUS M. LAFFERTY

1110½ Hay Street, Fayetteville, NC 28305 • preppub@aol.com • (910) 483-6611

OBJECTIVE

To continue contributing to the profitability and growth of the Sears and Roebuck Department Stores as a Divisional Merchandise Manager or in a key management role which could utilize my skills in team building, shoe merchandising, financial control, and strategic planning.

EXPERIENCE

Have excelled in this "track record" of advancement with Sears and Roebuck:
2002-present: DIVISIONAL MERCHANDISE MANAGER, SHOE DIVISION. Pittsburgh, PA. In addition to my responsibilities as Divisional Merchandise Manager, handle buying for Kids' shoes for 22 stores for more than two years.
- In a division with a total volume in 2004 of $18.6 million, increased merchandise margin dollars by $280,000 through my prudent decisions related to the merchandise mix of athletic and brown shoes; increased markup by 1.5%.
- Supervise two buyers and an associate buyer; pride myself on the "esprit de corps" and spirit of teamwork I create as I challenge buyers to plan strategically and focus on store needs.
- On my own initiative, established a "non-returnable-to-vendor" credit program which generated $25,000 in bottom-line credits.
- Am highly skilled in utilizing software to improve management decision making; proficient with software including Microsoft Word, Access, and Excel; skilled with merchandise systems POM, Markdown, IMS, Store SKU Database, MPO, and SAR.

2000-2002: DIVISIONAL MERCHANDISE MANAGER, SHOE DIVISION. Pittsburgh, PA. For 27 stores, provided merchandising leadership while undertaking several new initiatives which improved profitability; developed and managed three buyers.
- On my own initiative, developed a process to identify and eliminate aging inventory; this improved stock rotation by ensuring the "first in, first out" stock rotation method.
- Created a seasonal Buying Guide for 27 stores which enabled us to remain within our "open to buy" and stay rigorously within our budget.
- Produced a Standards and Information Guide to assist with the merger of 27 stores.

1997-2000: DIVISIONAL MERCHANDISING MANAGER, SHOE DIVISION, LADIES ACCESSORIES & INTIMATE APPAREL. Supervised five buyers and a merchandise secretary for 11 stores.
1996-1997: DIVISIONAL MERCHANDISE MANAGER, SHOE DIVISION. Supervised three buyers while providing merchandising leadership for 11 stores.
1994-1996: GROUP BUYER, SHOES. Excelled as Group Buyer for 11 stores.
1992-1994: GROUP BUYER, SHOES. Group Buyer for 13 stores in Pittsburgh, Easton.
1984-1991: BUYER/MANAGER. York, PA. Buyer/Manager for Kids and Intimate Apparel.
1982-1984: BUYER/MANAGER. Easton, PA. Buyer/Manager of Men's/Boys Apparel, Men's/Kids Shoes, and the Home Store.

EDUCATION

B. S. in Business Administration, University of Pittsburgh, Pittsburgh, PA, 1997.

AFFILIATIONS

Deacon, Joshua Baptist Church; am a member of the Children's Ministry Committee, past member of the finance committee, and other church activity involvement.

HONOR

Named "Best Seller" Divisional Merchandise Manager, 1999.

PERSONAL

Outstanding reputation. Truly thrive on the fast pace of the retail environment. Am known for my ability to react quickly and decisively to emerging trends. Have an ability to anticipate consumer desires.

Exact Name of Person
Title or Position
Name of Company
Address (number and street)
Address (city, state, and zip)

DIVISIONAL MERCHANDISE MANAGER
for Macy's Department Store

Dear Exact Name of Person: (or Sir or Madam if answering a blind ad.)

With the enclosed resume, I would like to make you aware of my interest in confidentially exploring the possibility of joining your management structure.

From my enclosed resume you will see that I am handling responsibilities equivalent to those of a General Merchandise Manager for the Macy's Department Store. I supervise a 20-store operation and manage a staff of buyers and assistant buyers while handling responsibility for sales and gross margin, merchandise mix, and advertising.

In my previous retail management experience, I enjoyed a track record of promotion with J C Penney Department Store, where I began as a Department Manager, was promoted to Assistant Buyer and then to Buyer, directed the company's strategic moves as its Market Research Director, and became Divisional Sales Manager. I was subsequently recruited by Macy's and have been in my current job since 2003.

Although I am held in high regard by the Macy's organization and can provide excellent references at the appropriate time, I am aware of your company's fine reputation and feel that my impeccable retailing credentials could be a valuable addition to your organization. My experience at J C Penney's and Macy's has taught me many truths about business and retailing including these:

- Doing an average job in retailing will put you out of business.
- You usually grow your business by taking business away from someone else.
- Innovative marketing, creative problem solving, and aggressive merchandising are the keys to outperforming your competitors.
- Determine what your customers want and give them more of it.
- Effective communication is the key to effective execution.

If you can use a successful retailing executive who could bring added strengths and creativity to your strategic initiatives, I hope you will contact me to suggest a time when we could talk about your needs. I would certainly enjoy the opportunity to meet you in person.

Yours sincerely,

Brock D. Ellerman

BROCK D. ELLERMAN

1110½ Hay Street, Fayetteville, NC 28305 • preppub@aol.com • (910) 483-6611

OBJECTIVE

To benefit a company that can use an innovative retailer who has excelled professionally utilizing my strategic planning ability, strong bottom-line orientation, solid management skills, and proven ability to produce captivating merchandising experiences for the consumer.

MY PHILOSOPHY OF RETAILING & MANAGEMENT

- Doing an average job in retailing will put you out of business.
- You usually grow your business by taking business from someone else.
- Innovative marketing, creative problem solving, and aggressive merchandising are the keys to outperforming your competitors.
- Consistency in attitude and demeanor is a key to leadership.
- Effective communication is the key to effective execution.
- Determine what your customers want and give them more of it.

EXPERIENCE

DIVISIONAL MERCHANDISE MANAGER, Macy's Department Store, Home Store Division and Children's Division, Nashville, TN (2002-present). Am excelling in handling responsibilities equivalent to those of a General Merchandise Manager while supervising a 20-store operation; received a Macy's Award of Excellence 2003 for my community leadership as a member of the board of directors, Habitat for Humanity.

- Supervise a staff of buyers, associate buyers, and a Pool Stock Supervisor.
- Am responsible for generating sales and gross margin, merchandise mix, and advertising.
- Achieved eight percent average annual sales growth with no sacrifice of margin percent.
- Negotiate special events and promotions, including:
  Nico Settles Master Cutter Showcase
  Lenox China Command Performance
  Personal appearances by Nathan Kim, Isaiah Davidson, Eileen Owens, and
    Miss Teen USA
  Carl Ewing Shop and personal appearance
  Donna Karan designer special event presentation

DIVISIONAL SALES MANAGER, JC Penney's Department Store, Homestore and Mens, Nashville, TN (2001-02). Supervised a staff of up to 60 personnel which included four Area Sales Managers. Increased sales, reduced shrinkage, and managed stock content and inventory levels at optimum levels. On my own initiative, developed exciting new sales and motivational presentation which improved performance and morale.

BUYER, MANAGER, & MARKET RESEARCH DIRECTOR. JC Penney Department Store, Nashville, TN (1994-2000). Excelled in the following track record of promotion:
1990-99: Buyer, Towel and Bath Shop. Had complete financial and merchandising responsibility for a $3.8 million 16-store operation; generated sales and developed gross margin and profit.

- Planned and directed an improved marketing strategy which included more contemporary and targeted merchandise. Improved annual sales by 20%.

1986-89: Market Research Director. Played a significant role in many new JC Penney initiatives while directing the company's strategic planning and strategic thinking.

- Performed analysis of financial, statistical, and marketing data including sales and stock planning, new store site selection, demographic studies, profit analysis, and sales promotion budgeting.

EDUCATION

B.S. degree in Business Management, Vanderbilt University, Nashville, TN, 1985.

Exact Name of Person
Title or Position
Name of Company
Address (no., street)
Address (city, state, zip)

**ELECTRONICS
DEPARTMENT
MANAGER**
for K-Mart

Dear Exact Name of Person: (or Dear Sir or Madam if answering a blind ad.)

I would appreciate an opportunity to talk with you soon about how I could contribute to your organization through my background in sales and management as well as through the outstanding planning, organizational, communication, and problem-solving skills that have made me very valuable to my current employer.

As you will see from my resume, I have excelled for the last seven years in a "track record" of promotion within the K-Mart Corporation, where I began working at the age of 19. While excelling in my full-time job, I simultaneously obtained my B.S. degree in Business Administration and also found time to donate my time to charities including the Special Olympics. In May 2003, I was promoted to manage the electronics department at one of K-Mart's largest stores, and I am being groomed for entry into the company's formal Management Training Program after completing six months as a department manager.

Although I respect the K-Mart Corporation greatly and enjoy my challenging management responsibilities, I am writing to your organization because I am attracted to your company's fine reputation and respected product line, and I feel I could make valuable contributions to your bottom line through my strong sales and management skills. I would enjoy an opportunity to meet with you to explore the possibility to putting my experience and talents to work for your company. I can provide outstanding personal and professional references; I am single and will travel and relocate according to your needs.

I hope you will welcome my call soon to arrange a brief meeting at your convenience to discuss your current and future needs and how I might serve them. Thank you in advance for your time.

Sincerely yours,

Kenneth McQueary

Alternate last paragraph:
I hope you will call or write me soon to suggest a time convenient for us to meet and discuss your current and future needs and how I might serve them. Thank you in advance for your time.

KENNETH MCQUEARY

1110½ Hay Street, Fayetteville, NC 28305   •   preppub@aol.com   •   (910) 483-6611

OBJECTIVE   To contribute to the bottom line of an organization that can use a hard-working and resourceful young manager who offers proven abilities in sales, personnel supervision, and operations management and who also offers excellent planning, organizational, communication, and problem-solving skills.

EDUCATION   **B.S. degree in Business Administration**, The University of Tampa, Tampa, FL, 2001. Completed this degree while excelling in my full-time job in retailing. A member of National Businessmen Association, received the prestigious Award of Merit for leadership potential and academic excellence in my advising position in our local Tampa Chapter.

EXPERIENCE   *Began with K-Mart Stores, Inc.. when I was 19 years old, and have been promoted into increasingly responsible positions:*
2003-present: DEPARTMENT MANAGER, ELECTRONICS. K-Mart on Rivers Avenue, Tampa, FL. Was promoted to this position in May and am responsible for training, motivating, scheduling, and supervising eight employees.
- Work with dozens of vendors to negotiate terms of trade, select merchandise, develop marketing plans, and determine pricing policy. Develop special promotions to create consumer demand for clothing and accessories; implement modular set-ups.
- Am continuously in the process of strategic planning; plan for seasonal events and set/order special features.
- Improved the appearance of the department by organizing the risers, flagging merchandise, and assuring that every item is properly labeled.
- Have utilized my extensive computer knowledge to develop a more informed staff and to boost sales of computers and computer accessories.
- Am respected for my excellent problem-solving and decision-making skills.
- Have been appointed to serve on key corporate committees including the Promotional Committee, Hiring Committee, Safety Team, and Support Team (a support team is authorized to make management decisions).

2001-03: SALES CLERK, ELECTRONICS. K-Mart on Dorchester Road, Tampa, FL. Used my computer knowledge to boost sales while stocking counters, setting features, operating the cash register, ordering merchandise, and maintaining a perpetual inventory.
- On my own initiative, developed several new measures that established better security and which reduced theft and pilferage.
- Became known for my exceptionally strong customer service skills.

1997-01: SALES CLERK, LAWN & GARDEN CENTER AND PET CENTER. K-Mart on Reynolds Avenue, Tampa, FL. While providing excellent customer service, discovered ways of preventing loss from plants dying and from exterior theft; set up modulars, ordered regular and seasonal merchandise. Handled ordering for the paint and hardware departments.

VOLUNTEER   Even while excelling in my full-time job and simultaneously earning my college degree, volunteered my time generously to worthy projects:
- *Special Olympics:* Prepared children for events; monitored the events.
- *Public Television fund raiser:* Worked telephones in Tampa, FL, 2000.
- *ROTC projects:* Sponsored a needy family at Christmas, held Easter egg hunt for preschoolers, and collected canned goods for the poor.

PERSONAL   Can provide outstanding personal and professional references. Will relocate.

Exact Name of Person
Title or Position
Name of Company
Address (no., street)
Address (city, state, zip)

FASHION
MERCHANDISER
for a Home Decor
company

Dear Exact Name of Person: (or Dear Sir or Madam if answering a blind ad.)

Can you use a creative hard worker who has a flair for merchandising, retailing, and sales?

With a 2000 B.S. degree in Fashion Merchandising from Colgate University, I have had experience in creating displays while working side-by-side with retail store owners and buyers.

Employers have often praised me for my ability to work easily with customers as well as fellow employees.

A fast learner with unlimited management potential along with a "bottom-line" orientation, I thrive on the challenge of helping my employer prosper in highly competitive conditions. I am customer service oriented!

I hope you will welcome my call soon to arrange a brief meeting at your convenience to discuss your current and future needs and how I might serve them. Thank you in advance for your time.

Sincerely yours,

Hannah E. Sampson

Alternate last paragraph:
I hope you will call or write me soon to suggest a time convenient for us to meet and discuss your current and future needs and how I might serve them. Thank you in advance for your time.

HANNAH E. SAMPSON

1110½ Hay Street, Fayetteville, NC 28305　•　preppub@aol.com　•　(910) 483-6611

OBJECTIVE　　To benefit an organization in need of a creative, service-oriented young professional who offers a "newly minted" degree in fashion merchandising along with a customer service orientation and strong communication abilities.

EDUCATION　　Earned a **Bachelor of Science (B.S.) degree in Fashion Merchandising** with a minor in Interior Design, Colgate University, Hamilton, NY, 2000.
- Held membership in the American Home Economics Association (AHEA).
- Elected by the membership as the Personnel Director for Kappa Si Sorority: counseled students with personal or school problems while creating and directing group activities.
- Completed specialized course work in areas including:
- Learned retail operations management skills.
- Developed creative displays through effectively coordinating themes, color, and styles.
- Gained an understanding of the psychological relationship of clothing to human behavior.
- Became familiar with the application of the most effective advertising media to promote fashion ideas

EXPERIENCE　　**FASHION MERCHANDISING INTERN.** Beacon's Home Décor, Brooklyn, NY (2003-present). Work closely with the buyer and owner while becoming familiar with the day-to-day details of operating a retail store.
- Receive and in-process merchandise shipments.
- Accept payments and processed charge purchases.
- Price and mark down items on display.
- Make sales including working the cash register and handling charge account purchases.
- Contribute my talents in skillfully displaying merchandise as well as choosing the most attractive accessories for each outfit.
- Refined my knowledge of retail operations while becoming known for my outstanding customer service and communication skills.

MERCHANDISING ASSISTANT and **CUSTOMER SERVICE SPECIALIST.** Carlyle Floral Designs, Hamilton, NY (2001-03). While working in the gift shop, helped customers choose gifts and decorative party accessories.
- Earned recognition for my creative abilities in designing displays, wrapping gifts, and finding interesting ways to organize merchandise.
- Used my knowledge of color to create attractive party decoration packages by coordinating invitations, favors, and balloons.
- Advised customers choosing stationery on the color and style most suitable for their needs.

Other experience: Gained valuable experience in part-time and summer jobs:
- As a Cashier, became experienced in handling funds and balancing daily receipts.
- As a Nurse's Assistant/Medical Secretary, was known for my attention to detail and communication skills in a job which included maintaining medical files and making appointments.

PERSONAL　　Offer experience in designing creative merchandising displays. Have a talent for relating to people and making them comfortable. Will relocate.

Exact Name of Person
Title or Position
Name of Company
Address (no., street)
Address (city, state, zip)

**FASHION
MERCHANDISING
STUDENT**
working at
a retail store

Dear Exact Name of Person: (or Dear Sir or Madam if answering a blind ad.)

Can you use a dynamic and hard-working young professional who offers a proven ability to "get things done" in the hectic and fast-changing environment of retailing?

As you will see from my enclosed resume, I have received several honors related to fashion merchandising and have recently completed a year of college-level studies in merchandising at the American Business Fashion Institute in Indianapolis. I have worked since I was 16 years old and I have excelled in every job I have held. My experience includes working with buyers and assistant buyers of swimwear, working with medical professionals purchasing uniforms and specialty items, and working with customers in all kinds of departments — women's, boys, men's, infants, shoes, housewares, and others.

You would find me to be an enthusiastic and reliable person, and I would be delighted to provide outstanding personal and professional references.

I hope you will welcome my call soon when I try to arrange a brief meeting to discuss your personnel needs and how I might fit into them. I believe I could be a valuable addition to your company's work force.

Yours sincerely,

Molly Anne Dyer

MOLLY ANNE DYER

1110½ Hay Street, Fayetteville, NC 28305 • preppub@aol.com • (910) 483-6611

OBJECTIVE   To contribute to an organization that can use a dedicated, hard-working young sales and marketing professional who offers excellent communication skills along with extensive knowledge of retail merchandising and operations.

EDUCATION   Am currently enrolled in studies leading to an **Associate of Science degree in Fashion Merchandising**, Ivy Tech State College, Indianapolis, IN, 2000.
Completed one year of college studies in **Business Management**, Butler University, Indianapolis, IN, 1999.
Graduated from Perimeter High School, Indianapolis, IN, 1997.

EXPERIENCE   **SALES ASSOCIATE** and **CASHIER**. Dillard's, Indianapolis, IN (2003-present). Contribute to increased efficiency and profitability while working in the Men's, Boy's, and Infant's departments of this major retailer.

DISPLAY ARRANGER. TJ Maxx, Indianapolis, IN (2002-03). Created exciting swimsuit displays used by assistant buyers and buyers in making their purchasing decisions. Gained insight into the variables and influences considered by buyers in purchasing fashion.

SALES ASSOCIATE. Belk, Indianapolis, IN (1999-00). Helped to set up this new store "from scratch" in this mall location; worked in Women's Apparel and Men's Shoes.

SALES ASSOCIATE. Best Buy, Indianapolis, IN (1998-99). Worked at the main service desk and in the computer department for this major electronics retailer.

SALES ASSOCIATE. Uniforms Inc., Indianapolis, IN (1996-98). Learned medical terminology while working with doctors and nurses in providing medical uniforms and tools.

Other experience:
COMPUTER OPERATOR. J. C. Magnolia High School, Indianapolis, IN (1996). Worked part-time as an administrative aide for the faculty and staff of this high school; worked with junior and senior high school students in the guidance department.
- Refined my communication and problem-solving skills, and was commended for my maturity and poise when counseling students.

PERSONAL
- Am a creative young professional who believes that hard work and persistence are keys to success.
- Have an excellent understanding of the buying, inventory control, sales, and customer service functions associated with retailing.
- Can provide outstanding personal and professional references upon request.

ACCOMPLISHMENTS
- At graduation, was named "Student of the Year" and "Student of the Year in Fashion Merchandising and Marketing," 1997: these distinctions were based on my outstanding grade point average.
- Produced two high-quality fashion shows at my high school.
- Was named Tennis Player of the Year, 1996: played tennis for four years and was tennis team manager for three years.
- Was active in Distributive Education Clubs of America (DECA), Future Homemakers of America (FHA), and Vocational Industrial Clubs of America (VICA).

CAREER CHANGE

Date

Exact Name of Person (if known)
Title or Position
Name of Company
Address (no., street)
Address (city, state, zip)

FINANCIAL PLANNER
for a major retail
organization

Dear Exact Name of Person: (or Dear Sir or Madam)

With the enclosed resume, I would like to introduce you to the considerable financial planning skills which I would like to utilize for the benefit of your organization. I am making a career change from financial management in the retail world to financial management in the financial services field, and I can assure you I have much to offer.

After earning my college degree in Communications, I began working for the Rich's organization and have excelled in an unusually rapid track record of advancement to Buyer. In my position, I am responsible for a $10 million sales volume, and much of what I do is similar to managing a portfolio of commercial accounts. In 2003, I increased volume by over 4% while also increasing profit margin dollars, and in 2001 so far, I am showing a 26% increase in sales compared to 2002.

While handling multimillion dollar responsibility related to 14 departments in 22 stores, I conducted extensive negotiations with vendors in Jackson, Cleveland, and New York City, as well as performing liaison with store managers throughout Mississippi. In handling my financial responsibilities, I work extensively with financial software. I am highly proficient with Microsoft Word and Excel and use them on a daily basis to analyze data for stores, vendors, and product lines.

I believe the primary reasons for my success have been my communication skills as well as my ability to establish and maintain excellent working relationships. Each time I have been reassigned responsibility for a new area within Rich's, my reputation has preceded me and I have been enthusiastically welcomed by store managers who had heard "through the grapevine" that I am a true professional who can be counted on to help them achieve outstanding bottom-line results.

Although I could remain with the Rich's organization and am held in high regard, I have decided that I wish to make a change into the financial services industry. I thrive on the fast pace and highly competitive nature of retailing, and I am certain I would thrive on the fast pace, aggressive sales orientation, and highly competitive environment of the financial services industry. With my strong communication, sales, and financial management skills, I feel certain I could make valuable contributions, and I would hope to rise into the ranks of management based on my accomplishments. I hope you will contact me to suggest a time when we might meet to discuss your needs and how I might meet them. Thank you in advance for your time.

Sincerely,

Veronica J. Hart

VERONICA JANE HART

1110½ Hay Street, Fayetteville, NC 28305 • preppub@aol.com • (910) 483-6611

OBJECTIVE

I want to contribute to an organization that can use a skilled financial manager and planner who thrives on meeting ambitious sales goals and financial objectives in a fast-paced, competitive environment where building strong relationships is essential to success.

EDUCATION

Earned **Bachelor of Science in Communications** with a Minor in **Public Relations**, Jackson State University, Jackson, MS, 1994.

Excelled in extensive training sponsored by the Rich's organization related to financial accounting, inventory control, and financial planning as well as sales, merchandising, and customer service.

EXPERIENCE

Have excelled in the following "track record" of advancement with Rich's Department Stores:

2002-present: FINANCIAL PLANNER and **BUYER.** Cleveland, MS. Was promoted in an unusually short time frame from Associate Buyer to Buyer, and then received in 2003 the prestigious Goldman Award; have excelled in managing an annual volume of $10 million while directing the planning, development, presentation, and profitability for the Women's Better Sportswear Departments in 22 stores.

- In 2002, increased volume by over 4% while also increasing profit margin dollars; in 2003 so far, am showing a 26% increase in sales over 2002.
- As a buyer, travel to New York 15 times a year; to the corporate office in Charlotte six times a year; and to stores throughout eastern Mississippi in order to re-merchandise stores, retrain sales personnel, and consult with store managers.
- Negotiate prices with vendors from companies including Donna Karan, Ralph Lauren, Coach, and Gucci; am known for my skill in negotiating the best price to ensure an optimal markup and gross margin.
- Aggressively manage my financial plan for 14 departments in 22 stores.
- Extensively communicate with vendors and store managers.
- Have earned an excellent reputation among vendors and store managers; each of the three times I was reassigned to a new buying area, my reputation as a vibrant communicator and strong manager preceded me and I was enthusiastically welcomed by the store management for whom I was assigned to perform buying.
- Am highly creative and resourceful by nature, and am continuously engaged in a process of developing new projects and contests to increase sales; have sponsored numerous sales contests.

2000-02: ASSOCIATE BUYER. Cleveland, MS. Assisted four buyers with buying.

1998-00: AREA SALES MANAGER. Cleveland, MS. Was responsible for sales associates' schedules; responded to customer inquiries and concerns.

- Conducted monthly department meetings; interviewed and trained new sales associates.
- Increased volume by 1.5%; exceeded personal sales goal by 61%.

1994-98: SALES ASSOCIATE. Cleveland, MS. Was rehired by Rich's because of my outstanding performance as a Sales Associate in Jackson, MS.

COMPUTERS

Highly proficient in utilizing computers in order to analyze financial data; on a daily basis use Microsoft Word and Excel to analyze sales, vendor, and store data.

PERSONAL

Can provide outstanding references. Offer a reputation as an outgoing communicator with an ability to establish and maintain excellent working relationships.

CAREER CHANGE

Exact Name of Person
Title or Position
Name of Company
Address (no., street)
Address (city, state, zip)

FOUNDER/MANAGER
for an established floor
covering company

Dear Exact Name of Person: (or Dear Sir or Madam if answering a blind ad.)

I would appreciate an opportunity to talk with you soon about how I could contribute to your organization through my business management, sales, and communication skills.

As you will see from my resume, I have founded successful businesses, tripled the sales volume of an existing company, and directed projects which required someone who could take a concept and turn it into an operating reality. While excelling as a retailer and importer of products that included oriental rugs and Italian antiques, I have become accustomed to working with a discriminating customer base of people regionally who trust my taste and character. In addition to a proven "track record" of producing a profit, I have earned a reputation for honesty and reliability. I believe there is no substitute in business for a good reputation.

I am ready for a new challenge, and that is why I have, in the last several months, closed two of my business locations in Vermont and turned over the management of the third operation to a family member. I want to apply my seasoned business judgement, along with my problem-solving and opportunity-finding skills, to new areas.

If you can use the expertise of a savvy and creative professional who is skilled at handling every aspect of business management, from sales and marketing to personnel and finance, I would enjoy talking with you informally about your needs and goals. A flexible and adaptable person who feels comfortable stepping into new situations, I am able to "size up" problems and opportunities quickly through the "lens" of experience. I pride myself on my ability to deal tactfully and effectively with everyone.

I hope you will welcome my call soon to arrange a brief meeting at your convenience to discuss your current and future needs and how I might serve them. Thank you in advance for your time.

Sincerely yours,

Carl D. Winchell

Alternate last paragraph:
I hope you will call or write me soon to suggest a time convenient for us to meet and discuss your current and future needs and how I might serve them. Thank you in advance for your time.

CARL D. WINCHELL

1110½ Hay Street, Fayetteville, NC 28305   •   preppub@aol.com   •   (910) 483-6611

OBJECTIVE

To add value to an organization that can use a resourceful entrepreneur and manager who offers a proven ability to start up successful new ventures and transform ailing operations into profitable ones through applying my sales, communication, and administrative skills.

EDUCATION

Earned **B.A. degree in Sociology**, University of Vermont, Burlington, VT.

AFFILIATIONS & COMMUNITY LEADERSHIP

Have served by invitation on the Board of Directors of the following organizations:

Waterbury Business Guild   American Heart Association
The Burlington Association   Burlington Family Life Center
Clemmons Hill Children's Foundation   Zion Methodist Association

- Have earned a reputation as a creative strategist with the ability to transform ideas into operating realities and leadership skills necessary to instill enthusiasm in others.

EXPERIENCE

FOUNDER/MANAGER. Bluestein's Floor Coverings, Inc., Burlington, Waterbury, and Northfield, VT (1992-present). Established "from scratch" this business which grew to two locations with sales in the mid six figures; developed a product line of oriental rugs which I bought from sources worldwide, and developed a customer base which included discriminating purchasers from all over the southwest.

- From 1995-2000, simultaneously acted as an Importer and management consultant for an Italian antiques business; traveled to Italy three times a year as an importer.
- From 1992-1995, after being specially recruited as Development Director by the New Englanders Antique Convention, took on the paid job of coordinating the pledging and collection of $1.5 million to construct a dormitory and cafeteria for the New Englanders Antique Convention; set up all systems and procedures and managed the distribution of funds until construction was finished.
- Recently closed down the Burlington and Waterbury location, and have turned over the Burlington location, now known as Y. L. Simone, Inc., to a family member.

ENTREPRENEUR. Winchell's Gift Shop, Inc., Waterbury, VT (1987-1992). After extensive market research to determine the viability of establishing a business in the gifts and accessories niche, set up a store in the affluent Waterbury community which rapidly became successful through innovative promotions, vigorous marketing, and word of mouth.

- Recently turned the full-time management of this business over to a family member.

EXECUTIVE VICE PRESIDENT & SALES MANAGER. M. Dumas Carpet Co., Burlington, VT (1982-1987). Took over the management of an existing business and, in five years, tripled the sales volume while increasing the staff from four to 11 employees.

- Used radio and newspaper in innovative and memorable ways. Supervised a five-person sales staff and trained them in techniques related to prospecting and closing the sale.

Other experience:
COLLEGE INSTRUCTOR. Community College of Vermont, Waterbury, VT (1981-1982). Was an instructor for the college on a part-time basis. Taught classes on leadership development and business management. Counseled student on entrepreneurial plans, preparations, and the risks involved.

PERSONAL

Offer a proven ability to manage several functional areas and projects at the same time. Am confident that I can turn any solid concept into a profitable business through the knowledge and experience I have acquired. Am creative, and enjoy the thrill of "making things happen."

Date

Exact Name of Person
Exact Title
Exact Name of Company
Address
City, State, Zip

FURNITURE SALES ASSOCIATE

for Rhodes Furniture

Dear Exact Name of Person (or Dear Sir or Madam if answering a blind ad):

With the enclosed resume, I would like to introduce you to a highly motivated, experienced customer service and retail professional with exceptional supervisory, communication, and organizational skills and a background in retail furniture sales, customer service management, and customer service coordination.

At Rhodes Furniture, I am currently excelling as a Sales Associate, providing the highest possible levels of customer service both during and after the sale. I regularly contact outside vendors in order to secure special order items, and make follow-up calls after the sale to ensure that my customers are completely satisfied. I am responsible for merchandising all display areas of the store and through my efforts I have been able to achieve and often exceed sales goals; in 2002, I was recognized for having the highest carpet sales in my district.

In a previous position as Customer Service Manager at Staples, I handled all customer and employee complaints and ran the front end and copy shop for this high-volume office supply store. In addition to interviewing, hiring, and training of new employees, I was also responsible for controlling inventory stock levels and labor hours in the cash wrap and copy shop areas of the store. I wrote weekly schedules, prioritized and assigned daily tasks, and prepared all operational paperwork.

Although I am highly regarded by my present employer, and can provide excellent references at the appropriate time, I feel that my strong customer service background is under-utilized in a retail environment, and my exceptional communication and telephone skills would be better suited to a direct service position.

If you can use a highly experienced, self-motivated customer service and retail professional, I look forward to hearing from you soon to arrange a time when we could meet to discuss your present and future needs, and how I might meet them. I can assure you in advance that I have an outstanding reputation, and would quickly become a valuable asset to your organization.

Sincerely,

Brittany Meyers

BRITTANY MEYERS

1110½ Hay Street, Fayetteville, NC 28305   •   preppub@aol.com   •   (910) 483-6611

OBJECTIVE

To benefit an organization that can use a retail and customer service professional with exceptional supervisory, communication, and organizational skills and a background in customer service, furniture sales, and data entry.

EDUCATION

A.S. degree in Business Management, Sinclair Community College, Dayton, OH, 2001. Currently enrolled in University of Dayton and working toward a **B.S. degree in Business Administration**; degree anticipated in 2003.

EXPERIENCE

FURNITURE SALES ASSOCIATE. Rhodes Furniture, Dayton, OH (2002-present). Provide customer service and perform merchandising and display tasks for this busy furniture retailer.
- Assist customers in selection and purchase of merchandise; process credit applications.
- Perform follow-up calls to ensure customer satisfaction after the point of sale.
- Direct warehouse personnel to restock floor from existing back stock.
- Consistently received outstanding marks on all performance appraisals.
- In 2002, was recognized for having the highest carpet sales in the district.

CUSTOMER SERVICE MANAGER. Staples, Dayton, OH (2001-02). Directed all aspects of the operation of the front end and copy center areas of this large office supply wholesaler, supervising 15 cashiers and copy center employees.
- Interviewed, hired and trained all new personnel; performed employee evaluations.
- Prepared and maintained operational paperwork, including inventory logs, computer printouts, copy machine usage logs, and management reports.
- Wrote weekly schedules, prioritized and assigned daily tasks for employees in my area.
- Performed periodic stock checks, inventory control, and ordering to ensure a strong in-stock position on fast-moving items.

PATIENT REPRESENTATIVE. The Medical Center of Dayton, Dayton, OH (1998-01). Acted as liaison between patients, family members, medical staff, and health agencies in the emergency room of this busy medical center. Counseled family members, logged in patients, and entered patient information into the hospital's computer system.

CUSTOMER SERVICE COORDINATOR. Nextel, Inc., Dayton, OH (1994-1998). Performed a wide variety of customer service tasks, as well as some clerical and secretarial duties in this fast-paced cellular phone service center.
- Received and processed customer orders for new service and equipment installation, cessation of existing service, and changes to existing service and equipment.
- Collected money for payment of current and delinquent bills and accounts; investigated complaints about bills and service; arranged for adjustments and extensions of credit.
- Prepared and maintained sales proposals for account executives and managers, as well as studies of WATTs lines.

Other Experience:
QUALITY ASSURANCE SPECIALIST AND ASSISTANT SUPERVISOR. Life Insurance of Ohio, Inc., Dayton, OH (1992-1994). Supervised five data entry clerks providing customer service. Excelled as a troubleshooter for correcting policies rejected by the computer.
SWITCHBOARD OPERATOR. Ohio Telephone & Telegraph, Dayton, OH (1994-1995). Routed and connected a large volume of incoming local and long-distance calls.

PERSONAL

Excellent personal and professional references are available upon request.

Exact Name of Person (if known)
Title or Position
Name of Company
Address (no., street)
Address (city, state, zip)

GENERAL MANAGER
for a successful import
corporation

Dear Exact Name of Person: (or Dear Sir or Madam)

    With the enclosed resume, I would like to make you aware of my background as a seasoned retail manager with exceptional communication and organizational skills. I offer proven abilities in human resources recruiting and training as well as purchasing, loss prevention, inventory control, and customer service.

    As the General Manager of Bethune Imports Inc., of Spokane, I supervised a staff of 16 associates while overseeing the operation of this busy retail outlet. Through innovative marketing and merchandising strategies as well as through emphasizing the highest levels of customer service, I was able to grow the store's annual sales to more than $1.2 million in a highly competitive market. I aggressively implemented state-of-the-art scanning and bar coding technology which resulted in numerous efficiencies and cost savings, and I automated management reporting. Because of our outstanding reputation in the market and our highly efficient operating systems.

    In an earlier position with Burlington Factory Outlet, I advanced from an entry-level position as a Sales Clerk to General Manager, responsible for the operation of four retail locations and a warehouse distribution center. I managed a combined staff of 20 employees at several different locations, conducting all interviews as well as hiring and training personnel.

    If you can use a sales and retail professional with exceptional leadership ability and problem-solving skills, then I hope you will give me a call to suggest a time when we might meet in person. I can assure you in advance that I have much knowledge which could be beneficial to your organization, and I am seeking an opportunity to put my experience and knowledge to use in ways that will maximize profitability and efficiency.

    Sincerely,

Taylor F. McLemore

TAYLOR F. MCLEMORE

1110½ Hay Street, Fayetteville, NC 28305   •   preppub@aol.com   •   (910) 483-6611

OBJECTIVE

To benefit an organization that can use an articulate and experienced retail professional with exceptional organizational skills who offers a track record of success in operations management, human resources and staff development, purchasing, and inventory control.

EDUCATION

A.S. in Business Management, Spokane Falls Community College, Spokane, WA, 2002.

EXPERIENCE

GENERAL MANAGER. Bethune Imports of Spokane, Spokane, WA (2003-present). Contributed to the growth of sales of more than $1.2 million annually. Oversee and direct all areas of this busy retail store to include managing human and fiscal resources, loss prevention, purchasing, training, inventory control, merchandising, and customer service.
- Provide leadership in implementing state-of-the-art scanning and bar code technology at the earliest opportunity; this technology improved efficiency and reduced inventory loss.
- Lead by example, supervise up to 25 associates; as a matter of personal and company philosophy, we aim for the highest standards of customer service.
- Create innovative and effective marketing and merchandising strategies which resulted in doubling sales from $300,000 to more than $11 million annually.
- Interview and hire potential employees; evaluate all personnel.
- Train all associates; author detailed training manuals designed to provide step-by-step instruction in all functional areas of performance.
- Computerized all reporting procedures at the management level, including payroll, accounts payable, accounts receivable, purchasing and order tracking, etc.
- Conduct store meetings in order to motivate staff members and foster a team atmosphere while improving and maintaining customer service standards.
- Perform regular inspections of the store to ensure compliance with company policies, appearance standards, and merchandising plans.

Began with Burlington Factory Outlet as a Sales Clerk and advanced:
2001-03: **GENERAL MANAGER.** Spokane, WA. Promoted to General Manager after ably serving the company; within two years of assuming a leadership role, transformed an organization that had not shown a profit in five years into a profitable operation.
- Entrusted with total responsibility for the operation of four retail stores and a warehouse distribution center; managed as many as 20 associates at several different locations.
- Interviewed, hired, and trained all personnel; conducted employee performance appraisals and counseled employees to improve performance.
- Oversaw all aspects of purchasing and inventory control, contacted and conducted negotiations with various vendors.

1998-01: **SALES CLERK.** Spokane, WA. Excelled in this entry-level position while still in high school; quickly evidenced a strong aptitude for retail merchandising, providing the highest possible levels of customer service.
- Assisted customers in the selection and purchase of merchandise; increased sales by suggesting related items.
- Stocked and shelved stock and performed shipping and receiving functions; displayed merchandise to present a full and attractive appearance.

PERSONAL

Excellent personal and professional references are available upon request.

Exact Name of Person (if known)
Title or Position
Name of Company
Address (no., street)
Address (city, state, zip)

GENERAL MANAGER
for a home decor
company in Iowa

Dear Exact Name of Person: (or Dear Sir or Madam)

With the enclosed resume, I would like to formally express my interest in the job of District Sales Manager with Foster Home Decor, Inc.

As you will see from my resume in 2000, I took over the management of a company which sells, installs, and repairs blinds, and I increased sales and net worth dramatically. In 2002, I received a Certificate of Achievement as a Fabricator from the Foster Home Decor Shutter Training, and in both 2002 and 2003, I was recognized for outstanding sales achievement as a Foster Home Decor Fabricator.

In my previous job, I also excelled in sales management and was cited as the most productive sales and service manager in the company.

With a reputation as a powerful motivator who believes in "leadership by example," I am known for my high energy level, positive and enthusiastic attitude, extroverted personality, persistence in all tasks, as well as for my highly organized approach to work and my relentless follow through on the details of any job.

You would find me in person to be a dynamic communicator who believes that excellent customer service is one of the keys to success in the marketplace. I can provide outstanding personal and professional references at your request.

I hope you will call or write me soon to suggest a time convenient for us to meet and discuss your current and future needs and how I might serve them. Thank you in advance for your time.

Sincerely yours,

Jesse D. Williams

JESSE D. WILLIAMS

1110½ Hay Street, Fayetteville, NC 28305 • preppub@aol.com • (910) 483-6611

OBJECTIVE

To contribute to an organization that can use a dynamic sales manager who offers a proven ability to improve "bottom-line" results, cement customer relations, and motivate others.

EDUCATION

B.S. in Business Management with concentration in Marketing, Drake University, Des Moines, IA, 2000.

In numerous Casey Treat and Paula White seminars, have studied "closing the sale," "motivation in sales and service," and "personal motivation in job performance."

EXPERIENCE

GENERAL MANAGER. Foster Home Decor, Inc., Des Moines, IA (2000-present). Took over the management of a company with no financial stability and reorganized it so that, within two years, the company's net worth increased from $21,000 to $190,000 while total average yearly sales increased from $190,000 to its current level of $450,000.

- Produced a 190% sales gain in two years; am still producing a 5% sales gain monthly.
- In 2002, received a Certificate of Achievement as a Fabricator from the Foster Home Decor Shutter Training Program.
- In 2002 and 2003, was recognized for Outstanding Sales Achievement as a Foster Home Decor Fabricator.
- Train sales representatives in opening new accounts, schedule appointments, perform highly effective telemarketing, and provide the kind of customer service designed to produce repeat business and generate word-of-mouth referrals.
- Restructured the corporate budget and have managed the company's accounting functions and tax preparation/reporting.
- Developed a new sales staff which pushed revenues up 30% the first year and 45% the second year; redefined sales goals and quotas; then conducted highly effective sales meetings to generate enthusiasm and to teach effective sales and marketing techniques.
- Have "turned around" this company so that it now enjoys an outstanding reputation for quality installation and repair. Revamped the customer service format to allow the company to offer a quality blind at manufacturer's prices with guaranteed service!

GENERAL MANAGER/STAFF MANAGER. Montclair & Camelot Fitness Centers, Des Moines, IA (1997-00). Began with this company as a Sales and Service Instructor in 1997, and was then promoted to Staff Manager, 1998, and then to General Manager in 2000.

General Manager (2000-2002), Montclair Fitness Center:
- In 2000, was promoted to supervise the total operations of these two health spas which have a combined net worth of $6 million and a net income of $3.2 million a year from the sales department alone.
- Managed and motivated four company managers, four assistant managers, one aerobics coordinator, one maintenance manager, 20 sales representatives, 20 health and fitness instructors, and 20 aerobics instructors.

Staff Manager (1998-2000), Camelot Spa:
- Was named "Regional Manager of the Year" for two straight years increasing overall sales 16% and for being the most productive sales and service manager in the company; personally achieved a sales quota of $10,000 cash sales per month and motivated two assistant managers and six sales representatives to meet or achieve their sales goals.
- While managing six health instructors, led them to earn the top awards in their fields.

PERSONAL

Am known for my positive and enthusiastic attitude, high energy level, extroverted personality, tenacious and assertive disposition, and for my well organized approach to every job as well as for my relentless persistence and follow through on every task.

Exact Name of Person
Title or Position
Name of Company
Address (no., street)
Address (city, state, zip)

GENERAL MANAGER

for Quixtar Nutri-System
organization

Dear Exact Name of Person: (or Dear Sir or Madam if answering a blind ad.)

I am writing in response to your ad in the *Boise Courier*. I am planning to relocate to the Boise area and am sending you a copy of my resume so that you can assist me in my search for a challenging and rewarding management position in this area.

As you will see from my resume, since early in 2002 I have been successful in a management position with Quixtar, the nationally known Nutri-System organization. Despite the fact that this corporation has declared bankruptcy and more than 800 locations have had to close, I have been able to not only keep my Twin Falls, ID, locations open but have increased sales. I edged out some tough competition to earn the respected "Manager of the Year Award" from among approximately 1,600 other professionals.

My degree is in Psychology and Sociology and I offer additional experience as a Social Worker. After demonstrating that I could handle a case load of 120-150 clients and consistently complete my cases ahead of schedule, I was promoted to Eligibility Specialist in the Department of Housing and Urban Development.

I have managed a staff of up to 25 and all aspects of operations in a facility which reached the $200,000 level in annual sales and serviced as many as 200 clients a week.

I am an enthusiastic, energetic, and well-organized professional. I offer a talent for getting the most from employees and finding effective ways to keep things running smoothly and productively — even under very unsettled circumstances.

I hope you will welcome my call soon to discuss how you might be able to help me in my job search in your area. Thank you in advance for your time.

Sincerely yours,

Gwyneth R. Oliver

GWYNETH REBECCA OLIVER

1110½ Hay Street, Fayetteville, NC 28305 • preppub@aol.com • (910) 483-6611

OBJECTIVE

To offer my superior communication and motivational skills to an organization that can use an experienced management professional who has demonstrated a bottom-line orientation and a talent for selling concepts and services through an enthusiastic and energetic style.

EXPERIENCE

GENERAL MANAGER and **SALES AND CUSTOMER RELATIONS ADVISOR.** Quixtar (Nutri-System), Twin Falls and Boise, ID (2002-present). Continue to set sales records and steadily increase the customer base despite the fact that the parent corporation declared bankruptcy in 2001 and more than 800 locations nationwide have been forced to close.

- Singled out as "Manager of the Year" from among 1,600 qualified professionals nationwide, displayed knowledge of every aspect of Nutri-System operations.
- Increased sales by more than 50% during reorganization following a corporate takeover.
- Handle a wide range of functional activities ranging from setting sales and service goals, to developing business plans, to recruiting/training/supervising employees.
- Oversee daily operational areas including financial management, inventory control, and customer follow up procedures.
- Handpicked for my effectiveness in running the Twin Falls site, was selected to open the Boise location and hold the position of interim area manager.
- During a two-month period prior to opening the Boise center, hired and trained personnel and set up their operation.
- Applied my knowledge of marketing techniques while developing campaigns which used successful clients in radio ads and placed "lead boxes" throughout the city.
- Supervise up to 25 employees in a facility which caters to 50 to 100 clients a week and makes over $200,000 in its peak years before corporate reorganization.
- Maintained a $1500,000 to $200,000 level with approximately 75 clients a week and about 12 employees in 2003.
- Through personal attention and rapport with clients, built a strong customer base which continues to generate about four new clients a week.

ELIGIBILITY SPECIALIST. Department of Housing and Urban Development, Twin Falls, ID (2000-2002). Through my ability to communicate effectively with others and quickly establish rapport, was effective in working closely with agency clients to assess their needs and using established guidelines to determine their eligibility for various types of aid.

- Was promoted after managing a case load of from 120 to 150 clients and displaying my ability to organize and deal with a heavy schedule by always completing my cases on schedule and pitching in to help other social workers with theirs.

EDUCATION

B.S., Psychology and Sociology, College of Southern Idaho, Twin Falls, ID, 2001.

- Earned recognition in "Who's Who Among American College Students" on the recommendation of Sociology Department faculty members.
- Maintained a 3.8 GPA and was one of the top two students in my graduating class.
- Received "Special Honors" and "Highest Academic Honors" upon my graduation.
- Founded and then served as president of the University's Sociology Club; planned and coordinated a wide range of campus activities for the Student Activities Committee.
- Completed independent study in Europe on the use of alternative medicines.
- Served as a volunteer counselor at a domestic abuse house.

PERSONAL

Am an energetic and enthusiastic individual with a flair for handling human, material, and fiscal resources. Contribute to my community through my church's Outreach Ministries Committee which is very active in assisting the homeless and disadvantaged.

Exact Name of Person (if known)
Title or Position
Name of Company
Address (no., street)
Address (city, state, zip)

GENERAL MANAGER
for Best Buy
with
previous banking
experience

Dear Exact Name of Person: (or Dear Sir or Madam)

With the enclosed resume, I would like to make you aware of my background as a seasoned retail manager with exceptional communication and organizational skills. I offer proven abilities in human resources recruiting and training as well as purchasing, loss prevention, inventory control, and customer service.

As the General Manager of Best Buy, I was selected to oversee all aspects of day-to-day operations from accounting and financing, to customer service and sales, to collections, to personnel management. I supervise four employees, conduct periodic performance reviews, respond to employee grievances, and interview and hire new employees.

In an earlier position as a Sales Associate for Sears and Roebuck, I discovered my talent in sales and became aware of the importance to listening the needs of my customers. I also handled all stages of new and used car sales from initial sales presentations at Northwestern Nissan as a Sales Representative.

If you can use a sales and retail professional with exceptional leadership ability and problem-solving skills, then I hope you will give me a call to suggest a time when we might meet in person. I can assure you in advance that I have much knowledge which could be beneficial to your organization, and I am seeking an opportunity to put my experience and knowledge to use in ways that will maximize profitability and efficiency.

Sincerely,

Magdalena A. Obas

MAGDALENA A. OBAS

1110½ Hay Street, Fayetteville, NC 28305   •   preppub@aol.com   •   (910) 483-6611

OBJECTIVE   To contribute an organization that can use a mature, honest professional who can contribute financial expertise, sales experience, and strong interpersonal skills refined in environments where customer confidence was of major importance.

EDUCATION   Earned associate's degrees in **Business Administration** and in **Banking and Finance,** Metropolitan Community College, Omaha, NE, 2002. 3.6 GPA.

EXPERIENCE   *Advanced in this track record of promotion with Best Buy,* **Omaha, NE,** *while refining my skills in finance, business operations, sales, and customer service:*
2003-present: GENERAL MANAGER. After two years as a top sales professional, was promoted in 2003 to oversee all aspects of day-to-day operations from accounting and financing, to customer service and sales, to collections, to personnel management.
- Collect and maintain data used while preparing daily and monthly financial reports and sales figures.
- Supervise four employees: conduct periodic performance reviews, respond to employee grievances, and interview and hire new employees.
- Prepare monthly projections of expected sales for the store as a whole and for each member of the sales staff.
- Operate with an "open door" policy which allows employees to feel comfortable coming to me to discuss ways to make the business operate smoothly and to support my decisions on operational matters which affect the company's profitability.
- Schedule employee work hours; take care of opening and closing the store; and make bank deposits on a regular daily basis.
- Acted as the Assistant Manager for six months before taking over the top management role: assisted in opening and closing, managed the $400 petty cash fund.

2001-03: SALES ASSOCIATE. Discovered a talent for sales and became aware of the importance of listening to the customer and finding the product that met their needs.
- Developed a strong repeat customer base while earning a reputation for my honesty.

Highlights of earlier experience in sales and bank operations positions:
ACCOUNT EXECUTIVE. WGKE 98 FM Radio, Omaha, NE, (1999-2001). Sold radio advertising time to a wide range of area businesses; made cold calls on potential customers.

SALES REPRESENTATIVE. Northwestern Nissan, Omaha, NE, (1996-1999). Handled all stages of new and used car sales from initial sales presentations, to closing the sales, to arranging financing, to ensuring the customer had proper licensing and insurance.

BRANCH MANAGER, HEAD TELLER, and **LOAN OFFICER.** Omaha Federal Credit Union, Omaha, NE, (1995-1996). Supervised three employees while contributing in several functional capacities in this full service financial institution.
- As Loan Counselor, developed a keen eye for detail while accepting and processing loan applications from customers: verified all information on the application.

ASSISTANT MANAGER and **SALES CLERK.** JCPenney and Sears, Omaha, NE (1994-1995). Supervised employees, sold women's clothing, controlled inventory in two stores.

PERSONAL   Am known for my honesty and personal integrity. Offer well-developed managerial skills along with an aptitude for the financial aspect of running a successful business.

Date

Exact Name of Person (if known)
Title or Position
Name of Company
Address (no., street)
Address (city, state, zip)

GENERAL MANAGER

for Condon's department store

Dear Exact Name of Person: (or Dear Sir or Madam)

With the enclosed resume, I would like to make you aware of the considerable sales, management, and marketing skills I could offer your organization.

As you will see from my resume, I have excelled most recently in managing a women's clothing store. As General Manager, I hire and train employees, handle accounts payable and receivable, and coordinate with a variety of vendors while handling the buying function.

In my previous position as Marketing Director and Events Coordinator with Collins & Rhodes Office Automation, I was involved in a wide range of management and marketing activities and was credited with playing a key role in the rapid growth of this multimillion-dollar company. I managed up to 10 branch managers while developing and coordinating advertising, marketing, and special events.

In a prior job with Baton Rouge Area Broadcasting as an Advertising Consultant, I created effective advertising and became skilled in cold-calling business owners to sell them on radio advertising. While working with Baton Rouge Area Broadcasting, I was active with community organizations including the Chamber of Commerce.

If you can use a vibrant and hard-working professional with versatile sales and marketing skills, I hope you will contact me to suggest a time when we could meet to discuss your needs and how I might meet them. I feel certain that I could make valuable contributions to your organization through my diversified marketing and management experience as well as through my creativity, aggressive sales skills, and highly positive personal attitude. I can provide excellent references at the appropriate time.

Sincerely yours,

Amanda J. Holladay

AMANDA JO HOLLADAY

1110½ Hay Street, Fayetteville, NC 28305 • preppub@aol.com • (910) 483-6611

OBJECTIVE   To contribute to an organization that can use an experienced manager who offers a background in managing retail and marketing operations, buying and controlling inventory, supervising and managing personnel, as well as in handling public relations.

EDUCATION   **GENERAL MANAGER.** Condon'sDepartment Store, Baton Rouge, LA (2003-present). As the General Manager of this 25-year-old high-end women's fashion store, am in charge of all areas of operation.

- Interview, hire, and train all employees; managed three people. Prepare business plans four times a year and review goal accomplishments on a monthly basis.
- Handle accounts payable and accounts receivable; reconciled invoices. Reconcile daily, weekly, and monthly receipts with actual deposits; handle all liaison with the bank.
- Make buying decisions and order inventory; coordinate with vendors and perform extensive liaison with suppliers and manufacturers who acted as vendors.
- Purchase and distribute the full line of beauty control make-up products; create innovative and effective sales and marketing strategies.

MARKETING DIRECTOR & EVENTS COORDINATOR. Collins &-Rhodes Office Automation, Hammond, LA (2001-03). Joined one of the state's fastest-growing companies with sales of $8 million annually; played a key role in its impressive growth to well over $12 million; utilized my previous advertising sales and copy writing experience to create effective advertising and marketing concepts.

- Developed a news letter of current events which acquainted the business community and employees with Collins & Rhodes business strategy and successes.
- Assumed a variety of management roles within this fast-growing company; managed 10 branch managers located throughout southeast Louisiana.
- Created and managed special events which celebrated company milestones and which established excellent public relations.
- Designed and directed innovative marketing activities; handled the development of co-op advertising for all branches and assisted the branches in developing their budgets.
- Traveled extensively to coordinate with branch managers and others.
- Became known for my enthusiastic and outgoing personality, and learned that a positive attitude is essential in developing an attitude of teamwork.

ADVERTISING CONSULTANT. WSKR 105.5 FM of Baton Rouge Area Broadcasting, Hammond, LA (1998-2001). While working with this popular radio station, excelled in numerous roles including working as an on-air personality in the News/Talk format.

- Prepared proposals for advertising plans and established projected budgets and goals for local businesses. Performed on live remotes to promote products.
- Wrote effective advertising copy including jingles which became memorable.

EDUCATION   B.A. in Business Management, Southeastern Louisiana University, Hammond, LA, 2002.
Completed extensive training related to marketing, management, sales, and other areas sponsored by employers including Baton Rouge Area Broadcasting.
Completed numerous college courses at Louisiana State University in Baton Rouge, LA.

AFFILIATIONS   Active in numerous community and civic organizations including the Chamber of Commerce.

PERSONAL   Can provide excellent personal and professional references. Am highly creative and enjoy new challenges. Enjoy the challenge of representing a quality product or service.

Exact Name of Person
Exact Title
Exact Name of Company
Address
City, State, Zip

**GROCERY STORE
MANAGER**
for Piggly Wiggly

Dear Exact Name of Person (or Dear Sir or Madam if answering a blind ad):

With the enclosed resume, I would like to make you aware of my background as an experienced manager with a track record of success in building sales and profitability while also maintaining focus on customer service and satisfaction.

As you will see, I have advanced with the retail supermarket chain Piggly Wiggly while becoming recognized as a professional who could be counted on to provide sound control over wages, inventory, supplies, and shrinkage. Presently a Store Manager in Roanoke, I have increased sales and profitability in a store with $14 million in average annual sales. I am leading this location to excellent results which include year-to-date rates of 21% increase in sales and a shrinkage rate of +0.14%.

I began my career with Piggly Wiggly as a Stocker in 1994 and soon advanced to Grocery Manager, then to Assistant Manager, and to Store Manager and have held this top management role in three area locations. In each store I have provided leadership which has led to my recognition with numerous "Outstanding Performance Awards" for sales increases and expertise in inventory control as well as for receiving high ratings in customer satisfaction surveys.

If you can use an experienced manager who is known for the ability to identify and solve problems and to lead employees to outstanding results in all measurable areas of operations, please contact me to suggest a time when we might meet to discuss your needs. I can assure you in advance that I could rapidly become an asset to your organization.

Sincerely,

Donald T. Miller, III

DONALD T. MILLER, III

1110½ Hay Street, Fayetteville, NC 28305   •   preppub@aol.com   •   (910) 483-6611

OBJECTIVE

To benefit an organization that can use a mature professional who offers a strong management background and expert knowledge of inventory, wage, and shrinkage control as well as a well-developed sense of the value of customer service and satisfaction.

TRAINING

Continually add to my knowledge by reading and taking tests which have earned me approximately 1,000 continuing education units awarded by the Piggly Wiggly corporation.

EXPERIENCE

Have built a track record of advancement with a large retail supermarket chain, Piggly Wiggly, which is headquartered in Roanoke, VA:

2002-present: GROCERY STORE MANAGER. Roanoke, VA. Increased sales and profitability in a store with $14 million in annual sales while managing six department heads and overseeing the day-to-day performance of 70 employees.

- Am providing the leadership which has allowed this location to see a year-to-date shrinkage rate of +0.14% and a 21% sales increase. Increased store profitability 4%.
- Oversee all phases of store operations ranging from wage control and processing, to inventory control and supply, to utilities, to maintenance, to security and safety, to cleaning and sanitation, to merchandising. Hire, train, and schedule employees.

2000-02: STORE MANAGER. Petersburg, VA. Increased sales 8% a year in a store which had an average annual sales volume of $10 million while supervising five department heads and 50 employees.

- Demonstrated my dedication to the success of store operations by working an average of 60 to 70 hours a week. Maintained outstanding results in all measurable areas of wages, shrinkage reduction, and bottom-line profitability.
- Oversaw all operational areas to include wage control and payroll actions, inventory control and supply, utilities management, building maintenance, security and safety, cleaning and sanitation, and merchandising as well as hiring, training, and scheduling.

1998-00: STORE MANAGER. Chester, VA. Supervised five department heads and 50 employees in a store which made an average of $9 million annually.

- Increased sales; learned to share responsibilities with my department heads while still working an average of 60-70 hours a week; and maintained high levels in all measured areas of operation (wages, shrinkage, and profitability).

1996-98: ASSISTANT MANAGER. Richmond, VA. Supervised one department head and seven employees in the grocery department while working as acting manager in his absence for a store with a $10 million annual sales volume. Was recognized for my excellent inventory control abilities as well as for my skills in scheduling, ordering, and building displays.

1994-96: GROCERY MANAGER. Richmond, VA. Recognized for my attention to detail as a Stocker in Richmond, VA, from 1994-1995, was promoted to oversee a grocery department in 1996. Supervised stockers; maintained a well-organized stock room and sales floor.

Highlights of earlier experience:
FLOOR MANAGER. Richmond, VA. Excelled in providing sound management and customer service skills in a small family-owned business, Doscher's Grocery Store in Richmond, VA.

PERSONAL

Numerous "Outstanding Performance Awards" based on sales, inventory control, and customer surveys. Have not missed one day of work due to illness in ten years with Piggly Wiggly.

Exact Name of Person
Exact Title
Exact Name of Company
Address
City, State, Zip

GROCERY STORE MANAGER
for Bi-Lo Inc.

Dear Exact Name of Person: (or Dear Sir or Madam if answering a blind ad)

With the enclosed resume, I would like to make you aware of my background as an experienced manager with excellent communication, organizational, and motivational skills as well as my background in operations management, staff development, and customer service.

I started with Bi-Lo as a meat cutter and advanced to Assistant Manager positions after being selected for the Store Manager Training Program, which is normally reserved for employees who have held a Department Manager position. In my present position as Store Manager for the Milwaukee location, I am responsible for all aspects of the operation of a $9.5 million store. I supervise as many as 52 employees, including six department managers, and direct the implementation of company programs, policies, and procedures. Through my initiative, the store's product levels and cleanliness have increased by 10%, and net contribution for the Milwaukee location has risen by 2.3%.

As you will see, I have earned a Associate of Science in Retail Management from the Madison Area Technical College. In addition, I have completed the Bi-Lo Store Manager Training Program and quickly mastered the proprietary computer system utilized by the company. I feel that my strong combination of education, initiative, and management experience would make me a worthy addition to your company.

If you can use a positive, results-oriented manager with a strong background in customer service, operations management, and staff development, then I look forward to hearing from you soon to arrange a time when we might meet to discuss your needs. I can assure you in advance that I have an excellent reputation and would quickly become a valuable asset to your company.

Sincerely,

Terrence G. Powell

TERRENCE G. POWELL

1110½ Hay Street, Fayetteville, NC 28305　　•　　preppub@aol.com　　•　　(910) 483-6611

OBJECTIVE

To benefit an organization that can use a manager with a positive, results-oriented leadership style and exceptional communication, organizational, and motivational skills as well as a background in operations management, staff development, and customer service.

EDUCATION

Earned a **Associate of Science degree in Retail Management**, Madison Area Technical College, Madison, WI, 2000.
Completed Bi-Lo Inc., Store Manager Training Program, Madison, WI, 1998.

EXPERIENCE

With Bi-Lo Inc., have excelled in areas of Customer Service, Inventory Management, and Staff Development while advancing in the following "track record" of increasing responsibilities for this 1,200-store retail grocery chain:
2003-present: **GROCERY STORE MANAGER.** Milwaukee, WI. Have been placed in charge of all operational aspects for this $9.5 million store.
* Supervise up to 52 employees, including six department managers.
* Increased store product levels and cleanliness by 10% while raising this location's net contribution by 2.3%.
* Hold final accountability for managing store inventory levels and controlling shrinkage.
* Interview prospective employees and consult with department heads to advise on final hiring decisions.
* Oversee the training efforts of the department managers, ensuring that all employees are adequately prepared to perform the duties required of them.
* Direct the implementation of company programs, policies, and procedures.

2001-03: **ASSISTANT STORE MANAGER.** Janesville, Fond Du Lac, Waukesha, WI. Transferred from the Madison store, supervised as many as 50 employees and oversaw store operations in the absence of the manager.
* Provided direct supervision to the Grocery Manager; was responsible for the grocery department operations and inventory control. Due to my initiative, inventory levels for the grocery department were within appropriate ranges for a store of our size and volume.
* Learned to use the in-store proprietary computer system.

1998-01: **STORE MANAGER.** Madison, WI. Promoted to this position after serving as Assistant Manager at various locations; responsible for all aspects of store operations at this $8 million location. Was fully accountable for inventory control, loss prevention, and shrinkage figures as well as overall profitability of the operation.
* Supervised up to 50 employees, including five department heads.
* Attended the University of Wisconsin on a full-time basis during the evenings.

1996-98: **ASSISTANT MANAGER.** Several locations throughout Wisconsin. Started with the company as a Meat Cutter and advanced to Assistant Manager positions after completing Bi-Lo Store Manager Trainee program; was selected to attend management training normally reserved for employees who had held a Department Manager position.

Other Experience: ROUTE SALES. Radefeld's Bakery, Madison, WI, (1995-1996). Excelled in this position selling and delivering bread and other baked goods; serviced 36 grocery, convenience store, and restaurant accounts in the Milwaukee area.

PERSONAL

Excellent personal and professional references are available upon request.

Exact Name of Person
Title or Position
Name of Company
Address (no., street)
Address (city, state, zip)

GROCERY STORE
MANAGER
for Publix

Dear Exact Name of Person: (or Dear Sir or Madam if answering a blind ad.)

I would appreciate an opportunity to talk with you soon about how I could contribute to your organization through my experience and personal qualities. With the enclosed resume, I would like to make you aware of my background as an experienced manager with excellent communication, organizational, and motivational skills as well as my background in operations management, staff development, and customer service.

I started with Publix as a bag boy and head stocker, and then I advanced to a Grocery Manager because of my hard work and dedication to the company. In my present position as Store Manager for the Augusta location, I am responsible for overseeing the implementation of a new Inventory Management System (IMS) which establishes an automatic reorder point for all products. I supervise up to 90 people, have rapidly developed the store into one of Publix's most profitable locations. I have also earned superior scores on three consecutive "surprise" audits.

As you will see, I have participated in many management training programs offered by Publix Inc. in areas involving customer service, strategic planning, quality control and others courses as well. I feel that my strong combination of management training and experience would make me a worthy addition to your company.

If you can use a positive, results-oriented manager with a strong background in customer service, operations management, and staff development, then I look forward to hearing from you soon to arrange a time when we might meet to discuss your needs.

Sincerely yours,

Harris J. Dew

Alternate last paragraph:
I hope you will welcome my call soon to arrange a brief meeting at your convenience to discuss your current and future needs and how I might serve them. Thank you in advance for your time.

HARRIS JAMES DEW

1110½ Hay Street, Fayetteville, NC 28305 • preppub@aol.com • (910) 483-6611

OBJECTIVE

To benefit an organization that can use an experienced manager who offers a "track record" of accomplishments in producing profits, managing operations, controlling costs, training employees, and increasing sales.

EXPERIENCE

Have built a track record of advancement with a large retail supermarket chain, Publix, Inc., **in Georgia and Alabama:**

2002-present: GROCERY STORE MANAGER. Publix, Inc., stores in GA and AL. After starting in the lowest-entry job as a "bag boy," have excelled as store manager of seven different stores in this thriving grocery retail chain with more than 1,000 stores nationwide.

- Am currently store manager of a store in Augusta, GA, that has been opened for more than five years; while supervising up to 90 people, have rapidly developed the store into one of Publix's most profitable, and have earned superior scores on three consecutive "surprise" audits.
- Am overseeing the implementation of a new Inventory Management System (IMS), and this store will be the training site for other stores in the region; IMS establishes an automatic reorder point for all products.
- Earned an Outstanding Performance Award for being the best in the area at returning unauthorized items to the reclaim center.
- Was recognized for achieving sales increases of 13.42% for the third quarter, 2003.
- Was specially selected to manage a store in Birmingham, AL, which was a "takeover" situation; trained "Five Star" employees in Publix's policies and methods of operation.
- In Marietta, GA, managed a store that was a takeover from Winn Dixie; retrained employees.
- Once managed the company's highest volume store in Atlanta, GA.
- On one occasion, was sent to manage a store in Macon, GA which had experienced an instantaneous doubling of its volume when a competitor suddenly closed down; learned to manage a nearly out-of-control growth situation.
- Deal with distributors and food vendors selling beer, wine, milk, bread, ice cream, and all types of grocery products; deal with national companies including Kelloggs, Kraft, Nabisco, and others.
- Have trained and developed many store managers who have become some of Publix's "superstar" managers; helped them refine their supervisory skills.
- Have become skilled in managing a multimillion-dollar profit center for a corporation with a reputation as a well organized giant known for low prices and thrifty management.
- Have learned to control expertly every variable and controllable cost including wage percentages, labor schedules, supplies, and all budgeted items.

1999-02: BAG BOY/STOCKER. Publix, Inc. Promoted rapidly from bag boy, to stocker and head stocker, to grocery manager because of hard work, determination, and dedication.

EDUCATION TRAINING

Participated in training programs with Publix in these and other areas:

customer service	strategic planning	sales
quality control	personnel administration	finance

PERSONAL

Have been singled out for particular recognition because of my stores' performance in customer courtesy and cost control. Offer outstanding problem-solving and decision-making skills. Am creative in working with people and in finding innovative approaches to training and supervision.

Date

Exact Name of Person
Exact Title
Exact Name of Company
Address
City, State, Zip

Dear Exact Name of Person: (or Dear Sir or Madam if answering a blind ad):

I am writing to express my strong interest in the position of Buyer/Assistant Manager. With the enclosed resume, I would like to make you aware of my experience in all aspects of purchasing, sales forecasting, events planning and development of promotions, and merchandising, as well as my analytical, planning, and negotiation skills.

As you will see from my resume, I have recently been excelling as a Buyer for Parisienne Department Store, where I was handpicked for my most recent position due to my analytical and problem-solving abilities. Assuming control of an area that was consistently overstocked by at least $500,000, I quickly reined in the excesses, and within six months Intimate Apparel was within established inventory guidelines for the Group.

Throughout my career in retail, I have applied my strong aptitude for creative and analytical thinking to problems related to increasing sales while maximizing profitability. An articulate communicator, my strong negotiation skills have resulted in acquiring the best prices and terms for my employers in interactions with national vendors.

If you can use a self-motivated professional whose abilities have been proven in a number of challenging environments, I hope you will write or call me soon to suggest a time when we might meet to discuss your needs and goals and how my background might serve them. I can provide outstanding references at the appropriate time.

Sincerely,

Denise Hardaway

DENISE HARDAWAY

1110½ Hay Street, Fayetteville, NC 28305   •   preppub@aol.com   •   (910) 483-6611

OBJECTIVE

To benefit an organization that can use a self-motivated, articulate professional with strong analytical, planning, and negotiation skills who offers a background in purchasing, sales forecasting, promotions and events planning, and merchandising.

EXPERIENCE

With Parisienne Department Stores, excelled in challenging positions as Group Buyer for Accessories and Intimate Apparel:

2003-present: **GROUP BUYER.** Intimate Apparel, Newark, NJ. Was handpicked to assume control of this troubled division which was consistently overstocked by $500,000 to $1 million; brought the group into compliance with inventory guidelines within six months.
- Manage a total sales volume of more than $10.6 million dollars while handling all aspects of merchandise selection for the Intimate Apparel departments in 22 stores.
- Analyze sales figures and budgetary requirements for each department against current year sales trends, generating sales forecasts and projections.
- Using sales projections and my industry experience, make buying commitments for the group; decided on merchandise purchased for all departments for a 4-6 month period.
- Track merchandise sales, analyzing department and group trends to identify items that needed to be marked down; determined percentage or amount of the price reduction.
- Monitor shipping and receiving, cross-checking with store personnel to ensure that items shipped by the vendor matched the merchandise ordered.
- Interact with store managers and associates, providing direction to store personnel regarding merchandising, upcoming events, new product information, and promotions.
- Generate 4.5% of total store volume for all stores in the group; facilitate an average yearly sales increase of 5%. Serve on the J. R. Heimer Committee for Foundations and Daywear and Sleepwear and Robes; received two Medallion Achievement Awards.

2000-03: **GROUP BUYER.** Accessories, Hosiery, Handbags, & Jewelry, Newark, NJ. Oversaw all buying functions for the Accessories departments of 11 stores; held responsibility for a total sales volume of $4.5 million.
- Developed sales projections for the group based on analysis of previous year, year-to-date, and category trends, budgetary requirements, and other marketing data.
- Consistently generated an average annual sales increase of more than 5% while maximizing profit margin through careful management of inventory levels and expenses.
- Negotiated with vendors to acquire the best prices and terms on new product as well as obtaining monetary refunds or merchandise credits for product that was not selling.

Highlights of earlier experience: Excelled in a number of earlier positions as a Buyer or Assistant Buyer for various retail outlets and small department store chains; honed my analytical and decision-making abilities in a variety of challenging environments:
1997-00: **BUYER.** Northern Division Department Stores, Newark, NJ. Performed all buying functions for an 18-store regional chain; held final responsibility for annual total sales of up to $1.5 million.
1995-97: **BUYER** and **ASSISTANT BUYER.** Catherine's Boutique, Newark, NJ. Started with this small chain of premium ladies specialty stores as an Assistant Buyer and advanced to increasing responsibilities. Performed all buying functions in assigned departments for 14 stores; was responsible for total annual sales of more than $3 million.
1994-95: **ASSISTANT BUYER.** M. Ward's Department Store, Newark, NJ. Handled buying for six stores and an annual sales volume of $1.5 million.

PERSONAL

Excellent personal and professional references are available upon request.

Exact Name of Person
Title or Position
Name of Company
Address (no., street)
Address (city, state, zip)

GUN SHOP MANAGER

for a firearms shop in
Minnesota

Dear Exact Name of Person: (or Dear Sir or Madam if answering a blind ad.)

I am very interested in employment opportunities with your organization and have enclosed my resume for your review and consideration.

I have extensive and diversified experience in management. I have directed all aspects of gun shop operations, including inventory control, cost accountability, finances, and providing customer service to the areas surrounding Minneapolis and Saint Paul.

My experience includes a strong background in safety, security, and training. I have excellent communication skills and demonstrated abilities to achieve quality results in all endeavors. I am confident that my skills and experience can be applied productively to your company. You would find me to be a versatile professional with a "track record" of achievements. Thank you in advance for your time and consideration.

Sincerely yours,

Norman J. Fischer

NORMAN J. FISCHER

1110½ Hay Street, Fayetteville, NC 28305 • preppub@aol.com • (910) 483-6611

OBJECTIVE

To offer my experience and state-of-the-art training in security and intelligence operations to an organization seeking a versatile professional with skills in managing tactical operations, training, technical information collection, and strategic analysis.

EDUCATION

B.B.A., Business Management, Ridgewater College, Willmar, MN, 1992.

EXPERIENCE

GUN SHOP MANAGER. Mid-West Firearms Shop, Minneapolis, MN (2003-present). For 17 years, have directed all aspects of operation, including inventory control, cost accountability, finances, and personnel administration of this popular firearms supplier serving the population surrounding the Minneapolis area.

TECHNICIAN, Buchanan Arms Room, Minneapolis, MN (2001-03). Used highly technical equipment such as a magnometer to locate and remove unexploded munitions; escorted them to authorized sites for safe disposal.

DIRECTOR. K & K Electronics, Saint Paul, MN (1999-2001). Applied my expert technical knowledge and excellent customer service skills to promote and sell electronics to all clientele.

SECURITY SUPERVISOR. *Saint Paul Daily*, Saint Paul, MN (1997-99). Supervised 60 two-man teams that provided 24-hour surveillance on striking teamsters, union officials, and newspaper distributors as well as executive protection for the daily news editor and other key personnel.
- Organized and conducted training in surveillance, night vision devices, camera/camcorder operation, executive protection, and escape driving techniques.
- Coordinated work schedules, including times and places, and maintained time sheets.
- Reported directly to Director of Security, *Minneapolis Press* on a nightly basis.

SECURITY CONSULTANT. D.S.V, Saint Paul, MN (1996-97). Conducted training on security-related projects to private corporations and individuals.

SECURITY MANAGER. Moorhead Security Protection Corporation, Moorhead, MN (1995-96). Managed all operations of this security guard service; when business closed, license reverted back to the Minnesota Private Protection Service Board.

SECURITY OFFICER. Roberson Nuclear Plant, Moorhead, MN (1994-95). Effectively secured the premises of a highly classified nuclear site.

OPERATIONS OFFICER/ASSISTANT MANAGER. Willmar Area Security, Inc., Willmar, MN (1991-1994). Directed all aspects of an agency that specialized in security for industrial organizations.
- Interviewed and conducted background investigations on potential employees and managed other administrative paperwork.
- Trained, motivated, and supervised 152 security guards.
- Performed security surveys and presented written and oral proposals.

SECURITY TRAINING

Saint Paul Police Academy: Fire Arms Instructor, Fire Arms Instructor Review.
State of Minnesota Law Enforcement Division: Security Training.
Minnesota Disaster Relief Organization: Introduction to Disaster, Emergency Assistance to Families, and Damage Assessment. Security Systems Training.

Date

Exact Name of Person
Title or Position
Name of Company
Address (no., street)
Address (city, state, zip)

**JEWELRY SALES
ASSISTANT MANAGER**
for Gordon's Jewelers
in Ohio

Dear Exact Name of Person: (or Dear Sir or Madam if answering a blind ad.)

I am a proven sales performer who is interested in a pharmaceutical sales career with your company.

With a B.S. in Business Administration from Malone College in Canton, Ohio, I have excelled in both sales and management positions with my current employer, Gordon's Jewelers. Even with my current extensive management responsibilities, I am one of the company's leading sales producers and consistently achieve more than $300,000 in sales annually. In a previous job, I handled administrative responsibilities and served as Biochemical Test Coordinator for an alcohol and drug control office.

My retail and management experience has taught me the value of flexibility and adaptability. I am self motivating and well organized and work well under pressure. These traits coupled with my winning attitude, initiative, and dedication to conducting business in an efficient, professional manner will allow me to rapidly become a productive member of your team. I can provide outstanding personal and professional references.

I hope you will contact me soon to arrange a time convenient for us to meet and discuss your goals and vision for extending and enhancing human life through the successful sale of your pharmaceutical products, and how I can help you reach those goals and objectives. Thank you in advance for your time and consideration.

Sincerely,

Tamra M. Prescott

TAMRA MARIE PRESCOTT

1110½ Hay Street, Fayetteville, NC 28305 • preppub@aol.com • (910) 483-6611

OBJECTIVE

To fulfill my desire to participate and excel in a dynamic business environment while applying my strong sales and communication skills to achieve the rewarding challenges involved in a customer-focused profession.

EDUCATION

Earned a **B.S. in Business Administration**, Malone College, Canton, OH, 2002.
- Maintained a 3.33 GPA and excelled in specialized course work including:

  Principles of Marketing   Basic Advertising

  Managerial Accounting   Marketing Management

EXPERIENCE

JEWELRY SALES ASSISTANT MANAGER. Gordon's Jewelers, Canton, OH (2000-present). After gaining experience as a Jewelry Sales Representative (part-time 2000-2002), and full-time manager trainee (2002-2003), was selected to become the Assistant Manager of this $2 million store.
- Recognized as one of the elite few who consistently achieve more than $300,000 in sales annually.
- Use my public relations knowledge and skills to implement creative marketing plans for special events.
- Handle day-to-day activities including opening and closing the store, making nightly deposits, entering various types of transactions in the computer, overseeing credit transactions, and verifying daily business reports with customer receipts.
- Explain diamond and gold watch warranties to customers and ensure that they understand and maintain warranty standards.
- Follow-up with customers during and after the sale to ensure customer satisfaction and provide any special instructions for the care of high-dollar merchandise; also a liaison with buyers at the home office for custom-made merchandise.
- Conduct training for new employees and provide continual guidance on any area needing improvement; create and use various types of rewards to maintain a high level of motivation; coach in areas that need improvement; inform staff members of company benefits and maintain the confidentiality of personal information gained while having access to personnel records.
- Participate in controlling inventory by processing monthly inventory reports, reporting losses immediately, and preparing for and conducting inventories.
- Efficiently resolve customer complaints in a professional and diplomatic manner that is within company policy and that is also satisfying to the customer.

ADMINISTRATIVE ASSISTANT. Candelier Medical Services, Canton, OH (1996-2000). Performed regular secretarial duties such as greeting the public, answering phone and in-person inquiries, typing, filing, and word processing reports and documentation.
- Chosen to handle additional responsibilities as assistant Biochemical Test Coordinator, scheduled/coordinated urinalysis testing, conducted testing of specimens, and informed our clients when their job candidates tested positive. Assisted the education coordinator in the development of education programs focusing on substance abuse knowledge.

Highlights of other experience:
ACCOUNTING CLERK. JCPenney, Canton, OH (1993-1996). Held sales associate position then promoted to Merchandising Assistant (MA) in (1993-1994) and Accounting Clerk (1994-1996).

PERSONAL

Excellent personal and professional references available upon request. Am available for travel or relocation according to employer's need.

Date

Exact Name of Person
Title or Position
Name of Company
Address (no., street)
Address (city, state, zip)

**JEWELRY STORE
MANAGER**
for Friedman's Jewelers

Dear Exact Name of Person: (or Dear Sir or Madam if answering a blind ad.)

I would appreciate an opportunity to talk with you soon about how I could contribute my versatile skills related to jewelry sales and management.

With a B.S. in Business Administration from Sonoma State University in Rohnert Park, I have excelled in both sales and management positions as a Store Manager with Friedman's Jewelers. Even with my previous management responsibilities, I learned that maximizing business profitability is dependent on public relation skills and providing valuable products to customers.

My retail and management experience has taught me the value of flexibility and adaptability. I have a winning attitude, initiative, and dedication to conducting business in an efficient, professional manner will allow me to rapidly become a productive member of your team. I can provide outstanding personal and professional references.

I hope you will contact me soon to arrange a time convenient for us to meet and discuss your goals and vision for extending and enhancing human life through the successful sale of your pharmaceutical products, and how I can help you reach those goals and objectives. Thank you in advance for your time and consideration.

Sincerely,

Madeline G. Stovall

MADELINE GLYNNIS STOVALL

1110½ Hay Street, Fayetteville, NC 28305 • preppub@aol.com • (910) 483-6611

OBJECTIVE

To benefit an organization that can use a well organized, reliable, and outgoing professional who offers versatile skills in office administration, customer service, accounting and billing management, inventory control, and computer operations.

EDUCATION

B.S. in Business Administration, Sonoma State University, Rohnert Park, CA, 2003.

OFFICE SKILLS

Experienced in performing light bookkeeping, computer entry, purchasing, typing (50 wpm), scheduling of employees, and controlling inventory.

EXPERIENCE

JEWELRY STORE MANAGER. Friedman's Jewelers, Rohnert Park, CA (2003-present). Coordinate all the buying and oversee inventory control while performing light bookkeeping, handling accounts receivable and payable, and directing sales and advertising activities for a store which employs two people.

- Have significantly contributed to the business through my expert product knowledge, organizational abilities, and highly refined "people skills."
- Have transformed numerous disorganized areas of operation into efficient activities.
- Have strengthened the skills of employees in sales and customer relations while tightening up behind-the-scenes activities including billing and inventory control.

ASSISTANT MANAGER. Marks and Morgan Jewelry, Rohnert Park, CA (2002-03). Learned the operations of a business where maximizing profitability is dependent on the judgment of key managerial staff in assessing value of products offered for purchase.

- Performed light bookkeeping and approved invoices for payment.
- Handled sales and acted as purchasing agent; became very knowledgeable about diamond and color stones as well as about all areas of jewelry manufacturing and repair.
- Was in charge of scheduling the 18 employees who worked at the store.
- Boosted profitability by refining merchandising and showcases while also assuring that product purchasing was expertly handled.

ASSISTANT MANAGER. Lifestyle Christian Center, Claremont, CA (1999-02). Was in charge of hiring, training, and terminating employees at this retail book center; performed research into new books and back-list products and bought books for sale.

- Attended book conventions in order to examine new products and attend retailing workshops.
- Handled light bookkeeping, approved invoices for payment, and coordinated with vendors, publishers, and wholesalers.
- Was commended for transforming a disorganized inventory control system into an efficient operation.

Other experience:
PROPERTY MANAGER. Greentree Apartment Homes, Claremont, CA (1996-99). Began managing these apartments when they had a 35% occupancy rate and brought the occupancy rate to 100% while assuring no delinquent accounts/no past due rent; screened tenants carefully.

- Managed cleaning crews as well as work crews performing yard and pool maintenance; made sure that the pool and grounds were immaculately maintained.

PERSONAL

Known for my high energy and enthusiastic personality. Am single and have no children, and am willing to make enormous contributions to my employer.

Date

Exact Name of Person
Title or Position
Name of Company
Address (no., street)
Address (city, state, zip)

JUNIOR BUYER
for Bloomingdale's in
Illinois

Dear Exact Name of Person: (or Dear Sir or Madam if answering a blind ad.)

I would appreciate an opportunity to talk with you soon about how I could contribute to your organization through my exceptional personal initiative and public relations ability as well as through my versatile skills related to sales, finance, and management.

As you will see from my resume, I hold a Bachelor of Arts degree in Political Science and I am currently in the process of obtaining my Master of Arts degree in Public Administration from the Northeastern Illinois University. It is my goal to make significant contributions within the public sector although, as you will see from my resume, my experience so far has been in the private sector.

When you look at my resume you will also see that I am a hard-working young professional with a "track record" of getting promoted quickly because of my strong personal initiative and versatile abilities. For example, after excelling in a rigorous management training program sponsored by Bloomingdale's department store, I was promoted in half the usual time to a key position which involved overseeing a $10 million store while supervising 150 employees. In another job I demonstrated my ability to "catch on quickly" as a "rookie" sales representative in a highly competitive area. Although I had no formal training in the product line, I was able to produce a 15% increase in sales in one year while maintaining every single account that I started with.

I believe I could apply these same personal qualities and skills in the public sector, and I hope you will give me an opportunity in person to show you that I could contribute to your fine team and to your personal goals.

I hope you will welcome my call soon to arrange a brief meeting at your convenience to discuss your current and future needs and how I might serve them. Thank you in advance for your time.

Sincerely yours,

Darrel A. Sykes

Alternate last paragraph:
I hope you will call or write me soon to suggest a time convenient for us to meet and discuss your current and future needs and how I might serve them. Thank you in advance for your time.

DARREL ANTONIO SYKES

1110½ Hay Street, Fayetteville, NC 28305 • preppub@aol.com • (910) 483-6611

OBJECTIVE

To contribute to an organization that can use a talented young professional who offers a "track record" of rapid promotion based on hard work and initiative along with exceptionally strong abilities related to finance, sales, management, and public relations.

EDUCATION

Completing a **Master of Arts degree** in **Public Administration**, Northeastern Illinois University, Chicago, IL; degree expected 2004.
Bachelor of Arts degree, Political Science, Northern Illinois University, De Kalb, 2002.
Completed a three-month executive development and management training program sponsored by Bloomingdale's Department Store; studied "total operations management" techniques for a $10 million business.

EXPERIENCE

JUNIOR BUYER and **OPERATIONS MANAGER**. Bloomingdale's Department Store, Chicago, IL (2003-present). Entered as Operations Manager; promoted within five months to the corporate office as an Assistant Buyer for Junior's Department.

- Was promoted in half the usual time to a key position which involved overseeing a $10 million store while supervising 150 employees. Visit showrooms in Nashville, TN, Dallas, TX, and Miami, FL to buy clothing for stores, working with a $2 million budget.
- Analyze data to determine the needs of 57 department stores.

SALES REPRESENTATIVE. Vaden Electronics, De Kalb, IL (2000-03). Produced a 15% increase in sales in one year in a territory which averaged sales of $1 million annually; excelled in managing this territory despite the fact that I was operating in a highly competitive environment and had no formal training from De Kalb.

- Demonstrated my ability to make key decisions concerning promotional sales; rapidly became accepted as the "voice of authority" in matters related to product performance.

OPERATIONS MANAGER. Stein Mart, De Kalb, IL (1997-00). After excelling in a rigorous management training program, was rapidly promoted twice and advanced in only half the usual time to a position which involved overseeing all store operations while supervising 150 employees and department heads.

- Simultaneously handled responsibilities in a wide variety of areas including:

product merchandising	store maintenance
waste control	employee and customer complaints
budget control	financial planning

- Was commended for my extraordinary ability to relate to employees and motivate them to excel at their jobs. Learned to handle pressure with poise.

COMMISSIONED SALES REPRESENTATIVE. Circuit City, De Kalb, IL (1994-1997). Financed my college education by working for Circuit City for four straight years as a commissioned sales representative in the electronics area.

- While working for this master retailer, learned valuable skills in inventory control and customer service.
- Became knowledgeable about the technical features of computers, VCRs, and TVs.
- Was handpicked to attend numerous sales schools because of my sales ability and executive potential; was continuously groomed by Circuit City for increasing responsibilities. Always met or exceeded my sales quotas.

PERSONAL

Read/write Spanish. Love golf, fishing, basketball, and football. Am an articulate communicator, and work well with others. Always aim to be the best and do my best.

Exact Name of Person
Title or Position
Name of Company
Address (no., street)
Address (city, state, zip)

**LOSS PREVENTION
ASSOCIATE**

for Marshalls with
experience in security

Dear Exact Name of Person: (or Dear Sir or Madam if answering a blind ad.)

With the enclosed resume, I would like to make you aware of my interest in exploring employment opportunities with your organization. I am available for worldwide relocation and travel.

As you will see from my resume, I am currently employed with Marshalls, as a Loss Prevention Associate. I have used a variety of methods to detect shoplifters and internal pilferage within a shopping environment. I am also working on my Bachelor of Science degree in Sociology from Furman University in Greenville on a part-time basis.

I worked as a Security Specialist for seven years with Ashley Security Services. I contracted myself out to businesses within the local area. I supervised 15 armed guards providing security at college campuses, high schools, and mall environments. I investigated and detected shoplifting, internal pilferage, as well as insurance fraud. I also handled administrative responsibilities including monitoring invoices for incoming freight and overseeing the security of the organization.

If you can use a dedicated and hard-working individual who offers expert knowledge related to security, surveillance, loss prevention, and private protective services, I hope you will contact me to suggest the next step I should take in exploring employment opportunities with your company.

Sincerely,

Clint J. Evans

CLINT J. EVANS

1110½ Hay Street, Fayetteville, NC 28305 • preppub@aol.com • (910) 483-6611

OBJECTIVE

I want to contribute to an organization that can use a hard-working professional who offers extensive experience related to security, surveillance, loss prevention, and private protective services.

EDUCATION

Completing a **Bachelor of Science degree in Sociology,** Furman University, Greenville, SC.

A. A. in Criminal Justice, Florence-Darlington Technical College, Florence, SC, 2000.

EXPERIENCE

LOSS PREVENTION ASSOCIATE. Marshalls, Greenville, SC (2003-present). Use a variety of methods to detect shoplifters and internal pilferage. Set up and monitored cameras.
- Handle invoicing for freight after verifying accuracy of receipts.
- Detect and investigate insurance fraud.

SECURITY GUARD. Francis Marion University, Greenville, SC (2001-03). Supervised 15 armed guards providing security for this college campus.
- Recruited, trained, and managed new armed guards.

SECURITY SPECIALIST. Ashley Security Services, Inc., Florence, SC (1995-01). Contracted with various businesses within the local area. Installed and maintained security cameras and all surveillance equipment. Proficient at safeguarding classified and hazardous materials. Extensive experience in surveillance, undercover tactics, and crowd control.
- Assisted in internal and external protection of employees at retail chains, college campuses, high schools, and other areas.
- Worked closely with local and state law enforcement officials.
- Trained in all aspects of fraud and embezzlement in financial offices.
- Gained extensive experience in reducing shrinkage control.
- Maintained and controlled all narcotics in medical facilities.
- Oversaw daily, weekly, monthly, and yearly paperwork and documents for Ashley Security Services, Inc.
- Accountable for over $12 million in medical supplies and equipment.
- Supervised and trained in excess of 100 people.
- Excellent analytical and administrative skills: compared freight against invoices to detect any freight discrepancies.
- Assisted in organizing, maintaining, and rotating merchandise in stockroom for the different retail organizations.

COMPUTER SKILLS

Am familiar with Microsoft Word, Excel, and PowerPoint and PageMaker.

PERSONAL

Offer more than 20 years of experience in security and inventory control.
- Honest, loyal, and dedicated with a positive attitude.
- Attention to detail, highly organized, able to work independently.
- Work quickly and efficiently under highly pressured situations and tight deadlines.

Date

Exact Name of Person
Exact Title
Exact Name of Company
Address
City, State, Zip

MARKET LEADER
for an athletic store
in Boston

Dear Exact Name of Person (or Dear Sir or Madam if answering a blind ad):

With the enclosed resume, I would like to make you aware of my background as a manager with exceptional recruiting and staff development skills who offers a track record of accomplishment as well as the proven ability to train and motivate personnel and increase the profitability of retail operations.

As you will see, I have excelled in positions of increasing responsibility with R & M Athletic Store, Inc. In my present position as Manager Trainer and Market Leader for the Germantown Mall location in Boston, I oversee all operational aspects of a retail operation with annual sales of $3 million. In addition, I serve as Market Leader, mentoring five new managers and acting as District Merchandise Coordinator, tracking and redistributing key product for the 23 stores in our district. In 2002, my store had the highest profit percentage in my district, and I received an audit award for reducing inventory shrinkage from the previous audit score, which was an unacceptable .60%, to only .01%, and extraordinarily low shrink figure.

Prior to that, as Manager Trainer at English Oaks Mall, I produced the highest profit margin for 2001, won the Coaches Award for my excellence in recruiting and staff development, and was further rewarded for my outstanding performance in human resources management by a promotion to Manager Trainer. Six employees whom I recruited in Boston moved into the management trainee program as Assistant Managers, and I recruited eight new employees for three different stores in our district.

In an earlier position as Store Manager at Towne Square Mall in Amherst, MA, I was able to quickly revive an under-producing store, increasing sales by $142,000 and turning a troubled operation into the most profitable store in the district.

If you can use a positive, results-oriented manager with a strong bottom-line orientation and exceptionally strong recruiting and staff development skills, then I look forward to hearing from you soon to arrange a time when we might meet to discuss your needs. I can assure you in advance that I have an excellent reputation, and would rapidly become a valuable asset to your company.

Sincerely,

Kelly O'Keefe

KELLY JOSEPH O'KEEFE

1110½ Hay Street, Fayetteville, NC 28305　•　preppub@aol.com　•　(910) 483-6611

OBJECTIVE　To benefit an organization that can use an articulate, experienced manager with exceptional recruiting, staff development, and leadership skills who offers a strong bottom-line orientation and the proven ability to train and motivate personnel and increase retail profitability.

EDUCATION　Completing **Bachelor of Science, Industrial Science**, Suffolk University, Boston, MA. As a professional retailer, have training courses sponsored by R & M Athletics, including:

Executive Development Program	Behavior-based Interviewing
Fundamentals of Recruiting	Customer Responsive Selling
Preventing Sexual Harassment	Valuing and Managing Diversity
Rightful Discharge Procedures	Security and Shrinkage

EXPERIENCE　*With R & M Athletic Store, Inc. have progressed in the following "track record" of accomplishment, advancing to positions of increasing responsibility for this large nationwide chain of athletic wear retailers:*

2002-present: MARKET LEADER and **MANAGER TRAINER.** Germantown Mall, Boston, MA. Manage a $3 million dollar store including recruiting, staff development, merchandising, and inventory control in addition to training other Store Managers.

- As a Market Leader, serve as mentor to five store managers in addition to supervising 25-32 employees, ensuring the highest possible levels of customer service. Serve as District Merchandise Coordinator, overseeing t redistribution of key products among 23 stores.
- Compile figures necessary to generate profit-and-loss statements as well as directing shipping and receiving, product returns, and other inventory controls.
- Have been a member of the MVP Club (for stores with sales volume over $2.5 million) since 2002; achieved the **Best Profit Percentage Award.** Received an Audit Award for compliance with operational and loss prevention guidelines; reduced shrinkage to an all-time low of 0.01%.

2001-02: MANAGER TRAINER. English Oaks Mall, Boston, MA. Produced the best profit percentage for 2001 while managing this $2.1 million store; selected as a Manager Trainer in recognition of my leadership and recruiting skills.

- Have been promoted to the position of Manager Trainer because of my success in recruiting and training other managers; accomplishments have included twice winning the Coaches Award for Recruiting and the Sales Leadership Award multiple times.
- Received an Audit Award for producing exceptionally low shrinkage figures.

2000-01: STORE MANAGER. Towne Square Mall, Amherst, MA. Turned around this under-producing store after taking over as Store Manager; increased sales by $142,000 annually and transformed this $1.6 million location into the most profitable store in the district; trained new employees and provided refresher skills training to existing employees in order to create a sense of team pride which resulted in increased sales.

- Focused on strong merchandising, carefully managed profit & loss, and restored sales programs in order to achieve highest the profit margin in the district in 2002 and 2003.
- Won the Sales Leadership Award and had the Best Manager Sales Book in the district.

1998-00: ASSISTANT MANAGER. Pepper Ridge Shopping Center, Amherst, MA. Rapidly excelled in management positions; developed exceptional recruiting, staff development, training, and motivational skills while controlling profit & loss and overseeing store operations.

PERSONAL　Single and willing to relocate according to employer needs. Exceptional references.

Exact Name of Person
Title or Position
Name of Company
Address (no., street)
Address (city, state, zip)

MENSWEAR SALES REPRESENTATIVE

for a privately owned Missouri retailer

Dear Exact Name of Person: (or Dear Sir or Madam if answering a blind ad.)

With the enclosed resume, I would like to make you aware of my experience in (and love for) the business of merchandising and selling better men's wear.

As you will see from my resume, I have been involved in retailing fine men's clothing throughout my working career. With an excellent personal reputation, I have worked for two of my employers twice, and I can provide outstanding references from all of them, including from my current employer. I would ask, however, that you treat my letter of interest in confidence at this time, and please do not contact my current employer until after we speak.

I earned a B. A. in Public Relations from Missouri Western State College. I have gained leadership abilities and communication skills that have led to working for a prestigious southern retailer of better men's wear. I can assure the highest standards of elegant merchandising and personal service. I thoroughly enjoy all aspects of the business of selling and merchandising better men's clothing, which is why I continue to be in the business in spite of several attempts by companies (and customers!) to employ me in other types of work. Naturally outgoing with an instinctive sales personality and a flair for fashion merchandising, I am respected for my good taste.

I am highly regarded in my current position, and I feel confident that I could benefit your organization through my experience and knowledge. I have excelled in all aspects of buying, merchandising, and sales. I want to be associated with a name which is known as a barometer of good taste, and I would like to arrange a brief face-to-face meeting with you so that you can see what I have to offer your excellent company.

If my considerable talents and skills interest you, I hope you will contact me by phone to suggest a time when we might meet on Friday, March 5th. I do work most evenings and go to the gym early most mornings, but if you leave a message on my answering machine, I will certainly return your call so that we can coordinate. I am sure that it would be an honor to be associated with your fine company, and I hope I will have the pleasure of meeting you. Thank you in advance for your time and professional courtesies.

Yours sincerely,

Trent J. Howarth

TRENT J. HOWARTH

1110½ Hay Street, Fayetteville, NC 28305 • preppub@aol.com • (910) 483-6611

OBJECTIVE

I want to contribute to an organization that can use a fashion-conscious retailer and experienced sales professional who offers expert knowledge of as well as a flair for the business of buying, merchandising, displaying, and selling better men's clothing.

EDUCATION

B. A. in Public Relations, Missouri Western State College, Saint Joseph, MO, 2003. Completed numerous training programs related to merchandising, sales, operations management, buying, and other areas sponsored by retailers.

EXPERIENCE

MENSWEAR SALES REPRESENTATIVE. M. Dumas & Sons, Saint Louis, MO (2003-present). Was recruited by this well-known, privately-owned Missouri retailer of fine men's wear; had worked for the company eight years previously and was working in another city when M. Dumas and Son's sought me out and persuaded me to return to Saint Louis.
- Am highly respected by a regular clientele of upper-end men's clothing for my impeccable taste and creative flair;
- Travel to Los Angeles on buying trips.
- Although I enjoy my job and colleagues and am held in high regard, I am seeking a new challenge; can provide an outstanding reference.

SALES REPRESENTATIVE. Nordstrom's, Saint Joseph, MO (2001-03). Was immediately rehired by Nordstrom's based on my exemplary work performance in my prior employment with the company.
- In this mini-department store, was involved in merchandising, display, and sales of fine men's wear department.

SALES REPRESENTATIVE. The Cistern, Saint Joseph, MO (1998-01). In this two-person business which sold fine men's wear to a clientele of professional people and alumni of Missouri Western State College, was involved in all aspects of operations including buying, merchandising, sales, and operations management.

SALES & MERCHANDISING MANAGER. M. Dumas & Sons, Saint Louis, MO (1995-98). Became the "right arm" of the founder and manager of this popular Missouri retailer of fine men's wear.
- Gained the respect of upscale clients who sought my advice on matters of taste and fashion; learned the importance of personal service.

MERCHANDISING MANAGER & ASSISTANT MANAGER. Fine's Men's Wear, Saint Louis, MO (1993-95). Established and maintained an excellent working relationship with customers, vendors, co-workers, and with my employer.
- Became skilled in all aspects of buying, merchandising, and display.

PERSONAL

Single; will relocate. Have become skilled in knowing when to take markdowns and how to move merchandise. Am well acquainted with the importance of elegant display techniques. Physically fit; enjoy tennis.

Date

Exact Name of Person
Title or Position
Name of Company
Address (no., street)
Address (city, state, zip)

MERCHANDISE MANAGER

for a major retail corporation in Oklahoma

Dear Exact Name of Person: (or Dear Sir or Madam if answering a blind ad.)

With the enclosed resume, I would like to make you aware of my interest, skills and experience in exploring employment opportunities with your organization.

As you will see from the resume I am sending you, I have excelled in handling profit-and-loss responsibility in one of the toughest industries. Because of my ability to predict consumer interests and satisfy customer needs, I have been promoted ahead of my peers and am currently being groomed for top management within one of America's leading corporations. In every job I have held, I have exceeded management expectations in terms of sales and profitability, and I have always been able to produce top-quality results through people because of my ability to train and motivate employees.

It is not, however, only marketing ability and "people" skills I offer you. In this highly technical age, I believe that managers must be able to use computers skillfully and be able to handle complex financial analysis. I offer a proven ability to lower costs while strengthening quality through my knowledge of finance as well as through my ability to use computers for daily operations and strategic planning. Proficient with Microsoft Word, Excel, Access and PowerPoint and familiar with many popular software programs, I have a knack for easily mastering complex MIS programs and training others to use them.

If you are looking for a dedicated hard worker who could help your business prosper in the years ahead, I would appreciate an opportunity to talk with you at your convenience. Of course I would be able to provide impeccable personal and professional references at the appropriate time.

I hope you will welcome my call soon to arrange a brief meeting at your convenience to discuss your current and future needs and how I might serve them. Thank you for your consideration of my interest in your fine company.

Yours sincerely,

Steffan T. Flynn

STEFFAN THOMAS FLYNN

1110½ Hay Street, Fayetteville, NC 28305   •   preppub@aol.com   •   (910) 483-6611

OBJECTIVE

To contribute to an organization that can use a resourceful and hard-working young manager who offers exceptional written and oral communication skills along with an ability to inspire teamwork, handle profit-and-loss responsibility, and develop/improve software so that it becomes a highly effective tool for daily operations and strategic planning.

EDUCATION

B.S. degree in **Business Administration**, University of Tulsa, Tulsa, Oklahoma, 2002.
- Excelled in course work emphasizing management, marketing, finance, and economics.

EXPERIENCE

Am considered on the "fast track" within Sears and Roebuck, Norma and Tulsa, OK:

2003-present: MERCHANDISE MANAGER. Tulsa, OK. Was promoted to this position usually reserved for a very senior manager because of my proven ability to excel in handling profit-and-loss responsibility related to a $2.5 million inventory; am being groomed for top management and am playing a key role in leading this store to enjoy its record year in profitability.
- Train and supervise 18 people; have learned to use a variety of management styles in order to most effectively motivate employees.
- Develop a weekly and monthly advertising program that increased sales 7.5% in a sluggish economy; have planned and coordinated exciting promotional plans for magazine contests, "doorbusters," and other marketing activities.
- Conduct customer service surveys and interpreted their results in ways that boosted customer satisfaction; instilled in employees a dedication to quality service.
- Have earned respect for my decision-making skills in determining what items to advertise; these are the "life-or-death" decisions of the retailing industry!
- Handle extensive financial responsibilities; continuously monitor stock-to-sales ratios, and personally direct all buying for the boys and girls department.
- Have earned a reputation as a "whiz" in identifying customer needs and wants.

2000-03: MERCHANDISE MANAGER. Tulsa, OK. Was rapidly promoted to manage a second and third department after increasing sales and improving all operating areas of a 19-person department; "turned around" a poorly functioning sales force and improved sales in petite and women's clothing 15% through the design of a basic stock inventory program.
- Increased sales 18% despite adverse economic conditions when a large segment of the population was serving in the war in the Middle East.
- Held salary costs to 10.3% in a district averaging 15%; managed $2.2 million in sales.

1997-00: MERCHANDISE MANAGER. Tulsa, OK. While supervising eleven employees in a department of a $28 million store, implemented changes which increased 1999 sales 16%; produced a sales growth of 11% while total store sales growth was only 3%.
- Managed buying and inventory control for $1.5 million in merchandise.

1996-97: MANAGER TRAINEE. Norma, OK. Completed a year-long training program in 10 months; handled buying and inventory control for $1.15 million in merchandise.

Other experience: INVENTORY CONTROL SPECIALIST. Norma, Stillwater, Durant, and Edmond, OK (1995-1996). Financed most of my college education in this job.

PERSONAL

Proficient in using Microsoft Word, Excel, Access and PowerPoint. Have developed software programs for inventory control and forecasting. Have a knack for mastering complex MIS programs and training others to use them.

Date

Exact Name of Person
Title or Position
Name of Company
Address (no., street)
Address (city, state, zip)

Dear Exact Name of Person: (or Dear Sir or Madam if answering a blind ad.)

With the enclosed resume, I would like to make you aware of my interest, skills and experience in exploring employment opportunities with your organization.

As you will see from the resume I am sending you, I have excelled in handling profit-and-loss responsibility in my current position as Merchandiser for Dowling Industries. Because of my ability to predict consumer interests and satisfy customer needs, I have been promoted ahead of my peers and am currently being groomed for top management within one of America's leading corporations. In every job I have held I have exceeded management expectations in terms of sales and profitability, and I have always been able to produce top-quality results through people because of my ability to train and motivate employees.

I earned a Bachelor of Science degree in Business Administration from Kentucky State University, and completed a variety of leadership and personnel management courses which has provided the marketing ability and "people" skills that I can offer you. In this highly technical age, I believe that managers must be able to use computers skillfully and be able to handle complex financial analysis. I offer a proven ability to lower costs while strengthening quality through my knowledge of finance as well as through my ability to use computers for daily operations and strategic planning. I am proficient with Microsoft Word and Excel software programs and enjoy training others to use them.

If you are looking for a dedicated hard worker who could help your business prosper in the years ahead, I would appreciate an opportunity to talk with you at your convenience. Of course I would be able to provide impeccable personal and professional references at the appropriate time.

I hope you will welcome my call soon to arrange a brief meeting at your convenience to discuss your current and future needs and how I might serve them. Thank you for your consideration of my interest in your fine company.

Yours sincerely,

Bradley J. Heron

BRADLEY JAMES HERON

1110½ Hay Street, Fayetteville, NC 28305 • preppub@aol.com • (910) 483-6611

OBJECTIVE

To benefit an organization seeking a skilled professional experienced in motivating and supervising personnel, inventory control, and operations management, who possesses excellent communication, planning, and time-management abilities.

EDUCATION

B.S., degree in Business Administration, Kentucky State University, Frankfurt, KY, 2000. Completed a wide range of continuing education coursework, including classes in education, leadership and personnel management, human resources program development from the Outer Banks Manufacturing Company.

EXPERIENCE

MERCHANDISER. Dowling Industries, Inc., Louisville, KY (2003-present). Gained excellent marketing and sales experience while acting as a traveling sales representative for such clients as the Kentucky Derby related products.
- Oversee all supply ordering and accountability in addition to maintaining or exceeding company sales quotas.

ASSISTANT PLANT MANAGER. Cummings Manufacturing, Louisville, KY (2001-03). Learned entire process of clothing manufacturing while training, supervising, and evaluating 100 employees, as well as assisting in the daily operations of a busy sewing plant.
- Managed shipping and receiving, inventory control, and production orders tracking.
- Ensured quick, accurate completion of garments.

SALES MANAGER. Jennings Supplies, Louisville, KY (1998-01). Refined personnel management and planning skills working for this inside sales company marketing cleaning supplies; trained, supervised, and evaluated a staff of 40 sales representatives; controlled office inventory.
- Revamped sales training program, improving weekly gross sales by 25%.

INVENTORY CONTROL MANAGER. Outer Banks, Frankfurt, KY (1994-98). Polished attention to detail abilities directing the ordering, issuing, tracking, and accountability of a 3,000-item inventory worth over $5 million; trained and supervised 10 personnel in a manufacturing industry.
- Determined short and long term departmental logistic goals and needs.
- Acted as departmental Environmental Protection Officer, overseeing the proper disposal of hazardous materials, hazardous wastes, and other controlled materials.
- Cited by top-level official as a professional who "readily accepts the most difficult task and quickly develops a plan of action, executing that plan with exceptional results."
- Implemented and conducted a training program vital to the success of the action; controlled all equipment inventory, maintenance, and repair.

COMPUTER SKILLS

Working knowledge of Microsoft Word and Excel software programs.

PERSONAL

Am a versatile professional who enjoys problem-solving, decision-making, and maximizing resources. Am computer literate. Have consistently received outstanding work evaluations.

Date

Exact Name of Person
Exact Title
Exact Name of Company
Address
City, State, Zip

MERCHANDISING SPECIALIST

for a merchandising organization

Dear Exact Name of Person: (or Dear Sir or Madam if answering a blind ad)

With the enclosed resume, I would like to make you aware of my background as an articulate, reliable professional with exceptional communication and organizational abilities as well as experience in merchandising, sales, and customer service.

Recently, I have been excelling as a Merchandising Specialist for Brooks & Fields Merchandising Services, Inc. In this position, I serviced a variety of large corporate accounts, including Adonna, Panasonic, and Hillshire Farms, resetting stock and ensuring that their products were prominently and effectively displayed. I worked in retail outlets such as Walgreens, Eckerds, Family Dollar, and Publix, removing product lines that were being replaced and correctly merchandising new product according to planograms provided by the corporate customer. In earlier positions with Saragon Retailers and Phar-Mor, I merchandised health & beauty aids and pharmaceutical products for Advil, Tylenol, Black and Decker, Revlon and other major accounts.

Earlier I served as a Book Merchandiser for Midpoint Trade Books, restocking book displays in numerous retail locations. I pulled time-sensitive materials, such as monthly romances novels off the shelf and replaced them with current releases. In addition, I quickly developed a general knowledge of authors, as well as fiction, non-fiction, children's books, and medical titles, which allowed me to more efficiently merchandise book product.

As you will see from my enclosed resume, I hold an Associate's degree from Kansas City Community College.

If you can use an enthusiastic, hard-working professional whose highly-developed merchandising, sales, and customer services skills have been proven in challenging situations requiring tact and diplomacy, then I look forward to hearing from you soon. I assure you in advance that I have an excellent reputation, and would quickly become an asset to your organization.

Yours sincerely,

Jetta K. Warfield

JETTA K. WARFIELD

1110½ Hay Street, Fayetteville, NC 28305   •   preppub@aol.com   •   (910) 483-6611

OBJECTIVE   To benefit an organization that can use an articulate, hard-working professional with experience in merchandising, sales, and customer service.

EDUCATION   Completed **A.S. degree** at Kansas City Community College, Kansas City, KS, 2000.

EXPERIENCE   **MERCHANDISING SPECIALIST.** Brooks and Fields Merchandising Services, Inc., Kansas City, KS (2003-present). Service a wide variety of corporate accounts including Adonna bras, Panasonic batteries, and Hillshire Farms, ensuring that their merchandise is presented in full and attractive displays in prominent locations and merchandised properly according to corporate guidelines.
- Reset stock in major retail outlets such as Walgreens, Eckerds, and Family Dollar, removing product lines that are being replaced and correctly merchandising new product.
- Read planograms to ensure proper placement of product, and change all shelf labeling to correctly reflect the new merchandise.
- Change endcap, slat wall, and spinner displays, stocking all display areas as full as possible, fronting and blocking displays to present a full and attractive appearance.

MERCHANDISING SPECIALIST. Phar-Mor, Kansas City, KS (2002-03). Reset stock and restructured existing displays in order to add new products, merchandising health & beauty aids, household/domestics, and pharmaceutical products at a number of major retail outlets.

BOOK MERCHANDISER. Midpoint Trade Books, Kansas City, KS. (2001-02). Merchandised book displays for a number of major retailers, including Walgreens, Eckerds, and Family Dollar, pulling older titles from the shelf, prominently displaying newer titles, and creating endcap and table displays.
- Pulled time-sensitive materials, such as monthly romance novels and replaced the old titles with current releases.
- Read merchandising planners in order to ensure proper placement of all titles.
- Developed a general knowledge of authors, as well as fiction, nonfiction, children's books, and medical, which allowed me to merchandise books more efficiently.

HEALTH & BEAUTY MERCHANDISER. Saragon Retailers, Inc., Kansas City, KS (1999-01). Specialized in merchandising health & beauty aids and pharmaceutical products for major corporate accounts, such as Advil, Tylenol, Black and Decker, and Revlon.
- Reset stock and created displays of new merchandise, using a planogram to ensure that all products were correctly merchandised.
- Checked expiration dates on pharmaceutical products such as vitamins, and pulled any old stock off the shelf.

Other Experience:
AUDITOR. Consumer Data Services, Kansas City, KS (1996-99). Use a hand-held inventory computer/scanner to conduct integrity audits of major retailers; primary responsibility is for conducting quarterly audits of local discount stores.

PERSONAL   Pride myself on my positive attitude and determination. Have a strong desire to learn. Can develop extensive product knowledge and present this knowledge to others. Work well as a member of a team. Have received awards for outstanding job performance.

Date

Exact Name of Person
Title or Position
Name of Company
Address (no., street)
Address (city, state, zip)

MERCHANT MANAGER
for The Gap in Texas
and Arizona

Dear Exact Name of Person: (or Dear Sir or Madam if answering a blind ad.)

With the enclosed resume, I would like to make you aware of my interest, skills and experience in exploring employment opportunities with your organization.

As you will see from the resume I am sending you, I have excelled in handling sales and profit maximization in my current position as a Merchant Manager. Because of my ability to predict consumer interests and satisfy customer needs, I have been promoted ahead of my peers and am currently being groomed for top management within The Gap corporation. I have always been able to produce top-quality results through people because of my ability to train and motivate employees.

I earned a Bachelor of Arts degree in Business Administration from Northern Arizona University. In this highly technical age, I believe that managers must be able to use computers skillfully and be able to handle complex financial analysis. I offer a proven ability to lower costs while strengthening quality through my knowledge of finance as well as through my ability to use computers for daily operations and strategic planning. I am proficient with Microsoft Word and Excel software programs and enjoy training others to use them.

If you are looking for a dedicated hard worker who could help your business prosper in the years ahead, I would appreciate an opportunity to talk with you at your convenience. Of course I would be able to provide impeccable personal and professional references at the appropriate time.

I hope you will welcome my call soon to arrange a brief meeting at your convenience to discuss your current and future needs and how I might serve them. Thank you for your consideration of my interest in your fine company.

Yours sincerely,

Tanya D. Haynes

TANYA DENISE HAYNES

1110½ Hay Street, Fayetteville, NC 28305 • preppub@aol.com • (910) 483-6611

PROFILE

I want to contribute to organization that can use a dynamic, enthusiastic professional with extensive experience in sales, management, and customer service.

EDUCATION

Completing **Bachelor of Arts degree in Business Administration**, Northern Arizona University, Flagstaff, AZ, 2003.

Earned **Associate of Arts degree in Business Management**, Cochise College, Sierra Vista, AZ, 1999.

EXPERIENCE

With The Gap, have progressed in the following "track record" of accomplishment, advancing to positions of increasing responsibility for this large nationwide chain of stores while simultaneously attending college on a full-time basis:

2003-present: MERCHANT MANAGER. Dallas, TX. Train up to 105 associates in sales and customer service policies.
- Guide staff in sales generation.
- Responsible for basic operations of store.
- Handle customer praise as well as complaints.

2002-03: MERCHANDISE MANAGER. Flagstaff, AZ. While supervising eleven employees of a $12 million store, implemented changes which increased 2001 sales 16%; produced a sales growth of 11% while total store sales growth was only 3%.
- Managed buying and inventory control for $1.5 million in merchandise.
- Developed a stock program that resulted in a $150,000 sales increase.

1999-02: MANAGER TRAINEE. Flagstaff, AZ. Completed a yearlong training program in 10 months at the Gap; handled buying and inventory control for $1.15 million in merchandise.

Other experience:

AREA SALES MANAGER. M. M. Cohn Department Store, Azalea Shopping Mall, Sierra Vista, AZ (1997-1999). Managed a $5 million department and handled responsibility for maximizing profitability while directing 14 sales associates.
- Compiled and analyzed reports.
- Achieved a consistent sales increase in all areas of responsibility.
- Became highly qualified in all aspects of customer service and product knowledge.
- Demonstrated the highest standards of merchandise presentation by displaying classification, key items, and hot trends.

SALES CLERK. Claire's Boutique, Azalea Shopping Mall, Sierra Vista, AZ (1996-1997). In a European gift collectibles store, became knowledgeable of the history of numerous lines of collectibles while refining my sales skills.

SKILLS

Offer well developed skills in the following areas:

Customer Service	Employee Training and Development
Organizational Skills	Creation and Utilization of Reports
Maximizing Associate Productivity	Sales and Profit Maximization

COMPUTERS

Have working knowledge of Microsoft Word, Excel, and PowerPoint.

PERSONAL

Outstanding references are available on request.

Exact Name of Person
Title or Position
Name of Company
Address (no., street)
Address (city, state, zip)

MODEL
with theatrical training
in New York

Dear Exact Name of Person: (or Dear Sir or Madam if answering a blind ad.)

Can you use a dynamic and hard-working young professional who offers a proven ability to "get things done" in a competitive and fast-changing environment of modeling and acting?

As you will see from my enclosed resume, I have received a B. A. in Media Studies from Southern Arkansas University in Magnolia. Southern Arkansas has an outstanding fine arts department where I developed extensive acting and modeling skills.

I have worked since I was 16 years old and I have excelled in every acting and modeling job I have held. My experience includes working on various films and television shows such as Alias, Starship Enterprise, Universal Soldier, JAG, and many others. I am currently interested in relocating to the Los Angeles area in order to network with other professionals within the entertainment industry.

You would find me to be an enthusiastic person with profitable credentials, and I would be delighted to provide personal and professional references. I hope you will welcome my call soon when I try to arrange a brief meeting to discuss your personnel needs and how I might fit into them. I believe I could be a valuable addition to your client list.

Yours sincerely,

Kevin Carmichael

KEVIN CARMICHAEL
1110½ Hay Street, Fayetteville, NC 28305   •   preppub@aol.com   •   (910) 483-6611

Ht.: 6'1" Wt: 180 lbs   Phone: (910) 487-5533 hm
Hair: Brown   (910) 100-0000 cell
Eyes: Green

MODELING   Runway model in NY and Paris for Boss Models for six years.

FILM & TELEVISION

Alias	Featured	NBC
Kiss of the Dragon	Featured	Joseph Brenner
Starship Enterprise	Featured	Samuel Irving
Andromeda	Co-Star	Oscar Jennings
Midnight Summer	Co-Star	SAU Grad Film
Air Force One	Featured	Yancey Taylor
Shaft	Featured	John Singleton
JAG	Featured	Quincy Hessen
Chicago Hope	Featured	ABC
Law & Order	Featured	CBS
Beverly Hills 90210	Featured	TNN
Universal Soldier	Featured	SCI-FI

THEATRE

Romeo and Juliet	Romeo	Dock Street Theater
Lion King	Simba (lead)	Harding Theater of the Arts
Nutcracker Production	Small Soldier	SCAD
Othello	Extra	SAU Fine Arts Theatre
West Side Story	Extra	SAU Fine Arts Theatre

TRAINING

Ernest Sampson	Theatre Studies	New York, NY
Clifton Burgess	Script Readings	New York, NY
Frederick Harding	Advanced On-Camera	Savannah, GA
Butler Productions	On Camera/Commercial	Los Angeles, CA
Southern Arkansas University	BA/Media Studies	Magnolia, AR

SPECIAL SKILLS & ABILITIES
Soccer, Softball, White Water Rafting, Skydiving, Tennis;
Voiceovers, Dialects: Los Angeles, California

EDUCATION   Southern Arkansas University   B.A. Media Studies

Also Available:
Demo Reel
Commercial List

Date

Exact Name of Person
Exact Title
Exact Name of Company
Address
City, State, Zip

MODEL

with limited training
seeks his first
modeling jobs. You
could use a letter such
as this one to
approach agents.

Dear Exact Name of Person (or Dear Sir or Madam if answering a blind ad):

With the enclosed resume, I would like to express my interest in exploring employment opportunities with your organization related to modeling.

As you will see from my resume, I recently completed a six-month training program sponsored by the Creative Model and Talent Agency, and I was specially selected to perform as a runway model in a showcase held in Charlotte, NC. The showcase was attended by more than 400 people who included a select group of talent scouts and agents, and the written comments of the judges were complimentary of my style. Nearly unanimously the talent scouts and agents evaluated me as having a "highly commercial look." I have a complete portfolio which is available for your review.

Although I am currently enrolled as a sophomore at the University of North Carolina at Chapel Hill, I can arrange my schedule so that I can work full-time in the modeling field. I am confident that I could add value to a company in the fashion business which is interested in having its products represented with style and grace. I realize that I am a novice in the industry, but I am a hard worker and am fully committed to doing whatever it takes to make a career in the fashion and modeling business.

I have demonstrated my ability to make a commitment and do whatever it takes to see it through. As a youth, I was involved in Boy Scouts and persisted in Scouting until I achieved the Eagle rank, the highest rank in Scouting. I can provide excellent references from my manager at Creative (Joanna Green, a respected model herself) and from outside industry personnel.

I would appreciate your favorably considering me for any roles or positions you are currently attempting to fill. I hope you will contact me soon to arrange a brief meeting at your convenience to discuss your needs. Thank you in advance for your time, and I enclose a couple of professional photos along with my resume.

Yours sincerely,

Michael Knight

MICHAEL KNIGHT
910-483-6611
preppub@aol.com

HEIGHT: 5" 11"	Suit: 40R
WEIGHT: 135 lbs.	Shirt: 15.5 X 32
WAIST: 32	Eyes: Hazel
HAIR: Black	Inseam: 32
AGE: 18 (born Aug 10, 1983)	Shoe: 11

TRAINING:

Creative Model and Talent Management
Participated in a showcase as a runway
model in Jan 2003. On the written
comments made by the agents who
attended the showcase, the main opinion
expressed was "commercial look."

Joanna Green
910-483-6611

Training in forensics

Myers Park High School,
Charlotte, NC

Private speech and diction lessons

Mrs. Samantha Fisher,
Charlotte, NC

Debate Team

Charlotte, NC

Forensics Team, numerous competitions

Locations throughout NC

Multiple awards for original oratory
and public speaking

TRAINING UPCOMING:

Pursuing theater coursework at University of North Carolina at Chapel Hill.

SPECIAL SKILLS:

Martial arts training. Knowledge of Judo and Karate.
Accents: Jamaican and Southern. (Born in North Carolina)
Knowledgeable of West Indies culture and Southern culture.
Some proficiency in Spanish and German.
Avid sports fan: skilled in tennis, soccer, baseball, basketball.
Played varsity tennis and soccer in high school. Computer enthusiast.
Deep-pitched radio voice. Lean, athletic build.

Exact Name of Person
Title or Position
Name of Company
Address (no., street)
Address (city, state, zip)

MODEL & ACTOR
seeking a career in
film and television

Dear Exact Name of Person: (or Dear Sir or Madam if answering a blind ad.)

Can you use a creative and persistent young actor, model, and singer who offers versatile knowledge of acting, directing, producing, playwriting, staging, and photography?

As you will see from my resume, I have demonstrated in many ways a commitment to a career in films and television.

- Recently while earning my B.A. in Dramatic Art from a major university, I won "rave reviews" for my acting performances.
- With a reputation as a cheerful hard worker who enjoys lending a helping hand to others, I offer an intellect trained by study as well as a "stage presence" that audiences enthusiastically respond to.

I hope you will welcome my call soon to arrange a brief meeting at your convenience to discuss your current and future needs and how I might serve them. Thank you in advance for your time.

Sincerely yours,

Travis R. Price

Alternate last paragraph:
I hope you will call or write me soon to suggest a time convenient for us to meet and discuss your current and future needs and how I might serve them. Thank you in advance for your time.

TRAVIS R. PRICE

1110½ Hay Street, Fayetteville, NC 28305   •   preppub@aol.com   •   (910) 483-6611

OBJECTIVE   I want to contribute to an organization that can use a talented young actor, model, and singer who offers a strong stage presence along with proven management ability and production operations know-how.

EDUCATION   Earned a **Bachelor of Arts (B.A.) degree in Dramatic Art**, University of Missouri, MO, Columbia, MO, 2002.
Earned an **Associate of Science Degree in Art History**, St. Charles County Community College, Saint Peters, MO, 1999.
- Completed this challenging course work while working part time and studying/rehearsing for different plays.

Acting: In several different courses, gained an understanding of the craft of acting by studying techniques of modern realism, character development, physical relaxation, and movement. Completed extensive training in voiceovers.
Playwriting/play production: Studied the art and craft of creating/ producing plays and learned about the materials, equipment, and processes in technical theater.
Directing: Learned principles of stage directing; analyzed production concepts and staging methodologies.
Scenery and costuming: Analyzed equipment and procedures related to the design and implementation of sound, scenery, lighting, and costuming.

HIGHLIGHTS OF ACTING EXPERIENCE
- Played lead role, Billy, in <u>Blues Maker:</u> was commended for my brilliant performance in this major production.
- Wrote a modified version of <u>Beauty and the Beast</u> and played the Beast.
- Played the lead role, Simba, in <u>The Lion King</u>: received this role as the result of my first audition.

LANGUAGE   Can read French.

EXPERIENCE   **FILM PROCESSING TECHNICIAN.** Hargray Studios, Columbia, MO (2003-present). Contribute my skills in photography and gained practical experience in the technical aspects of film development.
- Am recognized as a mature and dependable individual, was selected to relieve the manager of certain daily responsibilities such as opening and closing the store.

PHOTOGRAPHY ASSISTANT. Photo Plus, St. Peters, MO (2001-2003). Excelled in extensive professional training in the photography; provided assistant visual imagery acquisition and exploitation support.

LOOKS   Have been told that I am a Marlon Brando look-a-like.

PERSONAL
- Am known as a persistent young professional who is committed to succeeding and excelling in all I do.
- Believe that hard work is the key to success.
- Have a personality that others relate well to; am considered a cooperative, congenial person who enjoys lending a helping hand to others. Will relocate.

Exact Name of Person
Title or Position
Name of Company
Address (no., street)
Address (city, state, zip)

**MUSIC STORE
MANAGER**
for Millenium Music
in Las Vegas

Dear Exact Name of Person: (or Dear Sir or Madam if answering a blind ad.)

I would appreciate an opportunity to talk with you soon about how I could contribute to your organization through my sales and management experience along with my formal education and technical training.

As you will see from the enclosed resume, I earned a Associate of Arts degree in Restaurant and Hotel Management from the Community College of Southern Nevada. I have a reputation as a skilled store manager who is effective in turning around existing stores experiencing sales and profitability problems.

My resume also will show you my "track record" of achievement in sales and management. In my most recent position as a Store Manager for Millenium Music, I manage 10 other employees, decreased inventory shrinkage, opened new stores, converted acquisition stores to Millenium's systems and procedures, and was specially selected to manage a new "superstore" of more than 10,000 square feet.

I hope you will find some time in your schedule for us to meet at your convenience to discuss your needs and goals and how I might serve them. I shall look forward to hearing from you, and thank you in advance for your time.

Yours sincerely,

Darren M. Chapman

DARREN MICHAEL CHAPMAN

1110½ Hay Street, Fayetteville, NC 28305　•　preppub@aol.com　•　(910) 483-6611

OBJECTIVE　To contribute to an organization that can use a resourceful and congenial sales professional with excellent customer relations skills who offers a proven "track record" of accomplishment in both sales and operations management.

EDUCATION　**Associate of Arts degree** in **Restaurant and Hotel Management**, Community College of Southern Nevada, North Las Vegas, NV, 2001.
Completed renowned management training programs with an established restaurant, Hard Rock Cafe.

EXPERIENCE　**MUSIC STORE MANAGER.** Millenium Music, Las Vegas, NV (2003-present). Earned a reputation as a skilled store manager who was equally effective in **starting up new retail** operations, "turning around" existing stores experiencing sales and **profitability problems,** and managing "superstores."
- After managing three Millenium Music retail stores in Las Vegas, **was selected to manage a new 10,000 square foot freestanding "superstore."**
- Responsible for opening new stores and converting acquisition stores to Millenium's procedures, methods, and systems.
- Devise and implement effective merchandising techniques.
- Specialize in maintaining superior inventory conditions.
- Achieve consistent sales increases and ranked among the chain's highest volume stores.
- Diminish shrinkage and substantially increased profits.
- Implement effective off-site sales locations utilizing radio and television as well as popular musicians and bands at successful local events.

Other experience:
ASSISTANT MANAGER. Hard Rock Café, Las Vegas, NV (1999-03). After earning my Associate of Arts degree, excelled in restaurant management and was selected for management training programs.
- Worked in Hard Rock Cafe and was selected for their corporate training program while working as a waiter at the Las Vegas, Nevada location.
- Promoted to an assistant manager after completing their corporate training program.

SUMMARY OF EXPERIENCE
- Eight years of restaurant and retail management experience.
- Skilled in hiring, training, scheduling, and maintaining sales staff dedicated to superior customer relations.
- Proven commitment to meeting deadlines and serving customers.
- Exceptionally strong analytical and problem-solving skills.
- Known for my positive attitude and cheerful disposition.

PERSONAL　Am an accomplished guitarist and musical collector. Was born and raised in the Las Vegas area. Excellent health. Single.

Exact Name of Person (if known)
Title or Position
Name of Company
Address (no., street)
Address (city, state, zip)

OPERATIONS MANAGER
for a furniture sales
company

Dear Exact Name of Person: (or Dear Sir or Madam)

I would appreciate an opportunity to talk with you soon about how my excellent public relations skills and "results-oriented" approach to management could benefit your organization.

As you will see from my resume I offer extensive management and personnel supervisory experience from my current position as an Operations Manager with REX Furniture Sales. Also, I feel certain that you would find me to be a hard-working and reliable professional who prides myself on doing any job to the best of my ability.

In addition, my experience in sales management has provided me with a keen appreciation of the outstanding results that can be achieved when a flexible, creative, and empathetic approach is brought to managing and motivating others. This, I think, is one of the toughest, yet most rewarding challenges any manager can face.

I hope you will find some time in your schedule for us to meet at your convenience to discuss your needs and goals and how I might serve them. I shall look forward to hearing from you, and thank you in advance for your time.

Sincerely,

Frederick Earl Byers

FREDERICK EARL BYERS

1110½ Hay Street, Fayetteville, NC 28305 • preppub@aol.com • (910) 483-6611

OBJECTIVE

To contribute to an organization that can use an enthusiastic, energetic, and articulate young professional who offers a work history which includes the development of outstanding sales, managerial, and customer service skills.

EDUCATION

B. A. in Public Relations, Coppin State College, Baltimore, MD, 2001.

EXPERIENCE

OPERATIONS MANAGER. REX Furniture Sales, Baltimore, MD (2003-present). Exceeded the store's first-year sales goals while leading a newly opened facility to an exceptional record of becoming almost totally self-supporting in its first year of operations.
- Led the staff to $125,000 in sales — $29,000 over the projected figure for a store of this size which was establishing its place in the community.
- Oversee all phases of store operations from sales, to scheduling deliveries, to customer relations, to accepting payments, to making bank deposits. Handle customer complaints in a fair manner and act as liaison between customers and major companies such as Beautyrest and Restonic. Develop interesting and attractive merchandise displays.

SALESPERSON. Henry Cox Auto Sales, Baltimore, MD (2001-03). Consistently set sales records while selling and displaying used automobiles and becoming familiar with the procedures and methods which led to success in this industry.

SALES REPRESENTATIVE. Furniture Wholesales, Baltimore, MD (1999-01). Won several sales contests and earned recognition as the top salesman while gaining recognition as a knowledgeable professional.
- Gained exposure to operations including merchandising, ordering regular and special order stock, and coordinating deliveries.

AUTOMOBILE SALESPERSON. Automaxx, Baltimore, MD (1998-99). Was recognized with three company-wide monthly sales awards within a chain which, at that time, had approximately 25 locations.
- Gained experience in all phases of the collections process.
- Worked closely with customers during the process of getting credit approval and held the authority to approve or disapprove car loans.

RESTAURANT MANAGER. Backstage Deli, Baltimore, MD (1996-98). Learned the true value of maintaining high levels of customer service while developing effective managerial and supervisory skills overseeing the store's overall operations.
- Ensured payroll to sales ratios were in the proper ratio to ensure a profitable bottom line.

MANAGER TRAINEE. Sbarro's Pizza, Baltimore, MD (1994-96). Selected for a management training program, was exposed to all functional areas of operations from scheduling and supervising employees, to making bank deposits, to controlling inventory.

Highlights of earlier experience: Gained familiarity with the sale and marketing of home improvement products and services with one company; in an appliance store, discovered my aptitude for setting up displays and developing merchandising strategies.

PERSONAL

Displayed leadership skills and a talent for public speaking which led to election as senior class president and Lt. Governor for a two-state district of the Government Club in high school. Am known for my ability to respect others and treat everyone I meet with dignity.

CAREER CHANGE

Date

Exact Name of Person
Exact Title
Exact Name of Company
Address
City, State, Zip

**OWNER/GENERAL
MANAGER**

for an exclusive
women's boutique

Dear Exact Name of Person: (or Dear Sir or Madam if answering a blind ad)

I am writing to express my strong interest in a position as a **Pharmaceutical Sales Representative** with your organization. As you will see from the enclosed resume, I have excelled throughout my career in sales and teaching positions which required strong communication and negotiation skills.

I earned a Bachelor of Arts in German Language and Literature and have developed and presented German Language instructional materials as a Department of Health and Human Services employee in San Antonio. I worked with the Human Services Language Institute with University of Texas on a multimedia series of German language lessons that were later published on CD-ROM. While providing translation services for visiting German delegates, I demonstrated my strong ability to communicate effectively with individuals at every organizational level.

Although I have been highly successful in my entrepreneurial endeavors and could continue in my present career, I have decided to pursue my long-term interest in the field of pharmaceutical sales. Through the local physicians who patronize our business, as well as our sponsorship of numerous charity events, I have developed a solid network of contacts within the medical community from San Antonio to Dallas, Texas, which I feel would make me a great asset to any pharmaceutical company.

If you can use a dynamic communicator with a talent for establishing effective relationships and managing profitable business activities, I hope you will call or write me to suggest a time when we might meet in person to discuss your needs. I can provide outstanding references at the appropriate time.

Yours sincerely,

Delores P. Austin

DELORES P. AUSTIN

1110½ Hay Street, Fayetteville, NC 28305   •   preppub@aol.com   •   (910) 483-6611

OBJECTIVE   To benefit an organization that can use a motivated professional with exceptional communication and organizational abilities who offers a strong bottom-line orientation and a "track record" of accomplishment in sales and management, education, and accounting.

EDUCATION   Earned **Bachelor of Arts in English Literature**, The University of Texas at San Antonio, 2003. Excelled in specialized language development and German translation training courses from St. Phillips College, San Antonio, TX, 2000.

COMPUTERS   Familiar with most popular computer operating systems and software, including: Microsoft Word, Excel, and Access; and PageMaker.

EXPERIENCE   **OWNER** and **GENERAL MANAGER.** Sandy's Corner, San Antonio, TX (2003-present). Manage all phases of the opening and operation of this exclusive women's boutique; interview, hire, train, and now supervise the sales staff, ensuring that each customer receives the highest possible levels of customer service.
- Monitor daily, weekly, and monthly sales of all merchandise, oversee all purchasing and inventory control to guarantee a strong in-stock position on popular items.
- Oversee advertising and promotions for the store; negotiate with sales representatives from print, radio, and television media to obtain the best possible advertising rates.
- Direct all visual merchandising efforts, design and implement creative and effective displays throughout the store.

LANGUAGE INSTRUCTOR and **COURSE DEVELOPMENT MANAGER.** Department of Health and Human Services, San Antonio, TX (2001-03). Served as subject matter expert for the German language; developed course materials and conducted formal classroom training and platform instruction for students at the Calhoun Language and Arts Center.
- Coordinated with the Human Services Language Institute (HSLI) while developing and reviewing the Language and Translation Course in both English and German translations.

LANGUAGE INSTRUCTOR. St. Phillips College, San Antonio, TX (1999-01). Instructed college students and teachers in pronunciation, comprehension, and grammar of German.

Highlights of earlier experience:
BOOKKEEPER and **ADMINISTRATIVE ASSISTANT.** Stein Mart, San Antonio, TX (1998-1999). Provided accounting services to this upscale men's clothing store, performing accounts payable, accounts receivable, and general ledger bookkeeping; managed more than 200 customer accounts.
- Processed weekly payroll and calculated withholding taxes, FICA, and payroll taxes for employees; prepared a variety of financial statements for the store.

GENERAL MANAGER. Talbot's, San Antonio, TX (1996-1998). Oversaw all aspects of the planning, opening, and operation of this successful women's clothing store; handled purchasing, inventory and financial controls, interviewing and staff development, and advertising. By providing exceptional customer service and management of inventory and costs, the business turned a profit in its first year despite competition from more established boutiques.

PERSONAL   Excellent personal and professional references are available upon request.

Date

Exact Name of Person
Title or Position
Name of Company
Address (no., street)
Address (city, state, zip)

**PAWN SHOP MANAGER
& LOAN SPECIALIST**

for Crowell Pawn in
Aberdeen, SD

Dear Exact Name of Person: (or Dear Sir or Madam if answering a blind ad.)

I would appreciate an opportunity to talk with you soon about how I could contribute to your organization through my education in business management along with the natural leadership skills I have refined from gaining experience in customer service and sales.

While currently attending Northern State University in Aberdeen, SD, I have received numerous honors while pursuing a B.A. degree in Business Management. As an Assistant Manager, I was singled out for this role because of my leadership, maturity, and responsible attitude while working at Crowell Pawn Shop.

You would find me to be an intelligent and articulate young professional, known for my maturity and dedication to excellence. I am certain that I am capable of meeting the challenges of assuming managerial roles where I could make important contributions to a company's bottom line and continual high quality customer service. With my enthusiasm, motivational abilities, empathy, and compassion for others I can make valuable contributions to an organization that seeks a professional with these qualities.

I hope you will welcome my call soon to arrange a brief meeting at your convenience to discuss your current and future needs and how I might serve them. Thank you in advance for your time.

Sincerely yours,

Kareem F. Robinson

Alternate last paragraph:
I hope you will call or write me soon to suggest a time convenient for us to meet and discuss your current and future needs and how I might serve them. Thank you in advance for your time.

KAREEM F. ROBINSON

1110½ Hay Street, Fayetteville, NC 28305 • preppub@aol.com • (910) 483-6611

OBJECTIVE   To benefit an organization that can use an intelligent and articulate young professional who offers a background of excellent performance combining practical planning, customer service, and sales experience with a background as an award-winning scholar-athlete.

EDUCATION   Pursuing a B.A. in Business Management, Northern State University, Aberdeen, SD.
A.A. in General Studies, Aberdeen Community College, Aberdeen, SD, 1998.
- Placed on the Dean's List for my high GPA.

EXPERIENCE   *Refined my managerial and sales abilities in the following full-time and summer jobs:*
PAWN SHOP MANAGER and **LOAN SPECIALIST**. Crowell Pawn Shop, Aberdeen, SD (2003-present). In mid-May 2003, was selected for promotion to Assistant Manager, and am now in charge of three people; was groomed for rapid advancement based on my skill in providing excellent customer service which ensured repeat business while attending college on a part-time basis.
- Achieved the level of top salesman for the month in only my second month with the company — sold more than $14,000 worth of merchandise.
- Learned to accurately judge the value of items brought in and determine how much could be paid for them and still make an accurate profit.
- Was cited as a key player in the 68% profit margin for that month.
- Became skilled in making decisions on what items such as TVs, jewelry, guns, and stereo systems were worth.
- Became familiar with timesaving methods for using computers to track and search for inventory.

CUSTOMER SERVICE SPECIALIST. A. W. Schucks, Aberdeen, SD (2000-03). Gained insight into the value of providing courteous customer service while seating and waiting on people of all ages and social backgrounds in this resort-town restaurant.

SALESPERSON. Jennite Wholesale Company, Aberdeen, SD (1999-00). Learned the value of planning and using time wisely while processing contracts for new and existing customers. Processing orders online and by telephone for local business owners.

SALES ASSOCIATE. Office Depot, Aberdeen, SD (1998-99). Earned a reputation as a conscientious worker while providing customer service, processing online orders and seeing that they were complete and accurate along with ensuring that they went out on time.

COMPUTER SKILLS   Have experience in working with computers using Microsoft Word, Excel, and Photoshop.

PERSONAL
- Earned numerous athletic and scholastic honors including: was named captain of the varsity men's baseball team, 1997-1998, placed on the all-conference team — two seasons was named to the NCAA Division II All-Region team — two seasons.
- Became a baseball Academic All-American in recognition of my above-average GPA while participating in varsity sports, 1996-1997 was Honorable Mention on the All-American baseball team.
- Am a natural leader who is effective at guiding and teaching others. Have excellent time management skills. Will travel. Will relocate.

Date

Exact Name of Person
Title or Position
Name of Company
Address (no., street)
Address (city, state, zip)

PAWN SHOP SALES ASSOCIATE

for a shop in Rhode Island

Dear Exact Name of Person: (or Dear Sir or Madam if answering a blind ad.)

I would appreciate an opportunity to talk with you soon about how I could contribute to your organization through my strong interest in the field of law enforcement and my reputation as a mature, creative, and dependable professional who excels in dealing with the public.

You will see from my resume that I am an adaptable hard worker who has always done well in positions of responsibility. In my present position in sales and consulting for a pawn shop, I deal with law enforcement professionals, professional shooters, and the general public on a daily basis. A competitive marksman, I have become familiar with the qualities of firearms and am involved in giving advice to customers on firearms and accessories.

In earlier jobs while earning a A.A., in Parks and Recreation Administration, I was often singled out for advancement. These jobs in inventory control, irrigation installation and lawn maintenance, carpet and tile sales, and pawn shop sales and service allowed me to take on responsibility beyond my age and actual years of experience.

Because my father is a 35-year veteran with the Rhode Island Highway Patrol, I have been exposed to the realities of law enforcement. This has given me the opportunity to realize the need for dedicated professionals in every aspect of law enforcement, from game wardens and park rangers, to each level of local, county, and state patrol and investigative fields. I feel that through my interests, exposure, abilities, and knowledge I have a great deal to offer.

My versatile background also includes using heavy materials-handling equipment as well as using and maintaining radio communications equipment. Through training programs sponsored by the American Red Cross among other organizations, I have earned certification as a hunting safety instructor, water safety instructor, lifeguard, and in CPR and Basic First Aid.

I hope you will welcome my call soon to arrange a brief meeting at your convenience to discuss your current and future needs and how I might serve them. Thank you in advance for your time.

Sincerely yours,

Reggie Curtman

REGINALD D. CURTMAN ("Reggie")

1110½ Hay Street, Fayetteville, NC 28305   •   preppub@aol.com   •   (910) 483-6611

OBJECTIVE

To offer my reputation as a creative, mature, and trustworthy individual to an organization that can benefit from my strong interest in and exposure to law enforcement along with my knowledge of firearms and ability to get along with the public, my peers, and superiors.

EDUCATION

A.A., Parks and Recreation Administration, Bryant College, Smithfield, RI, 2001.
Studied Civil Engineering, Norwalk Community-Technical College, Norwalk, CT, 1999.

EXPERIENCE

PAWN SHOP SALES ASSOCIATE. B & B Pawn Shop, Inc., Bristol, RI (2003-present). Work closely with customers in law enforcement professionals and professional shooters, providing them with advice on the proper firearms for their own particular use.
- Excelled in providing personalized attention and sound advice.
- Became familiar with the values and characteristics of a wide range of firearms in order to evaluate their potential for resale.
- Offer suggestions on the reorganization of functions within the company and have seen many of my ideas successfully put into place.
- Earned the owner's trust and soon was locking up at the end of the day, setting security alarms, and handling large sums of money and valuable jewelry and firearms.

Gained experience in dealing with the public, supervising others, selling, and managing my time for peak productivity while attending school and succeeding in the following jobs:
LAWN MAINTENANCE TEAM SUPERVISOR. Trent Landscaping, Bristol, RI (2001-03). Chosen to supervise a team of up to three other employees, became familiar with the installation of irrigation systems, lawn maintenance, and estimating job costs.

INVENTORY AND WAREHOUSE SPECIALIST. Catskills Supplies, Inc., Smithfield, RI (1999-01). Became familiar with proper methods of storing, distributing, and transporting a large inventory of equipment and supplies while making deliveries and pick ups at maintenance sites throughout the college campus.
- Implemented timesharing ideas for storing large bulky items.

SALES ASSOCIATE. Millington Pawn and Loan Shop, Smithfield, RI (1997-99). Earned a reputation for my skills in dealing with the public and earning customer trust while becoming known as a dependable and honest young professional.
- Handled large sums of money while cashing checks for customers.

SALES ASSOCIATE. Carpet Wholesales, Norwalk, CT (1996-97). Gained experience in areas including direct sales of carpet and tile, measuring new homes for tile, carpet, and wallpaper installation, answering phone inquiries, and placing orders by phone for new inventory items.
- Hired under a high school vocational education program, was asked to remain on a permanent basis because of my work ethic and level of productivity.

CERTIFICATIONS

Completed training courses which led to certification in these areas:
- American Red Cross CPR, Lifeguard, Water Safety Instructor, and Advanced and Basic First Aid — 1998
- Wildlife Association Hunter Safety Instructor — 1997

PERSONAL

Am an avid outdoorsman who enjoys a challenge. Like meeting people and being exposed to new ideas and situations. Am very patient and willing to learn from others.

Date

Exact Name of Person
Exact Title
Exact Name of Company
Address
City, State, Zip

**PHARMACY
MANAGER**

for Eckerds drug store

Dear Exact Name of Person: (or Dear Sir or Madam if answering a blind ad)

I would appreciate an opportunity to talk with you soon about how I could contribute to your organization through my exceptionally strong "track record" in management and sales as well as through my customer service and pharmacy background.

As you will see from my resume, I have earned a doctorate in Pharmacy from the University of California in Irvine. Most recently, as a Pharmacy Manager for Eckerds, I have been commended for exceptional performance which has included, filling over a 140 prescriptions per day, performing administrative management, personnel management, and building a trusting relationships with new and existing customers.

During my fourth year clinical rotations and clerkships, I have gained knowledge in working with geriatric patients at the Faber Grove Retirement Community. I have counseled patients, worked closely with physicians and mid-level practitioners, provided clinical pharmacy services with Walgreens and Eckerds Drug Stores, as well as monitored inpatients on a general medicine ward at Roper Hospital.

I believe that my exceptionally strong management "track record" is due to a combination of natural ability, excellent training which I received from my employers, and a "hard-charging" personality that thrives on a fast pace. I offer a talent for training and motivating people, and experience has taught me how to handle "problem" employees and how to interact with the general public. I guarantee you can trust me to produce outstanding results with little or no supervision.

I hope you will call me soon to arrange a brief meeting at your convenience to discuss your current and future needs and how I might serve them. Thank you in advance for your time.

Sincerely yours,

Chester David Ayers

CHESTER DAVID AYERS ("Chet")

1110½ Hay Street, Fayetteville, NC 28305   •   preppub@aol.com   •   (910) 483-6611

OBJECTIVE

I want to contribute to an organization that can use a skilled health care professional who offers an extensive background as a pharmacist along with a strong bottom-line orientation.

EDUCATION

Doctorate of Pharmacy, University of California School of Pharmacy, Irvine, CA 2002.
- Graduated *magna cum laude*.

EXPERIENCE

PHARMACY MANAGER. Eckerds, Santa Monica, CA (2003-present). Fill an average of 140 prescriptions a day while handling a variety of managerial duties.

STAFF PHARMACIST. Johnson's Rx Family Pharmacy, Santa Monica, CA (2002-2003). Was involved with dispensing activities and advanced compounding.

FOURTH YEAR CLINICAL ROTATIONS & CLERKSHIPS:
- **Geriatrics (two rotations):** Faber Grove Retirement Community, Irvine, CA. Jan 2002 and Francis Xavier Medical Hospital, Irvine, CA, Feb 2002. Gained knowledge of geriatric patients.
- **Community Pharmacy:** Eckerd Drug Store, Irvine CA, Dec 2002. Gained experience in all aspects of the operation of a community pharmacy; learned techniques related to receiving and processing Rx orders; dispensing and checking prescriptions; counseling patients; and billing third party payers.
- **Ambulatory Medicine:** Walgreens, Irvine, CA, Nov 2001. Worked closely with physicians and mid-level practitioners and provided clinical pharmacy services; refined my skills in basic physical assessment; drug utilization reviews; and clinical pharmacy practice including patient chart reviews, interpretation of lab results, development of drug regiments, patient counseling, and kinetics service.
- **Drug Information:** University of California Drug Information Center, Irvine, CA Sep 2001. Received requests for information concerning drugs and drug therapy from physicians, pharmacists, and nurses; searched primary, secondary, and tertiary sources for information, to include computerized databases and online sources; compiled information into concise answers.
- **Community Pharmacy:** Bay Drug Store, Irvine CA, Aug 2000. Gained experience in all aspects of the operation of a community pharmacy; completed a school project in which data was collected and counseling given to patients concerning drug-drug interactions.
- **Internal Medicine:** Roper Hospital, Irvine, CA, Jun 1999. Monitored inpatients on a general medicine ward; member of a medical team consisting of an attending physician, a medical resident, an intern, and a student. Monitored patients through attending rounds, medical charts, and computerized databases. Advised physicians concerning pharmacotherapy and pharmacokinetic issues verbally and in writing.

ACHIEVEMENTS
- Elected officer in Kappa Phi Pharmacy Fraternity; inducted into Pre-Med Health Honor Society; Gamma Si Honor Society; Kappa Phi Honor Society.
- Named to Dean's List, President's List; awarded Presidential Scholarship; recipient of Dean's Academic Scholarship.
- Member of the Christian Pharmacist Fellowship International.
- Active in student life and community organizations: participated in annual Kappa Phi fundraiser for Wallace Irvine Elementary School and battered women's shelter.

PERSONAL

Outstanding references. Completed 16 hours of training in primary compounding.

Date

Exact Name of Person
Exact Title
Exact Name of Company
Address
City, State, Zip

**PHARMACY
MANAGER**

for a Rite-Aid drug
store in Albany

Dear Exact Name of Person: (or Dear Sir or Madam if answering a blind ad)

I would appreciate an opportunity to talk with you soon about how I could contribute to your organization through my exceptionally strong "track record" in management and sales as well as through my finance and customer service background.

As you will see from my resume, I have been promoted rapidly in every job I have ever held because of my proven leadership ability and willingness to assume responsibility. A self starter and fast learner, I have excelled most in retail management and was promoted to Sales Area Manager by Phar-Mor after beginning as a stocker and advancing rapidly to reorder associate. As Sales Area Manager I supervised a department of 13 employees and became skilled in hiring and interviewing. Most recently, as an Assistant Manager for Rite-Aid I have been filling in for the absent manager and have been commended for my exceptional performance which has included, managing finances including NSF check returns, performing administrative management, and personnel management.

I believe that my exceptionally strong management "track record" is due to a combination of natural ability, excellent training which I received from my employers, and a "hard-charging" personality that thrives on a fast pace. I offer a talent for training and motivating people, and experience has taught me how to handle "problem" employees and how to motivate marginal workers. I guarantee you can trust me to produce outstanding results with little or no supervision.

I hope you will call me soon to arrange a brief meeting at your convenience to discuss your current and future needs and how I might serve them. Thank you in advance for your time.

Sincerely yours,

Stacy W. Hubert

STACY W. HUBERT

1110½ Hay Street, Fayetteville, NC 28305　　•　　preppub@aol.com　　•　　(910) 483-6611

OBJECTIVE　　To offer my proven management, organizational, and sales skills to an organization that can use a fast learner and hard worker who thrives on serving customers and solving problems in a fast-paced, competitive environment in which I am handling lots of responsibility.

EDUCATION　　Completed extensive executive development training sponsored by Phar-Mor in these areas:
- Managing a department of employees
- Ordering/reordering merchandise throughout the U.S.
- Using the Phar-Mor computer system for retail sales, accounting, and control
- Was selected to attend specialized OSHA training for supervisors

EXPERIENCE　　**PHARMACY MANAGER**. Rite-Aid Drug Stores, Inc., Albany, NY (2003-present). Was rapidly promoted from Assistant Manager to single-handedly manage daily operations of this popular hard-line retail chain, including employee supervision, training, inventory control, merchandising, pricing, markdowns, returns, and discontinued items.
- Handle administrative functions such as working with vendor invoices, and complete daily/weekly/monthly paperwork.
- Perform general accounting procedures including controllable expenses, NSF check listings, cash control, and daily deposits.

SALES AREA MANAGER. Phar-Mor, Albany, NY (2001-03). Began with as a stocker and after two months was promoted to reorder associate; after less than ten months in that job was selected as Sales Area Manager, a position usually reserved for someone with much more experience.
- Received a cash bonus and Excellence Awards for superior performance, 2002.
- Was recommended through a formal letter from my supervisor for selection as Sales and Merchandise Manager because of my trustworthiness, ability to motivate a team, and willingness to tackle any responsibility.
- Supervised a department of 13 employees and learned how to adopt a neutral attitude with "problem" employees; became skilled in hiring and interviewing.
- Acquired considerable skills related to merchandise ordering, reordering, shipping, and markdowns. Was commended on my flair for creating eye-catching displays.
- Learned valuable techniques for maximizing the turnover of seasonal merchandise.
- Continuously assured correct merchandise pricing and stocking; set plan-o-grams.
- Gained extensive experience with retail hard lines.

ASSISTANT MANAGER. Dairy Queen, Albany, NY (1999-2001). Learned "the ropes" of managing a fast food service business.

STORE MANAGER. Circle K Convenience Store, Albany, NY (1998-1999). Always exceeded sales and inventory turnover goals, and earned a bonus with every paycheck I received from this company; handled the responsibility for making daily deposits of up to $8,000.

ASSISTANT MANAGER. Scotchman's Convenience Store, Albany, NY (1996-1998). Was groomed for eventual store management, and became knowledgeable about every job in this convenience store.
- Acted as cashier and made deposits; learned to order inventory and stock shelves; prepared plan-o-grams; trained and scheduled employees.

PERSONAL　　Sincerely thrive on a fast pace and work well under deadlines and pressures.

Date

Exact Name of Person
Exact Title
Exact Name of Company
Address
City, State, Zip

Dear Exact Name of Person: (or Dear Sir or Madam if answering a blind ad)

With the enclosed resume, I would like to express my interest in exploring management opportunities within your organization. Although I am held in high regard by my current employer and can provide outstanding references at the appropriate time, I would appreciate your holding my interest in your company in confidence at this time.

You will see from my resume that since 1999 I have excelled in a track record of promotion with ColorTyme, where I started as an Account Manager, was promoted to Assistant Manager, and then to Manager. In my current position, I manage six employees including three assistant managers and three account managers while overseeing 550 accounts.

I have led the store to achieve a year-to-date profit of 16% higher than the previous year, and the store has been named "Store of the Month" three times while also receiving three Customer Service Awards. I provide continuous training to account managers to assure that they are highly skilled in all aspects of sales, collections, and accounts management.

In prior positions, I worked as an Assistant Manager for Mitchell's Formal Wear and a sales associate for S & K's Menswear and Dillard's Department store. In these positions, I acquired customer service skills by working with clients to determine their needs, and I used state-of-the-art equipment to make bar codes and to take inventory with a scanning system.

If you can use a go-getter and self-starter known for my unlimited personal initiative and strong problem-solving skills, I hope you will write or call me to suggest a time when we might in person to discuss your needs. I can assure you that I could become a valuable member of your management team.

Yours sincerely,

Dean Windley

DEAN WINDLEY

1110½ Hay Street, Fayetteville, NC 28305   •   preppub@aol.com   •   (910) 483-6611

OBJECTIVE

To contribute to an organization that can use an experienced young manager who offers a strong bottom-line orientation and a proven ability to produce outstanding results.

EDUCATION

A. S. in Computer Science, Mercyhurst College, Erie, PA, 2001.
Completed course work related to computer operations, personnel management, office administration, and other areas.
Excelled in extensive training related to management, collections, and sales sponsored by ColorTyme Rentals.

EXPERIENCE

With ColorTyme Rentals, have excelled in the following track record of promotion based on my exceptionally strong managerial skills and bottom-line results:
2003-present: RENTAL STORE MANAGER. Erie, PA. Was promoted to manage three assistants and three account managers whose schedules I create and manage; oversee 550 accounts and assure timely payments and collections; prepare monthly budget.
- Achieved a year-to-date profit of 16% higher than the previous year.
- Have led the store I manage to receive three Customer Service Awards and to be named "Store of the Month" three times.
- Implemented new policies and procedures during a change in management.
- Train and develop two assistant managers who were promoted to manager.

2001-03: ASSISTANT MANAGER. Erie and Scranton, PA. Excelled in all aspects of my job while organizing administrative paperwork for the manager's approval; supervised three account managers.
- Assured that account managers completed all training requirements, and continuously updated their knowledge by training them on collections, sales, and customer service.
- Processed payroll and maintained both customer and employee files.

1999-01: ACCOUNT MANAGER. Erie, PA. Closed store accounts following strict company guidelines; collected merchandise from past due accounts.
- Excelled at in-store sales while providing excellent customer service.
- Handled the administrative paperwork to close sales, reviewed purchase agreements with customers, and delivered merchandise to customers' homes.

ASSISTANT MANAGER. Mitchell's Formal Wear, Erie, PA (1998-99). Served as an Assistant Manager for three stores after completing a rigorous six-month training program.
- Trained five personnel to be Assistant Managers.
- Led by example; motivated and brought team together to get the job done.
- Supervised up to 18 personnel and assisted the manager in payroll, filing rental contracts, inventory, and training.

Other experience:
SALES ASSOCIATE. Dillard's, Erie, PA (1997-98). Won numerous awards for sales and customer service expertise while advancing from selling and stocking the men's department to overseeing men's accessories.
- Worked with customers to help them find the items they were looking for in addition to handling inventory control.
- Learned procedures for operating cash registers, making sales, and providing good service in a retail environment.

SALESPERSON. S & K's Menswear, Erie, PA (1995-1997). Provided superior customer service while assisting customers in selection of fine men's suits.

Date

Exact Name of Person
Title or Position
Name of Company
Address (no., street)
Address (city, state, zip)

RETAIL MANAGER
for a retail operation
in Knoxville

Dear Exact Name of Person: (or Dear Sir or Madam if answering a blind ad.)

With the enclosed resume, I would like to formally inquire about employment opportunities within your organization where my experience in senior level retailing could be utilized for your benefit.

As you will see from my resume, I have spent an exciting career in retailing and have excelled in every aspect of it: setting up new outlets, closing down outlets and consolidating operations into superstore and mall environments, and generally creating environments which induce a customer desire to buy. In my most recent position as a Retail Manager for Target, I took a mall operation which was losing money while producing $11 million in sales annually, and I transformed it into an operation making 10% profit after expenses based on increased sales of $26 million annually.

In my prior job I took over a retail operation which was losing money and experiencing out-of-control accountability problems, and I boosted annual sales 250% to $15 million while restoring profitability.

Perhaps there is a little "bloodhound" in me, but I enjoy working in the security control and accountability part of operations management, and I am extremely knowledgeable of all aspects of security, accountability, and inventory control. Early in my retail career, I worked as a Loss Prevention Associate managing a force of other associates in Knoxville, Memphis, and Nashville troubleshooting theft and accountability problems. I recently updated my knowledge of security by completing security training with the Knoxville Police Department.

If you can use a seasoned professional who offers a proven ability to sense potential problems and opportunities in retailing and then develop and implement appropriate strategies and plans, I would be delighted to make myself available for a brief meeting at your convenience. I am approaching your organization because there are many things I admire about your style of retailing, and I feel there could be a fit between your needs and my expertise. Thank you in advance for your professional courtesies.

Yours sincerely,

Jay Ball

JAY CHRISTOPHER BALL

1110½ Hay Street, Fayetteville, NC 28305   •   preppub@aol.com   •   (910) 483-6611

OBJECTIVE

I want to contribute to an organization that can use an experienced professional with expertise related to the management of retailing and service operations as well as the design and implementation of systems designed for loss prevention, accountability, and control.

EXPERIENCE

Can offer a "track record" of experience with a Target retail operation in Knoxville, TN:
2003-present: RETAIL MANAGER, MAIN STORE. Was specially selected to take over a mall-type operation with total annual sales of $11 million which was losing between 4% and 10% yearly as a percentage of gross product; transformed this complex operation with 15 different facilities into an operation that, by 2004, was making an 8% profit after expenses with a more-than-doubled annual sales volume of $26 million.
- Directly manage 215 employees. Within a few weeks after taking the job, initiated changes which streamlined operations and reduced unacceptable accountability losses.
- Manage all aspects of this diversified mall operation including procurement, merchandising, and operations management while managing inventories of up to $37 million per year.
- Oversee vendor contact to assure timely stock replenishment of open-end and direct-delivery orders; supervise maintenance of inventory management documents.
- Improved the security of cash, fixed assets, and merchandise inventory.

2002-03: ASSISTANT RETAIL MANAGER. Took over an operation which was losing money and experiencing out-of-control accountability problems and produced sales increases of more than 250% while restoring profitability and acceptable levels of accountability; supervised 90 personnel.
- Boosted annual sales to nearly $15 million.
- Closed smaller outlets and consolidated categories of merchandise into one complex, thereby decreasing costs and improving consumer satisfaction.
- Maintained a very hands-on style in managing store renovations and which resulted in a greatly enhanced image and superior merchandising environments.
- Became known for my fair and straightforward management style, and for my knack for attracting reliable, conscientious individuals who became excellent retailers.

1999-02: Other TARGET experience: Retail operations in Knoxville, TN. Excelled in these and other positions while advancing into the top management positions above:
- As a Loss Prevention Associate, managed a force of 10 employees working at locations in Knoxville, Memphis, and Nashville to solve theft and other accountability problems at retail outlets of all sizes.

EDUCATION

Completed more than four years of executive development training in all areas of retailing and operations management including:

security management	surveillance	loss prevention
sales and merchandising	profit protection	customer service
softlines merchandising	hardlines merchandising	fashion merchandising
cashiering procedures	Phoenix funding	understanding diversity
financial management	retail accounting	developing subordinates
sexual harassment	AIDS in the workplace	ethics and responsibility

AWARDS

Received seven **Excellence** awards and five **Special Recognition** and **Superior Accomplishment** awards citing my extraordinary achievements in turning around troubled operations, boosting profitability, and generating enthusiastic merchandising presentations.

Date

Exact Name of Person
Title or Position
Name of Company
Address (no., street)
Address (city, state, zip)

SALES ASSOCIATE
for Sam's Wholesale

Dear Exact Name of Person: (or Dear Sir or Madam if answering a blind ad.)

I would appreciate an opportunity to talk with you soon about how I could contribute to your organization through my management experience and personal qualities. Mrs. Lizzie Collins has suggested that I send you a resume describing my background.

While working for Bi-Lo Inc., I supervised seven employees while working as an acting manager. I was recognized for my excellent inventory control abilities as well as for my skills in scheduling, ordering, and building displays.

I am especially proud of the fact that I have helped trained and developed many cashiers and sales associates through my training skills, motivational and counseling techniques. I have enjoyed the challenge of being in the college classroom and am pursuing a B.S. in Psychology at Barry University of Miami.

I can provide outstanding personal and professional references, and I can assure you that I could rapidly become an asset to your organization through my management experience. I hope you will write or call me soon to suggest a time when we might meet to discuss your needs and goals and how my strong planning, organizational, and supervisory experience could serve them. Thank you in advance for your time.

Yours sincerely,

Gregory H. Brandt

GREGORY HARRIS BRANDT

1110½ Hay Street, Fayetteville, NC 28305   •   preppub@aol.com   •   (910) 483-6611

OBJECTIVE

To offer my experience in sales and customer service to an organization that can use a hard-working professional with knowledge of serving the general public.

EDUCATION

Am pursuing a **B.S. in Psychology** by attending classes at Barry University, Miami, FL, in the night school; degree anticipated in 2005.
Studied **Industrial Management Technology** at Miami-Dade Community College including course work in operations management, computer applications, safety and health.

EXPERIENCE

SALES ASSOCIATE and **COLLEGE STUDENT.** Sam's Wholesale, Miami, FL (2003-present). Am sharpening my sales and customer service skills in processing memberships for this giant wholesale company while refining my time management skills while attending night-school classes.

SALES ASSOCIATE. Sears, Miami, FL (2002-03). Provided customer service in this well known department store. Performed opening and closing procedures. Stocked and displayed merchandise on a daily basis. Performed inventory duties. Authorized refund transactions and trained new associates on cash register procedures and customer service skills.

FLOOR SUPERVISOR. Bi-Lo, Miami, FL (2000-02). Supervised one department head and seven employees in the grocery department while working as acting manager in his absence for a store with a $10 million annual sales volume.
- Was recognized for my excellent inventory control abilities as well as for my skills in scheduling, ordering, and building displays.
- Recognized for my attention to detail as a sales clerk in from 2000-2001, was promoted to oversee all cashier operations.
- Supervised stockers; maintained a sanitary and well-organized stock room and sales floor.

CASHIER. IGA Groceries, Miami, FL (1998-00). Excelled in providing sound management and customer service skills in a small family-owned business, IGA. Performed open and close procedures. Operated registers and handled cash from daily transactions. Stocked merchandise.

Other experience:
COUNSELOR. Miami-Dade Community College, Miami, FL (1997-98). Counseled college freshman on making adjustments to college life. Organized group discussions covering topics that dealt with daily activities on college campuses.

ACHIEVEMENTS

Received Honor awards from Miami-Dade Community College. Graduated with a 3.4 GPA.

PERSONAL

Earned several respected medals for my professionalism, leadership, and managerial skills. Am accustomed to working long hours to see that the job is done. Excellent references.

Exact Name of Person
Title or Position
Name of Company
Address (no., street)
Address (city, state, zip)

SALES ASSOCIATE
for an Indiana
department store

Dear Exact Name of Person: (or Dear Sir or Madam if answering a blind ad.)

I would appreciate an opportunity to talk with you soon about how I could contribute to your organization through my excellent public relations and customer service skills.

As you will see from my resume, I have excelled in retail sales positions that have permitted me to develop public relations and customer service skills. In my present position as a Sales Associate at Burdines, I ranked #1 in sales per hour while excelling in creating attractive, eye-catching displays and operating an automated inventory control system.

I am currently working on a B. A. in Public Relations with a minor in Psychology from Indiana Wesleyan University. I believe that my education and experience makes a good candidate for the available Sales Associate position. You would find me to be a well-organized, reliable professional with a genuine customer-service orientation. Thoroughly flexible, I would cheerfully relocate according to your needs.

I hope you will welcome my call soon to arrange a brief meeting at your convenience to discuss your current and future needs and how I might serve them. Thank you in advance for your consideration.

Sincerely yours,

Woodrow C. Hollingsworth

Alternate last paragraph:
I hope you will call or write me soon to suggest a time convenient for us to meet and discuss your current and future needs and how I might best serve them. Thank you in advance for your consideration.

WOODROW C. HOLLINGSWORTH, JR.

1110½ Hay Street, Fayetteville, NC 28305   •   preppub@aol.com   •   (910) 483-6611

OBJECTIVE

To contribute to an organization that can use an intelligent young professional with a reputation as an innovative thinker who can motivate others to work toward common goals by applying natural leadership abilities.

EDUCATION

Earned a **Bachelor of Arts (B.A.) in Public Relations with a minor in Psychology**, Indiana Wesleyan University, Marion, IN, 2003. 3.5 GPA.

EXPERIENCE

SALES ASSOCIATE. Burdines, Marion, IN (2003-present). Ranked #1 in sales per hour while excelling in creating attractive, eye-catching displays and operating an automated inventory control system.

ADMINISTRATIVE ASSISTANT. Chamber of Commerce, Marion, IN (2002-03). Gained experience using computer programs while processing packets mailed to entrepreneurs.

Refined my skills in part-time and seasonal jobs:
RETAIL SALES ASSOCIATE. Service Merchandise, Marion, IN (1999-02).   Achieved outstanding results while polishing sales and customer service skills in the jewelry department of this major retail store.
- Was recognized as the most productive associate in the area of selling customers on the advantages of extended service plans on merchandise. Placed third in overall sales despite having less experience in sales of luxury items than most other associates.

STOCK ASSISTANT. The Closet, Grand Rapids, MI (1997-99). Learned to set up and coordinate pleasing merchandise displays; helped in all aspects of stock control from receiving and processing incoming stock to keeping stock on the floor.

CUSTOMER SERVICE SPECIALIST. Carrabbas Italian Restaurant, Grand Rapids, MI (1995-97). Earned a reputation as a mature individual with well-developed customer service skills and the ability to communicate effectively with other employees as well as the public.

TEAM LEADER. Wedgy's Pizza, Grand Rapids, MI (1994-95). Developed and refined personnel management abilities as well as customer service and organizational skills in this popular and busy food service location.
- Operated cash registers, made pizzas, and closed the store at the end of the day.

ACADEMIC & COMMUNITY INVOLVEMENT

As a student at Whitehaven High School, Grand Rapids, MI, participated in scholastic and extracurricular as well as community service activities including the following:
- Was named in Who's Who Among American High School Students and received recog nition from the Beta Club for my accomplishments and scholastic excellence in the field of mathematics.
- Held membership in the Beta Club and SAIL — a program for gifted students — as well as attending advanced placement courses.
- Was a member of the Vocational Club with a concentration in Engineering.
- Helped organize a chapter of SADD (Students Against Drunk Driving) which grew to 150 students and met at least once a month: created flyers and encouraged young people to avoid the dangers of driving or riding with anyone under the influence of alcohol/ drugs.

PERSONAL

Helped with roadside cleaning, lawn maintenance, and other services as a volunteer with a local fire department. Am able to easily handle deadlines and pressure.

Exact Name of Person
Title or Position
Name of Company
Address (no., street)
Address (city, state, zip)

SALES ASSOCIATE
for Hecht's department
store

Dear Exact Name of Person: (or Dear Sir or Madam if answering a blind ad.)

I would appreciate an opportunity to talk with you soon about how I could contribute to your organization as a sales associate through my experience in working with the general public my excellent communication, planning, and time-management abilities.

As you will see from my resume, I have a strong background in public relations which has allowed me to successfully interact the general public. In a previous position as a photographer's assistant with Olan Mills Photography Studios allowed me to discover my knack for quickly establishing a rapport with people of all ages.

You would find me to be a hardworking and reliable professional who prides myself on always giving "110%" to every job I undertake. I am currently employed by Hecht's and I can provide excellent personal and professional references upon request.

I hope you will call or write me soon to suggest a time convenient for us to meet and discuss your current and future needs and how I might serve them. Thank you in advance for your time.

Sincerely,

Melinda J. Hall

MELINDA J. HALL

1110½ Hay Street, Fayetteville, NC 28305 • preppub@aol.com • (910) 483-6611

OBJECTIVE

To benefit an organization in need of an enthusiastic, young professional knowledgeable and experienced in project management, public relations, inventory, and photography, who also possesses a knack for planning, problem-solving, and decision-making.

EDUCATION

A. S. in Business Administration, Hinds Community College, Raymond, MS, 2002. Have completed a wide range including classes in psychology, composition, history, and business administration.

EXPERIENCE

Polished my public relations and creativity in a fast-paced retail environment:
SALES ASSOCIATE. Hecht's, Raymond, MS (2003-present). Utilize my outstanding customer-service skills providing sales, merchandising, and inventory functions while working for this well known, upscale retailer; train and supervise new employees.

- Earned a reputation for easily establishing a rapport with people from diverse backgrounds.
- Manage the designer accessories department, consistently exceeding my own sales goals and assisting the department in achieving 106% above company sales quotas.
- Apply my product knowledge to successfully satisfy my customers' most challenging needs. Praised by top-level management for lowering departmental external and internal shrinkage rate.
- Have a knack for quickly and courteously resolving thorny customer-service problems.
- Liaison with headquarters for inventory and supply needs.
- Design displays and coordinate merchandise for customers.
- Presented the prestigious employee "Customer Service Award" for showing excellent sales and management abilities.

Discovered my talent for working one-on-one with children:
PHOTOGRAPHER'S ASSISTANT. Olan Mills Photography Studios, Raymond, MS (2001-03). Gained valuable experience working with children and refined my photography knowledge while assisting in the set-up, presentation, and development of children's portraits.

- Arranged lights and backdrops and posed children both in the studio and at a variety of area elementary, junior high, and senior high schools.
- Readied proofs and worked with parents to determine purchase shots.
- Used excellent attention-to-detail skills to ensure each portrait was perfect.
- Sharpened my ability to turn out quality work under tight deadlines.
- Developed an increased appreciation for well-rounded photography.
- Creatively interpreted photographer's requests to produce attractive portraits.

Highlights of other experience:
VOLUNTEER WORKER. Jenkins Orphanage, Raymond, MS (1999-2001). Volunteered at this orphanage acting as a role model and entertaining disadvantaged children during Christmas and other holidays; also worked with this civic group visiting and "adopting" senior citizens.

PERSONAL

Am a versatile professional who enjoys people. Can handle pressure and react logically to emergencies. Love working with children. Adapt easily to new situations and function smoothly in handling simultaneous responsibilities. Am a permanent resident of Raymond.

Date

Exact Name of Person
Title or Position
Name of Company
Address (number and street)
Address (city, state, and ZIP)

SALES CONSULTANT
for Victoria's Secret

Dear Exact Name of Person: (or Sir or Madam if answering a blind ad.)

I would appreciate an opportunity to talk with you soon about how I could contribute to your organization through my creative abilities and expertise in all aspects of public relations as well as through my sales and marketing experience.

I most recently accomplished outstanding results as a Sales Consultant for the rapidly growing national retail organization of Victoria's Secret. During their first season of existence, the Middlebury, VT, location exceeded corporate sales goals by 11% and is very productive in selling high quality products while emphasizing very personalized customer service.

Although I enjoyed my recent position and was successful in sales and managerial roles, I felt my creative abilities were not being utilized and I now wish to offer my talents and knowledge to an organization that will benefit directly from my versatile experience.

You will see from my resume that before building my sales, marketing, and management skills with Victoria Secrets and Express (ladies fashion store), I had held positions as a Editorial Assistant, Publicity Assistant, Public Relations Intern, and News Assistant for a ABC affiliate. While writing a column for the The Middlebury Herald, I earned recognition for good judgment in writing and editing features for the paper as well as earning a reputation for quickly and easily establishing a rapport with the large number of people from diverse backgrounds with whom I came into contact.

You will find me to be a versatile, creative, and innovative professional who thrives on the responsibility of new challenges. I am certain my background could significantly contribute to your organization's efforts.

I hope you will welcome my call soon to arrange a brief meeting to discuss your current and future needs and how I might serve them. Thank you in advance for your time.

Sincerely,

Maxine L. D'Errico

MAXINE L. D'ERRICO

1110½ Hay Street, Fayetteville, NC 28305 • preppub@aol.com • (910) 483-6611

OBJECTIVE
To offer my superior verbal communication and writing skills to an organization in need of a creative and versatile professional experienced in public relations, print and broadcast journalism, retail sales, and marketing.

EXPERIENCE
SALES CONSULTANT. Victoria's Secret, Middlebury, VT (2003-present). Play an important managerial role while contributing to team efforts which resulted in this store's exceeding projected corporate sales goals an impressive 11% and leading the district in sales during the store's first season of operations at this location. Was commended for my exceptional leadership and guidance as part of this fast-growing retail giant which had 500 stores late in 1995.
- Emphasize customer service and encouraged my staff to make sure that each customer's needs were met and that they were educated and informed on various products.
- Accepted into the management training program, use the knowledge gained to contribute to the store's success in all areas of operations.

SALES ASSOCIATE. Express, Middlebury, VT (2001-03). Helped with the opening of this popular store; wore many "hats" while demonstrating exceptional attention-to-detail skills and also complied with very strict company-wide guidelines.

EDITORIAL ASSISTANT. The Middlebury Herald, Middlebury, VT (2000-01). Recognized for subject expertise and promoted from reporter to columnist, was in charge of coordinating and writing a weekly current event sections for this 84,000-circulation newspaper.
- Organized material for calendar events, reunions, personnel close-ups, and sports events.
- Wrote the "In Our Town" column, detailing the concerns and experiences of local families and a wide range of other special story features.
- Received excellent feedback from readers through letters to the editor.
- Built a reputation for sound judgment and thorough reporting.

PUBLICITY ASSISTANT. Hudson County Housing Development, Burlington, VT (1996-00). Performed writing and public relations functions for an active community volunteer organization while also serving as a liaison between the housing development company and local media.
- Promoted special fundraising events and created press releases, slogans, and graphic designs. Wrote and released press releases to area newspapers and other local media.

PUBLIC RELATIONS INTERN. Department of Commerce, Jersey City, NJ (1994-1996). Wrote press releases on current events and issues concerning local area businesses.
- Acquired expert communication skills handling a wide range of functions including preparing press releases, a long-range marketing plan, and business announcements.

NEWS ASSISTANT. ABC Affiliate/WKEE-TV, Jersey City, NJ (1992-1994). Developed expertise in writing and public relations skills while working as an intern at a respected television news station.
- Produced, wrote, and directed an educational videotape: *Newsroom Guidelines.*
- Prepared daily news broadcast scripts.
- Gathered information for news reports by working with area law enforcement agencies.

EDUCATION
Bachelor of Arts degree in **Communication Arts**, with a concentration in Radio/ Television/ Film, University of Vermont, Burlington, VT, 2000.

Exact Name of Person
Exact Title
Exact Name of Company
Address
City, State, Zip

SALES CONSULTANT

with versatile experience
in selling home decor and
jewelry

Dear Exact Name of Person (or Dear Sir or Madam if answering a blind ad):

With the enclosed resume, I would like to make you aware of my interest in exploring employment opportunities with your organization.

As you will see from my resume, I am a versatile individual who has excelled in sales, management, and theatrical roles. Most recently I excelled as a Sales Consultant and Framing Designer for an established retailer which catered to a high-end clientele. I was especially involved in selling high-end home decorating items, jewelry, unique gifts, and oil paintings, and I became skilled at custom framing since many of our clients were avid art collectors and redecorating usually involved reframing.

In a previous position with Macy's in Los Angeles, I thoroughly enjoyed selling jewelry, and I established record sales figures.

I offer a true talent for establishing effective working relationships which derives to a large degree from my professional acting experience. I became involved in acting part-time while working for a public utility and subsequently worked full-time as a Professional Actor until shortly before I relocated permanently to Charlotte.

I consider myself a permanent resident of Charlotte, and I live in downtown Charlotte and do everything I can to support downtown development efforts. I am also a member of the Arts Council and Art Museum. I can provide outstanding personal and professional references, and I would enjoy an opportunity to explore your needs for a reliable hard worker with versatile sales and management skills.

Yours sincerely,

Frank McAlister

FRANK MCALISTER

1110½ Hay Street, Fayetteville, NC 28305 • preppub@aol.com • (910) 483-6611

OBJECTIVE   I want to contribute to an organization that can use an outgoing individual who offers versatile experience in sales, customer service, and business management.

EXPERIENCE   **SALES CONSULTANT & FRAMING DESIGNER.** Marty's Gifts & Antiques, Charlotte, NC (2000-03). Was involved in retail sales while working with a clientele interested in high-end home decorating items, custom jewelry, unique gifts, oil paintings; consulted with and advised customers on upholstery fabrics as well as custom furniture restoration.

- Became skilled in custom picture framing; many of my customers were avid art collectors with unusual framing needs.
- Played a key role in a 25% growth in the business. Attended buyer's markets including the High Point Furniture Market and Charlotte's Jewelry and Gift Show.
- Excelled in representing high-end items including jewelry, gifts, and home decorating items. Also sold retail items such as entertainment centers, bronze statues, and other exciting home pieces.

JEWELRY SALESMAN. Macy's, Los Angeles, CA (1999). Developed a true love and appreciation for jewelry of all types as I set sales records in multiple store promotions.

PROFESSIONAL ACTOR—Member, Screen Actors Guild (SAG). Los Angeles, CA (1986-99). I credit my acting experience with giving me the ability to excel in sales, because my acting experience trained me to appreciate the customer's point of view. I was successful in film, commercials (tv and radio), and theatre.

- Worked part-time as an actor from 1986-90; pursued acting full-time from 1990-99.
- In film, my roles ranged from star, to co-star, to extra, in films such as *The Louisiana Conspiracy, Portrait of a Nightmare, Boy from the Bayou, Private Life of Jean Le Fete, Future Tense, James Brady Story, Final Verdict,* and many other films.
- Played various roles in industrial training videos made for Houston Industries and Chrysler.
- Acted in commercials shown on CNN and Channel 13.
- Extensive theatre credits included major and minor parts in productions such as *A Christmas Carol, The Nutcracker, Sweet Charity, Hollywood Murders,* and many other stage events.
- Refined my communication skills through training in acting, dramatic interpretation, and dialects.

Highlights of other experience:
SPECIAL PROJECTS MANAGER. California Lighting & Power Company, Merced, CA Began with this major utility company as a Junior Draftsman involved in producing schematic drawings, graphs, and charts related to highways and road alignments. Was promoted to Draftsman in the Survey and Right of Way Department. Advanced to handle special projects which involved custom mapping, special graphics, special pipeline, and right-of-way.

EDUCATION   Completed courses at University of California and Methodist University in General Business, Psychology, and Art.
Completed three years of study in Architectural Design, Mechanical Drawing, and Art.

ACTIVITIES   I live in downtown Charlotte and am a staunch supporter of downtown development efforts and the Charlotte arts community. Member of the Arts Council and Art Museum.

CAREER CHANGE

Date

Exact Name of Person
Title or Position
Name of Company
Address (number and street)
Address (city, state, and zip)

SALES REPRESENTATIVE
for Belk in Ohio

Dear Exact Name of Person: (or Sir or Madam if answering a blind ad.)

I would appreciate an opportunity to talk with you soon about how I could contribute to your organization through my managerial abilities as well as through my reputation as a dedicated young professional with the ability to quickly learn and apply new ideas, concepts, and procedures.

Having polished my communication and public relations skills in a management training program with the retail giant, Belk, I am confident that I have expanded abilities which would allow me to be productive and effective in management roles in environments other than the retail industry. Other important aspects of being a Customer Service/ Sales Representative included troubleshooting problems and providing supervision over other sales and customer service personnel.

You will also see from my enclosed resume that I graduated from Ashland University with a B.A. in Industrial Relations and Speech Communications. While attending college I contributed my organizational and communication skills in activities including fund raising, library operations, counseling, and personnel recruiting. Known for my strong work ethic and high degree of self-motivation, I began working as a young teen in a summer youth program where my assignments included assisting in the offices of a hospital administrative office an a landscaping office as well as working as a warehouse clerk.

I hope you will welcome my call soon to arrange a brief meeting to discuss your current and future needs and how I might serve them. Thank you in advance for your time.

Sincerely,

Kevin A. Perry

Alternate last paragraph:
I hope you will call or write me soon to suggest a time convenient for us to meet and discuss your current and future needs and how I might serve them. Thank you in advance for your time.

KEVIN A. PERRY

1110½ Hay Street, Fayetteville, NC 28305 • preppub@aol.com • (910) 483-6611

OBJECTIVE   To use my oral communication and public relations skills to contribute to an organization that can use a hard-working, motivated young professional.

EDUCATION   Earned a **Bachelor of Arts (B.A.) degree in Industrial Relations** and **Speech Communications**, Ashland University, Ashland, OH, 2001.
- Refined my oral communication skills through numerous analytical and dramatic presentations and through class work in leadership and interpersonal communication.

EXPERIENCE   **SALES REPRESENTATIVE.** Belk, Columbus, OH (2003-present). Provide public relations while refining communication and troubleshooting skills for this leading retailer.
- Am known as a dependable team player who has not missed a day of work throughout several years of employment.

TELEMARKETING REPRESENTATIVE. United Way, Columbus, OH (2003). During a budget crisis, sharpened my communication skills as a telemarketer for a busy fund-raising office.
- Contacted alumni by phone, asking for pledges to support academics.
- Played a key role in an effort raising $15,000.
- Provided information about university activities to interested patrons.

MEDIA CLERK. Columbus Community Library, Columbus, OH (2001-03). While working in a specialized library, became known for strong planning and organizational skills.

Developed a "track record" of promotion while working with Ashland University in Ohio:
2000-01: ORIENTATION COUNSELOR. Guided and informed 15 incoming junior transfer students on university operations, history, and activities.
- Welcomed new students to the university with personal letters.
- Conducted tours of the campus and town to familiarize new students with their surroundings.
- Assimilated large amounts of information on the university to inform others.

1998-2000: PERSONNEL RECRUITER and **PLACEMENT ASSISTANT**. In the administrative office was selected to be a placement assistant; recruited potential candidates by sending brochures to area high schools and high school seniors.
- Earned trust of supervisors; was often left in charge of office.
- Performed word processing and telephone communication tasks.

Other experience:
VOLUNTEER WORK. Summer Youth Employment Program, Naples, Italy (1997-1998). Gained cultural, work, and other valuable experience while spending three summers working at an overseas Christian youth camp.
- **OFFICE ASSISTANT.** (1998). As the sole assistant in a busy hospital administrative office, was entrusted with correspondence duties.
- **WAREHOUSE CLERK.** (1997). Became familiar with inventory control and distribution while handling office and phone work.
- **OFFICE ASSISTANT.** (1997). Exhibited initiative by becoming proficient in both office duties and landscape work.

PERSONAL   Am highly motivated; began working as a young teen. Skilled at working with others or as an individual. Enjoy working with the public.

Date

Exact Name of Person
Title or Position
Name of Company
Address (number and street)
Address (city, state, and ZIP)

SALES REPRESENTATIVE

for Nextel's cellular
services

Dear Exact Name of Person: (or Sir or Madam if answering a blind ad.)

Can you use an assertive, enthusiastic, and productive sales professional who has been very effective in selling your product lines and who believes in Nextel's products and services?

I joined the Nextel sales staff in June 2002 and quickly saw that the other sales representatives were not "pushing" your products. On my own initiative, I became the resident expert on Nextel products and services. Earlier this week I was named "Salesman of the Month" in recognition of my accomplishments and bottom-line results.

I believe that through my experiences of the past few months I have proven that I offer a high level of self-motivation, initiative, and drive. As you will see from my enclosed resume, I spent approximately 7 years at The Columbian, a Vancouver, Washington publication, where I applied my skills in dealing with people while training, supervising, and motivating personnel. I earned a reputation as an adaptable and dependable professional who could be counted on for excellent results.

I believe in Nextel and am confident that I offer the type of expertise, skills, and product knowledge that could be applied directly to represent your company. I hope you will call or write me soon to suggest a time convenient for us to meet and discuss your current and future needs and how I might serve them. Thank you in advance for your time.

Sincerely,

Hernando Miguela

HERNANDO MIGUELA

1110½ Hay Street, Fayetteville, NC 28305   •   preppub@aol.com   •   (910) 483-6611

OBJECTIVE

To contribute sales and customer service skills to an organization that can use a proven sales professional with particular expertise in the sale of cellular services and who is dedicated to maximizing bottom-line results.

EXPERIENCE

SALES REPRESENTATIVE. Nextel, Vancouver, WA (2002-present). On my own initiative, became a Nextel product expert after noticing that of the ten other sales representatives, there was no one selling up to the potential of this product line, and in only a few months was formally recognized as "Top Salesman."
- Earned recognition for selling 128 cellular phones in October 2002 and 110 in January 2003.
- Display a high level of self motivation and initiative while having the vision to see that Nextel products needed to be emphasized and sold more aggressively.

CUSTOMER SERVICE SPECIALIST. *The Columbian* Vancouver, WA (1996-02). Earned numerous honors and awards for my accomplishments while becoming an effective customer service specialist for 7 years while providing administrative oversight for district managers that distributed this publication on a daily basis.
- Evaluated the performance of district managers and counseled them on ways to improve their skills and professional knowledge.
- Prepared daily reports for district managers and their assistants providing delivery locations for daily *Columbian* newspaper subscribers.
- Evaluated work requirements and made scheduling decisions while keeping the circulation budget restrictions and organizational objectives in mind.
- Learned to apply my effective communication skills and ability to deal with people of various cultural and national backgrounds while handling customer concerns and complaints.
- Trained personnel from on the proper use of equipment and methods while providing customer service.
- Became familiar with the full range of inventory control activities from the request process, through receipt and storage, to issuing and accountability for a wide range of office supplies and equipment.
- Developed telemarketing and public relation skills by utilizing various marketing strategies for increasing subscriptions.
- Became knowledgeable of computer operating systems and MS DOS systems to maintain up-to-date and accurate subscriber records.

INSURANCE REPRESENTATIVE. American Insurance Claims, Vancouver, WA (1995-96). Supervised four other employees while processing car and life insurance claims.
- Processed all paper work for accident and health claims, credit life claims, refinance contracts, repo notification, credit bureau inquiries, and small claims court.

EDUCATION

Studied **Computer Science** at Clark College, Vancouver, WA, 2001; completed 21 semester hours of course work.

AWARDS

Earned a reputation as a skilled and knowledgeable professional and was awarded several dedication awards including a 1999 United Way "Outstanding Service Award".

PERSONAL

Am an articulate, enthusiastic, and energetic individual. Feel that my skill in sales is being polished and refined. Insist on seeing that customers are well-informed and buy the right product to meet their needs.

Exact Name of Person
Title or Position
Name of Company
Address (number and street)
Address (city, state, and zip)

SALES TRAINER
for Barry's Menswear

Dear Exact Name of Person: (or Sir or Madam if answering a blind ad.)

I would appreciate an opportunity to talk with you soon about how I could contribute to your organization through my sales experience as well as through my reputation as a dedicated young professional with the ability to quickly learn and apply new ideas, concepts, and procedures.

Having polished my communication and public relations skills in a sales training program with Barry's Menswear, I am confident that I have expanded abilities which would allow me to be productive and effective employee. Other important aspects of being a Sales Professional/Consultant included troubleshooting problems and providing supervision over other sales and customer service personnel.

You will also see from my enclosed resume that I graduated from Upper Iowa University with a B.S. in Business Management. I have also been selected to attend a wide range of graduate level executive development courses in leadership and development. While attending college, I contributed my organizational and communication skills in Consulting and Sales Representative positions. Was known for my strong work ethic and high degree of self-motivation while working as a Sales Assistant for Anderson News.

I hope you will welcome my call soon to arrange a brief meeting to discuss your current and future needs and how I might serve them. Thank you in advance for your time.

Sincerely,

Christopher P. Sullivan

Alternate last paragraph:
I hope you will call or write me soon to suggest a time convenient for us to meet and discuss your current and future needs and how I might serve them. Thank you in advance for your time.

CHRISTOPHER P. SULLIVAN

1110½ Hay Street, Fayetteville, NC 28305   •   preppub@aol.com   •   (910) 483-6611

OBJECTIVE

To contribute to an organization in need of a resourceful problem solver and dynamic communicator who offers expertise related to sales and training along with strong planning, organizational, and management skills refined as a military officer.

EDUCATION

B. S. in Business Management, Upper Iowa University, Fayette, IA, 2001.
Currently selected to attend a wide range of graduate level executive development courses in leadership and management.

EXPERIENCE

Have built an excellent track record of advancement with Barry's Menswear, a custom-made men's clothing company located in Iowa City, IA:
2003-present: SALES TRAINER. Coordinate and conduct training for a team of 20 sales associates, including supervising and evaluating their progress during field training.

2001-03: SALES PROFESSIONAL/CONSULTANT. Provided image consulting to over 200 prominent political and business professionals in Iowa.
- Offered expert advice and critiques regarding wardrobe planning, custom clothing fit, body styles, fabric/patterns, and color coordination.
- Trained in prospecting, cold calling, personality traits, sales presentations, and other sales techniques.
- Completely handled all business aspects for my clientele, including measuring and delivering their clothing and processing all accounts receivable/payable.
- Generated over $310,000 in revenue during my two years in this position, in addition to averaging 20% new business a month and obtaining 112% in personal sales growth.

Other experience:
SALES AND CUSTOMER SERVICE SPECIALIST. Structure Men's Shop, Germantown Mall, Fayette, IA (1998-01). Worked with customers to help them find the items they were looking for in addition to handling inventory control. Learned procedures for operating cash registers, making sales, and providing good service in a retail environment.

SALES ASSISTANT. Anderson News, Fayette, IA (1997-98). Worked as a Wholesale Representative for this publishing distributor. Assisted the Territory Manager in managing a $125,000 budget while also planning traveling schedules for 13 other territory managers.
- Managed files of existing clients, and performed other administrative duties.
- Handpicked to formulate, evaluate, update, and selling techniques, concepts, and procedures.
- Prepared media kits for potential clients.
- Earned a reputation as a gifted salesperson.

TRAINING

Attended 30 hours of classroom training on sales presentation skills and associated sales techniques taught by Lawrence Brown, a motivational speaker; completed 40 hours of sales field training.

PERSONAL

Known for initiative, dedication, leadership, and high ethical and moral standards. Am a professionally trained Salesperson. Enjoy golf and traveling.

Exact Name of Person
Title or Position
Name of Company
Address (number and street)
Address (city, state, and zip)

**SALON GENERAL
MANAGER**
for Millenium Designs

Dear Exact Name of Person: (or Sir or Madam if answering a blind ad.)

I would appreciate an opportunity to talk with you about my desire to offer Sam's Club my considerable sales, management, and retailing background along with my proven ability to master the mechanics of the buying and purchasing function.

As you will see from my resume, I take pride in my work and I have a "track record" of excelling in everything I do. In my most recent job as a general manager, I have led my store to be ranked as 4th in sales throughout Idaho compared to other salons. I have earned a reputation as a skilled Salon General Manager.

In my previous job as a store manager I used my management skills to make my store "the best in the region" among all stores in the chain. I was named "Manager of the Region" for two years in a row, and I was credited with dramatically improving store profitability. In a previous job with Condon's, I was named "Associate of the Month" and I was cross trained in customer service and package pick-up.

You would find me to be a congenial professional who understands the importance of "listening" to the customer and of remaining calm when others are agitated. I greatly admire the operations of Sam's Club and feel that I could make significant contributions to your continued success.

Yours sincerely,

Erica Jasper

ERICA J. JASPER

1110½ Hay Street, Fayetteville, NC 28305 • preppub@aol.com • (910) 483-6611

OBJECTIVE   To contribute to an organization that can use an experienced sales professional who offers excellent decision-making, problem-solving, and customer service skills along with a proven ability to motivate, train, and manage personnel.

EDUCATION   Graduated with honors with an **A.A.S. degree in Marketing and Retailing**, Ricks College, Rexburg, ID, 2003.
Earned Diploma in Cosmetology, Rexburg Technical College, Rexburg, ID, 2002.
Completed training in sales, telemarketing, customer service, and merchandising.
Traveled around the country to various sales seminars.

EXPERIENCE   **GENERAL MANAGER**. Millenium Designs, Rexburg, ID (2003-present). While acting as general manager for a chain of salons, routinely manage the entire company comprised of six stores in Rexburg, Boise, and Lewiston; have led my store to be ranked as 4th in sales throughout Idaho compared to other salons.
- **Recruiting:** Act as liaison between beauty schools and Millenium Designs.
- **Operations:** Assure adequate staffing levels and appropriate levels of beauty supplies; ensure adherence to and continuously monitor work to assure high quality performance.
- **Business development:** Work with managers to develop and implement programs to improve productivity; conduct public relations.
- **Education:** Teach classes of up to 20 people related to sales techniques.
- **Troubleshooting:** Solve a wide range of store and customer problems.

STORE MANAGER. The Burlington Corporation, Rexburg, ID (2001-03). Was specially selected to train incoming managers and manager trainees while using my management ability to make this chain's Rexburg store the best in the region in 2001 and 2002; direct activities including:

sales/merchandising	finances	inventory control
personnel hiring/training	security	maintenance

- Was named "Manager of the Region" in 2002 and 2003.
- In less than one year, "turned around" a store making only 65% profit into one with profits of 88%. Refined my skills in forecasting customer needs and projecting sales.

SALES ASSOCIATE. Condon's Department Store, Lewiston, ID (1999-01). While selling products in all departments of this popular store, was cross trained to work in customer service and package pick-up; prepared merchandise for mailing and controlled cash registers.
- Was named "Associate of the Month."

PUBLIC RELATIONS LIAISON. Lewis-Clark State College, Lewiston, ID (1998-99). Met with a wide range of people while conducting educational surveys throughout the Lewiston area; excelled in interesting students in the benefits of a college education.

SALES COUNSELOR. Carlyle Jewelry, Lewiston, ID (1996-98). In addition to selling fine jewelry, created exciting merchandise displays and stocked cases and counters.

COSMETOLOGIST. Professional Results Beauty Salon, Lewiston, ID (1995-96). Styled hair, gave facials, and sold supplies; gave every customer "VIP" treatment.

PERSONAL   Operate IBM and Dell computers. Use various software programs such Microsoft Word, Excel, and PowerPoint. Work well with customers from all backgrounds.

Date

Exact Name of Person
Exact Title
Exact Name of Company
Address
City, State, Zip

SENIOR MERCHANDISE MANAGER

for a prominent retail corporation

Dear Exact Name of Person: (or Dear Sir or Madam if answering a blind ad)

With the enclosed resume, I would like to make you aware of the considerable skills I feel I could offer your organization.

As you will see from my resume, I have excelled since 1998 in a track record of advancement with the JCPenney's organization, where I started as a management trainee and advanced into a senior management position in charge of 25 individuals. After earning my undergraduate degree in Business Administration with a minor in Economics in 1998, I was attracted to the JCPenney's organization because of its tradition of regarding its managers as profit centers and treating them essentially as entrepreneurs. While hiring and supervising personnel, I handled general management responsibilities including preparing business plans four times a year, reviewing progress monthly toward goals, and performing extensive community relations and public relations. For example, I worked annually with the Girl Scouts of America to coordinate a special function for the children. I was also actively involved with the March of Dimes.

Although I was excelling in my job and held in high regard, I made the decision to resign from JCPenney's in late 2003 for two reasons: first, I wanted to spend a few weeks caring full-time for my widowed mother, who had undergone a serious operation, and second, I had decided that I wished to pursue a career outside retailing. I left on excellent terms and can provide outstanding personal and professional references within the JCPenney's organization including from my immediate supervisor, Charles Shedrick, who would gladly welcome me back at any time.

I feel certain that I could make valuable contributions to your organization through the diversified management experience I have gained as a Senior Manager at JCPenney's Department Store. Although I am only 34 years old, I have controlled buying decisions of more than $5 million annually while refining my skills in prospecting, customer service, public relations, financial forecasting and financial analysis, and budgeting.

I am single and would cheerfully travel as your needs require. If you feel that my skills and background might be of interest to you, I hope you will contact me to suggest a time when we might meet in person to discuss your needs. I can assure you in advance that I am a hard worker and have become an excellent problem-solver and negotiator through my nearly 13 years in retailing. Thank you in advance for your consideration of my skills, and I hope I will have the pleasure of meeting you.

Sincerely yours,

Duane Watson

DUANE S. WATSON

1110½ Hay Street, Fayetteville, NC 28305 • preppub@aol.com • (910) 483-6611

OBJECTIVE

To contribute to an organization that can use an experienced manager who offers a background in managing budgets and performing financial analysis, buying and controlling inventory, supervising and managing personnel, as well as in handling public relations.

EDUCATION

Bachelor of Arts, Business Administration major with a minor in Economics, Bellevue University, Bellevue, NE, 1998.
Currently pursuing a MBA from Creighton University, Omaha, NE.
Have completed extensive management training sponsored by JCPenney's Department Store.

EXPERIENCE

Excelled in a track record of promotion at JCPenney's Department Store, which is the largest in Nebraska:
2003-present: SENIOR MERCHANDISE MANAGER. Recently resigned from JCPenney's in order to devote my full time to caring for my widowed mother in the aftermath of a serious operation, and to seek a career outside retailing.
- Work with managers to develop and implement programs to improve productivity; utilize proper customer service and public relation skills.
- Resigned under excellent conditions; can provide an outstanding reference from Charles Shedrick, my immediate supervisor, as well as numerous other JCPenney's executives.

2001-03: MERCHANDISE MANAGER. Was promoted to manage 25 sales associates while controlling a $5 million inventory; this position placed me in charge of the largest volume Children's Department in Nebraska which includes 60 stores; also managed the Home Department and Infant Department.
- Interviewed and hired new sales associates. Increased department sales by 5% annually.
- In the JCPenney's environment, the Senior Merchandise Manager is in an essentially entrepreneurial role and, unlike most department stores, the Senior Manager undertakes the buying function; performed extensive liaison with suppliers and manufacturers who acted as vendors to JCPenney's.

1998-01: PROJECT MANAGER. Because of my reputation as an excellent communicator and public speaker, was selected to take on a special project related to implementing a new Programs; as coordinator of this program, traveled extensively throughout the Nebraska to talk with store managers.
- Throughout this nine-month project, was commended for my ability to articulate the concepts of this new program in ways managers could understand.

2001: MANAGER. Men's Clothing and Men's Accessories.
2000: MANAGER. Infant Department.
1999: MANAGER. Housewares Department.
1998-99: MANAGEMENT TRAINEE. Was attracted by JCPenney's outstanding management training program and by the opportunity as a manager to function in an essentially entrepreneurial role with broad decision-making abilities after advancing into management.

MERCHANDISE MANAGER. J.B. White's, Bellevue, NE (1996-98). Worked part-time at J.B. White's for two years while completing my college degree which I earned in 1998.

PERSONAL

Am seeking a career outside retailing primarily so I can attend classes two nights a week in pursuit of my MBA. Work well under pressure and am known for my attention to detail.

Exact Name of Person
Title or Position
Name of Company
Address (number and street)
Address (city, state, and zip)

SHOE STORE SALES ASSOCIATE

for a popular store in Baton Rouge

Dear Exact Name of Person: (or Sir or Madam if answering a blind ad.)

With the enclosed resume, I would like to introduce myself and make you aware of the considerable experience in sales, customer service, and retail management which I could put to work for you.

As you will see from my resume, I have developed extensive customer service and managerial skills while working for Rack Room Shoes for over 12 years. I began with as a Sales Associate and learned the ropes of retailing at the ground level. During that time, I also worked on my college degree, and I completed my B.S. degree in Retail Management. Although I earned a teaching degree, my first student teaching experience persuaded me that I was better suited for business management than for classroom teaching.

I became a Manager-in-Training with Rack Room Shoes in 1993 and then excelled in a variety of assignments ranging from managing newly started stores to closing stores in unprofitable locations and transferring inventory and employees to other locations. I am especially proud of the fact that, in a store I managed in Baton Rouge, LA, I hired and trained three employees who remained with me throughout my tenure at that store. I am grateful to several Rack Room managers for the many sound principles and techniques they taught me related to managing people and retail operations.

If you can use a reliable hard worker with proven management skills and a solid understanding of retail, I hope you will contact me to suggest a time when we could meet to discuss your needs and how I might serve them. I can provide outstanding personal and professional references. Thank you in advance for your time.

Sincerely,

Paulette D. Erwin

PAULETTE D. ERWIN

1110½ Hay Street, Fayetteville, NC 28305 • preppub@aol.com • (910) 483-6611

OBJECTIVE   I want to contribute to an organization that can use an experienced young professional who offers a track record of success in a variety of managerial positions which required excellent sales, problem-solving, decision-making, and customer relations skills.

EDUCATION   **Bachelor of Arts degree in Retail Management**, Louisiana Tech University, Ruston, LA, 1993.
- Earned a teaching degree which has helped me communicate effectively with people.

EXPERIENCE   *Have excelled in a variety of assignments with Rack Room Shoes:*
2003-present: SHOESTORE SALES ASSOCIATE. Baton Rouge, LA. Handle a special assignment troubleshooting a backlogged inventory, and play a key role in establishing appropriate inventory levels and assuring the store was stocked to meet customer demand.

2001-03: MANAGER. Baton Rouge, LA. Hired and trained three employees, and was successful in retaining those same three original employees during my tenure at this store.
- Developed employee work schedules which satisfied employee and employer needs.
- Controlled inventory and made recommendations to buyers based on customer feedback.
- Excelled in management in this relatively new store; at this Rack Room unit which was not expected to make a profit for several more months, was given a profit-loss goal of $10,000 and achieved a bottom-line result of $5,000.

1999-01: UNIT CLOSING MANAGER. Gazebo Mall, Baton Rouge, LA. Was specially selected for a three-month assignment which involved closing a store at an unprofitable location since Rack Room Shoes had opened a new unit in a high-traffic mall.
- Assisted in counseling and relocating employees. Developed employee schedules.
- Participated in the packing and transfer of store products to other stores.
- Exceeded the managerial profit goal assigned to me.

1997-1999: MANAGER. Slidell, LA. For a five-month period, worked in a newly started store and led the store to exceed all expectations for profit and shrinkage; produced a 5% increase in sales over the targeted goal and maintained shrinkage at less than 1%.
- Added a creative touch to the innovative merchandising plans established for this store.

1993-96: MANAGER-IN-TRAINING. Slidell, LA. Gained my first experience in managing a store closing during this seven-month assignment.
- Liquidated inventory from 6,000 pairs of shoes to 1,700 pairs.

1993: MANAGER-IN-TRAINING. Darienne Mall, Slidell, LA. Excelled in this two-month apprenticeship in which I was trained in nearly all aspects of retailing.

Other experience:
STUDENT TEACHER. Brennen High School, Ruston, LA (1990-1992). While obtaining my teaching certification, taught in an at-risk classroom; learned to evaluate student work, prepared daily and weekly lesson plans, and handled all classroom duties.
- During my student teaching experience, I decided that I wanted to work in the business world, not in the classroom.

PERSONAL   Can provide outstanding personal and professional references. Proven ability to establish and maintain excellent relationships. Have earned respect for my creativity and flexibility.

Date

Exact Name of Person
Exact Title
Exact Name of Company
Address
City, State, Zip

STORE MANAGER
for CVS Pharmacy

Dear Exact Name of Person (or Dear Sir or Madam if answering a blind ad):

With the enclosed resume, I would like to express my interest in exploring employment opportunities with your organization.

As you will see from my resume, I am an experienced retailer with store management experience. Although I am held in the highest regard by my current employer and am being groomed for further promotion, I am selectively exploring other opportunities. I can provide outstanding references at the appropriate time, but I would appreciate your not contacting my current employer until after we talk.

I was handpicked for my current position which involved starting up a Dollar General store for CVS Pharmacy. There are now 21 Dollar General stores in Virginia, and they offer discounted front-end drug store products as well as the expanded Dollar General trademarked line. Because of my outstanding communication skills and reputation as an innovative retailer, I was chosen as the spokesperson for the "Freewriter's Event" and I communicate the views of my peers to upper management in the parent organization. My store won the Customer Service Award of the Year, and I am also proud that the turnover in my store has been practically nonexistent. I have retained nearly all the employees I hired when I started the store, and I believe those employees would say that they feel well treated. Prior to my current position I excelled as an Assistant Manager in a large CVS Pharmacy location.

In prior experience, I excelled in outside sales positions in the business equipment industry and as a Realtor Associate. I offer exceptionally strong customer service and problem-solving skills.

If you can use an astute problem solver who is accustomed to contributing to the bottom line in an environment in which there is stiff competition and constant pressure on the profit margin, I hope you will contact me to suggest a time when we might meet. I would certainly enjoy discussing your needs.

Sincerely,

Marcia Price Fletcher

MARCIA PRICE FLETCHER

1110½ Hay Street, Fayetteville, NC 28305　•　preppub@aol.com　•　(910) 483-6611

OBJECTIVE　　I want to contribute to an organization that can use an experienced manager with exceptionally strong sales and communication skills along with a proven ability to identify new trends, solve complex problems, and develop junior employees.

EXPERIENCE　　*Have been promoted in the following "track record" based on accomplishments; am being groomed for further promotion:*
2003-present. STORE MANAGER. Dollar General Store (a division of CVS Pharmacy), Lexington, VA. Was specially selected to assume the responsibility of starting up a new Dollar General store within the CVS Pharmacy; CVS now operates 21 Dollar General stores in Virginia which offer discounted front-end drug store products and the expanded Dollar General trademarked line.

- Managed the transition when the CVS Pharmacy at this location relocated six blocks away and the site became the home of the Dollar General store; handled hiring and merchandising of this new value store.
- Hire and train the store's and maintain exceptionally low turnover; the staff feels well treated and they respond with loyalty.
- Received the Customer Service Award of the Year. My store has also received exceptionally high evaluations of merchandising and maintenance.
- Am the spokesperson for the "Freewriter's Event," a brainstorming tool used by CVS; am widely respected for my strong communication skills.
- Utilize a computer daily to access reports related to sales, gross margin percentages, UPCs, merchandise availability, and other matters. However, the Dollar General stores still rely on the store manager to order all merchandise since there is no automated reordering system. Am extensively involved in ordering merchandise, verifying invoices, and maintaining store records.

2001-03. ASSISTANT MANAGER. CVS Pharmacy, Lexington, VA. Was rapidly promoted in a store with 12 employees which included a pharmacy.
- Made contributions to the success of the store in special promotions and other areas.

Other experience:
OUTSIDE SALES REPRESENTATIVE & MAJOR ACCOUNT REPRESENTATIVE. Quincey O'Neill, Inc., Abingdon, VA (1995-2001). Was a top producer in this company which was bought in the 1990s by Epson Products.
- Set up numerous major new accounts including the Maxwell House account; managed the local Carlyle Industries account.
- Won numerous awards for sales achievements and customer service performance.
- Excelled in this industry at a time of dynamic change when there were multiple new product introductions of computers, copiers, faxes, and printers; became skilled in introducing new concepts and products.
- Participated in trade shows, and handled all aspects of organizing the booths.

ASSISTANT TO THE MANAGER. Collins Office Supplies, Inc., Abingdon, VA (1992-1995). Became the owner's managerial "right arm" as I ordered all office supplies for resell, typeset documents, and sold office supplies/equipment.

EDUCATION　　Extensive training in sales and management sponsored by CVS Pharmacy; Quincey O'Neill; and other organizations. Have attended numerous motivational and time management workshops of Martin Thompson, and others.
Completed one year of college, Virginia Highlands Community College, Abingdon, VA.

Date

Exact Name of Person
Title or Position
Name of Company
Address (no., street)
Address (city, state, zip)

STORE MANAGER
for Autozone auto
parts store

Dear Exact Name of Person: (or Dear Sir or Madam if answering a blind ad.)

    I would appreciate an opportunity to talk with you soon about how I could contribute to your organization through my experience in all aspects of management/auto advisor, including shouldering the full responsibility for profit and loss and for market share.

    I began my management career with NAPA Auto Parts, Inc. After only seven months as a sales representative, I was promoted to manage the store and, in my first year as a manager, took sales from $800,000 to $1,100,000 without any increase in payroll. I was selected Manager of the Year in 2001.

    Most recently while managing a "superstore" with four assistant managers and more than 30 employees, I produced dramatic increases in sales, increased profit as a percentage of sales, and cut payroll as a percentage of the operating budget. I became known for "setting the standard" for customer service and was even featured in written articles because of my commitment to outstanding customer service.

    You would find me to be an innovative and resourceful professional who has a congenial style of dealing with people. I am skilled at simultaneously coordinating numerous functional areas ranging from sales, to personnel training, to inventory control. I can provide exceptional personal and professional references upon request.

    I hope you will call or write me soon to suggest a time convenient for us to meet and discuss your current and future needs and how I might serve them. Thank you in advance for your time.

Sincerely yours,

Hector P. Tournado

HECTOR P. TOURNADO

1110½ Hay Street, Fayetteville, NC 28305 • preppub@aol.com • (910) 483-6611

OBJECTIVE   To contribute to an organization that can use a store manager with a proven ability to manage multiunit operations and start up new stores using my award-winning talents related to sales, customer service, financial control, employee supervision, and quality control.

EXPERIENCE   **STORE MANAGER.** Autozone, Stanton, DE (2002-present). Became known for "setting the standard" for customer service in this company, and was featured in publications because of my commitment to outstanding service; have come to believe that superior customer service is the key to competing in today's marketplace.

- Have excelled in customer service as well as these key management areas:

profit	inventory control	personnel development
sales	store appearance	gross markup

- In a unit which had two different sections — automotive retail and automotive repair — supervise four assistant managers and more than 30 employees.
- With a customer base of 150,000 customers per year, posted 2003 retail sales of $3.2 million.
- From 2002 to 2003, steadily increased profit from 9% to 16% as a percentage of sales.
- Cut payroll from 10.5% to 8.5% of the store's total budget.
- Produced a 26% increase in sales in 2002 compared to 2001.

STORE MANAGER. NAPA Auto Parts, Stanton, DE (2001-02). Began as a Sales Representative and, after only seven months, was promoted to manage the store; in my first year as a manager, took sales from $800,000 to $1,100,000 without any increase in payroll.

- Supervised a unit with more than 10 employees producing $1.2 million in annual sales on a customer base of 100,000 people a year.
- Was selected as "Manager of the Year", 2001, a selection made from among 15 other managers based on personnel development, shrinkage, sales, and profits.
- Was handpicked as Training Coordinator for Division Seven; oversaw the training of 150 people and was responsible for orienting/training all new employees.
- Was named to the company's Advisory Council in charge of long-range planning.
- Operated the company's 6th highest-volume store, and led it to consistently rank first out of 100 stores in the volume of special orders placed.

SALES PERSON. Livingston Parts and Services, Stanton, DE (2000-01). Learn the auto parts business and became an expert in consulting technical manuals related to parts; learned the terminology of the automotive/automotive parts business.

EDUCATION   Excelled in extensive sales and management training sponsored by:

Gregory Gerald Seminars   NAPA Auto Parts
Delaware Technical & Community College   Autozone

- Through formal course work, have become knowledgeable about numerous aspects of automotive service including engine repair, brakes, manual drive trains/axles, suspension and steering, and heating and air conditioning.
- Hold an Automotive Service Certificate, Delaware Technical & Community College, Stanton, DE.

PERSONAL   Offer the ability to get along with others. Am self-motivated and flexible. Will provide outstanding personal and professional references upon request.

Date

Exact Name of Person
Title or Position
Name of Company
Address (number and street)
Address (city, state, and zip)

**TERRITORY MANAGER &
SALES REPRESENTATIVE**
for McAllister Retail Group

Dear Exact Name of Person: (or Sir or Madam if answering a blind ad.)

I enjoyed speaking with you about opportunities available with Downing Solutions Inc. I am very interested in discussing further how I may contribute my versatile skills and abilities to your organization.

As you will see from my resume, I offer diversified skills related to sales, marketing, and advertising along with experience in all aspects of office operations. In addition, I offer superior time-management and organizational skills along with the ability to efficiently complete multiple, simultaneous tasks under tight deadlines.

Most recently, I am excelling as a Territory Manager/Sales Representative with the McAllister Retail Group. During my first year with the company, I not only exceeded sales goals but was also named "Salesman of the Year," in 2003. In this position, I have gained valuable skills at communicating with people on a variety of levels while serving as liaison between our company and as many as 40 retail stores throughout Wisconsin.

I am certain that you would find me to be a hard-working and reliable professional who prides myself on doing any job to the best of my ability. I can provide excellent personal and professional references if you require them.

I hope you will contact me soon to arrange a convenient time for us to meet and discuss your current and future goals and how I can help achieve them. Thank you in advance for your time.

Sincerely yours,

Pamela T. Montrose

PAMELA T. MONTROSE

1110½ Hay Street, Fayetteville, NC 28305 • preppub@aol.com • (910) 483-6611

OBJECTIVE

To benefit an organization through my versatile skills in sales and marketing and office administration, as well as planning and organizing.

EDUCATION

B.S. degree in Business Administration, St. Norbert College, De Pere, WI, 2001; achieved a 3.0 GPA while working full-time to finance my education.
- Minor in **Economics**; excelled in courses which included statistics, managerial economics, management, human resource management, cost and basic accounting, business law, business policy and strategy, business computer applications, and advertising.

EXPERIENCE

TERRITORY MANAGER and **SALES REPRESENTATIVE**. McAllister Retail Group, LaCrosse, WI (2003-present). Manage a territory of 40 retail stores throughout Wisconsin; conduct district-wide training seminars on product knowledge and equipment use.
- Provide training to all levels of store management and associates.
- Work closely with management teams to identify weaknesses in sales and merchandising.
- Coordinate promotional events and training seminars; have excelled in extensive corporate training classes.
- Exceeded all sales goals in the first year and was named "Salesperson of the Year" 2003.

MARKETING REPRESENTATIVE. E. B. White, Inc., La Crosse, WI (2001-03). Began with this company by working in the Borro County territory, and achieved more than 200% of targeted sales quotas. Produced new business in an assigned, unestablished territory.
- Developed a database on accounts; maintained contacts with accounts.

ADMINISTRATIVE ASSISTANT. Pittney, Fields, and Brennan Law Practices, De Pere, WI (1999-01). Worked full time in this job while obtaining my college degree; handled a wide variety of responsibilities for attorneys while routinely posting accounts receivable and payable, interviewing clients, performing clerical duties, and handling some purchasing.

CREDIT ASSOCIATE. Le Tourneau Loan Company, De Pere, WI (1998-99). Worked full time while completing courses at De Pere Community College prior to enrolling in St. Norbert College.

PROCUREMENT CLERK/CREDIT ASSOCIATE. Haverty's Furniture, De Pere, WI (1996-98). Began with this furniture company as a credit associate in De Pere; collected payment on delinquent accounts, prepared finance contracts, processed and analyzed credit reports, prepared necessary documents for court action against delinquencies, ordered merchandise, and posted accounts receivable.

Other experience:
- **Account Executive**. Coming Events Magazine/DRPR and Associates. Built and maintained an account base while performing advertising sales and coordination in Bloomingdale County.
- **Sales Associate**. Barry's Jewelers/Jewel Box. Provided superior customer service and assisted customers in selecting fine jewelry.
- **Co-Manager**. Simply Fashions. While in high school, was rapidly promoted into management for this discount ladies clothing store.

COMPUTERS

Proficient with Microsoft Word, Excel, and Access.

Date

Exact Name of Person (if known)
Title or Position
Name of Company
Address (no., street)
Address (city, state, zip)

**VICE PRESIDENT
OF OPERATIONS**

for Moore Drums
Industries

Dear Exact Name of Person: (or Dear Sir or Madam)

With the enclosed resume, I would like to make you aware of my interest in your organization. If you feel that my well-developed managerial skills could be of value to you, I would appreciate the opportunity to talk with you in person about my considerable background in training, team building, and customer service as well as my track record of achievement in retail operations.

As you will see from my resume, I am known for my team building, time management, and organizational abilities. I am currently employed as a Vice President of Operations with Moore Drum Industries. I established marketing procedures which increased sales by 11% and reduced freight expenses by 80% in 2003.

In prior positions with Media Play, I was singled out to manage complex projects including overseeing store openings from hiring and staffing locations, to opening them, to operational oversight. I have been involved in managing projects to remodel multiple stores and as well as in corporate strategic planning.

I have gained experience in all operational environments in retail settings: human resources and personnel management, purchasing and inventory control, customer service, public relations, merchandising, office operations, and loss prevention. I offer expertise in numerous areas and am confident that I am a professional capable of contributing successfully to your organization's "bottom line."

If my considerable talents and skills interest you, I hope you will call or write me soon to suggest a time convenient for us to meet to discuss your needs and how I might serve them. I can provide outstanding personal and professional references at the appropriate time. Thank you in advance for your time.

Sincerely,

Harry Miller Ridgeford

HARRY MILLER RIDGEFORD

1110½ Hay Street, Fayetteville, NC 28305   •   preppub@aol.com   •   (910) 483-6611

OBJECTIVE

To apply my versatile background in operations, material, logistics, and general management to an organization in need of a creative executive and resourceful problem-solver with superior strategic planning, decision-making, and motivational skills.

EDUCATION & EXECUTIVE TRAINING

B.S., Business Management, Muhlenberg College, Allentown, PA 2001.
Completed graduate-level technical and managerial training programs for business executives with an emphasis in management, corporate communication, and employee training.

EXPERIENCE

VICE PRESIDENT OF OPERATIONS. Moore Drum Industries, Chester, PA (2003-present). Contribute to the company's "bottom line" by developing and implementing numerous cost and timesaving procedures while directing and controlling all aspects of purchasing supplies and equipment in addition to supervising shipping and production.
- Guarantee that purchase orders are filled and shipped efficiently and on time for companies including Wal-Mart.
- Design and implement new management systems including a program of inventory management procedures. Take immediate action to correct problems after identifying both a $46,000 in excess inventory and a $19,000 shortage.
- Established procedures which increased sales by 11% and reduced freight expenses 80%, supply costs as much as 64%, and overall inventory 35%.

CONSULTANT. Neilson Marketing Research, Chester, PA (2001-03). Provided consulting while involved in a marketing project to analyze information and then developed/wrote realistic training scenarios for marketing executives.
- Applied my previous experience as a General Manager for Thunderstar determine the most successful target markets for small business throughout Pennsylvania.
- Gained experience in all operational environments: human resources and personnel management, purchasing and inventory control, customer service, public relations, merchandising, office operations, and loss prevention.

GENERAL MANAGER. Thunderstar Expeditions, Allentown, PA (1999-01). Learned how to establish and manage a profitable business by setting up and developing a thriving operation which specialized in providing guides for instructional fishing trips.
- Handled functional operations including preparing budgets and financial records and reports as well as purchasing supplies and equipment.
- Creatively restructured the local guide industry which enabled independent contractors to increase their income, thereby improving morale and the quality of services available.

Advanced in a track record of promotion with Media Play, Allentown, PA: (1992-99):
MARKETING MANAGER. (1997-99). Developed a management system which raised retail sales by 21% of their quotas to 38% in one year and to 42% in two years. Developed marketing and advertising strategies for a 200-person organization.
ASSISTANT MANAGER. (1993-97). Managed 42 employees; led my team to first place in competitions among elements of other media entertainment organizations.
MANAGER IN TRAINING. (1992-93). Trained and evaluated on public relations, store operations, problem solving, and management skills.

PERSONAL

Offer skills in operating Wang, IBM, and Tandy computers. Am known as an innovative problem solver who excels in finding new ways to save time and money. Can motivate others to set and strive for high goals.

ABOUT THE EDITOR

Anne McKinney holds an MBA from the Harvard Business School and a BA in English from the University of North Carolina at Chapel Hill. A noted public speaker, writer, and teacher, she is the senior editor for PREP's business and career imprint, which bears her name. Early titles in the Anne McKinney Career Series (now called the Real-Resumes Series) published by PREP include: *Resumes and Cover Letters That Have Worked, Resumes and Cover Letters That Have Worked for Military Professionals, Government Job Applications and Federal Resumes, Cover Letters That Blow Doors Open,* and *Letters for Special Situations.* Her career titles and how-to resume-and-cover-letter books are based on the expertise she has acquired in 20 years of working with job hunters. Her valuable career insights have appeared in publications of the "Wall Street Journal" and other prominent newspapers and magazines.

PREP Publishing Order Form

You may purchase any of our titles from your favorite bookseller! Or send a check or money order or your credit card number for the total amount*, plus $4.00 postage and handling, to PREP, 1110 1/2 Hay Street, Fayetteville, NC 28305. You may also order our titles on our website at www.prep-pub.com and feel free to e-mail us at preppub@aol.com or call 910-483-6611 with your questions or concerns.

Name: _____

Phone #:_____

Address: _____

E-mail address:_____

Payment Type: ☐ Check/Money Order   ☐ Visa   ☐ MasterCard

Credit Card Number: _____ Expiration Date: _____

Put a check beside the items you are ordering:

☐ Free—Packet describing PREP's professional writing and editing services

☐ $16.95—REAL-RESUMES FOR RESTAURANT, FOOD SERVICE & HOTEL JOBS. Anne McKinney, Editor

☐ $16.95—REAL-RESUMES FOR MEDIA, NEWSPAPER, BROADCASTING & PUBLIC AFFAIRS JOBS. Anne McKinney

☐ $16.95—REAL-RESUMES FOR RETAILING, MODELING, FASHION & BEAUTY JOBS. Anne McKinney, Editor

☐ $16.95—REAL-RESUMES FOR HUMAN RESOURCES & PERSONNEL JOBS. Anne McKinney, Editor

☐ $16.95—REAL-RESUMES FOR MANUFACTURING JOBS. Anne McKinney, Editor

☐ $16.95—REAL-RESUMES FOR AVIATION & TRAVEL JOBS. Anne McKinney, Editor

☐ $16.95—REAL-RESUMES FOR POLICE, LAW ENFORCEMENT & SECURITY JOBS. Anne McKinney, Editor

☐ $16.95—REAL-RESUMES FOR SOCIAL WORK & COUNSELING JOBS. Anne McKinney, Editor

☐ $16.95—REAL-RESUMES FOR CONSTRUCTION JOBS. Anne McKinney, Editor

☐ $16.95—REAL-RESUMES FOR FINANCIAL JOBS. Anne McKinney, Editor

☐ $16.95—REAL-RESUMES FOR COMPUTER JOBS. Anne McKinney, Editor

☐ $16.95—REAL-RESUMES FOR MEDICAL JOBS. Anne McKinney, Editor

☐ $16.95—REAL-RESUMES FOR TEACHERS. Anne McKinney, Editor

☐ $16.95—REAL-RESUMES FOR CAREER CHANGERS. Anne McKinney, Editor

☐ $16.95—REAL-RESUMES FOR STUDENTS. Anne McKinney, Editor

☐ $16.95—REAL-RESUMES FOR SALES. Anne McKinney, Editor

☐ $16.95—REAL ESSAYS FOR COLLEGE AND GRAD SCHOOL. Anne McKinney, Editor

☐ $25.00—RESUMES AND COVER LETTERS THAT HAVE WORKED. McKinney. Editor

☐ $25.00—RESUMES AND COVER LETTERS THAT HAVE WORKED FOR MILITARY PROFESSIONALS. McKinney, Ed.

☐ $25.00—RESUMES AND COVER LETTERS FOR MANAGERS. McKinney, Editor

☐ $25.00—GOVERNMENT JOB APPLICATIONS AND FEDERAL RESUMES: Federal Resumes, KSAs, Forms 171 and 612, and Postal Applications. McKinney, Editor

☐ $25.00—COVER LETTERS THAT BLOW DOORS OPEN. McKinney, Editor

☐ $25.00—LETTERS FOR SPECIAL SITUATIONS. McKinney, Editor

☐ $16.00—BACK IN TIME. Patty Sleem

☐ $17.00—(trade paperback) SECOND TIME AROUND. Patty Sleem

☐ $25.00—(hardcover) SECOND TIME AROUND. Patty Sleem

☐ $18.00—A GENTLE BREEZE FROM GOSSAMER WINGS. Gordon Beld

☐ $18.00—BIBLE STORIES FROM THE OLD TESTAMENT. Katherine Whaley

☐ $14.95—WHAT THE BIBLE SAYS ABOUT... *Words that can lead to success and happiness* (large print edition) Patty Sleem

_____ **TOTAL ORDERED**

_____ **(add $4.00 for shipping and handling)**

_____ **TOTAL INCLUDING SHIPPING**

PREP offers volume discounts on large orders. Call us at (910) 483-6611 for more information.

THE MISSION OF PREP PUBLISHING IS TO PUBLISH
BOOKS AND OTHER PRODUCTS WHICH ENRICH
PEOPLE'S LIVES AND HELP THEM OPTIMIZE THE
HUMAN EXPERIENCE. OUR STRONGEST LINES ARE
OUR JUDEO-CHRISTIAN ETHICS SERIES AND OUR
REAL-RESUMES SERIES.

Would you like to explore the possibility of having PREP's writing
team create a resume for you similar to the ones in this book?

For a brief free consultation, call 910-483-6611
or send $4.00 to receive our Job Change Packet to
PREP, 1110 1/2 Hay Street, Fayetteville, NC 28305. Visit our
website to find valuable career resources: www.prep-pub.com!

QUESTIONS OR COMMENTS? E-MAIL US AT PREPPUB@AOL.COM